D1211762

Alexander Calder
by James Johnson Sweeney

The Sculpture of John B. Flannagan
edited by Dorothy C. Miller
with an introduction by Carl Zigrosser
and a statement by the artist

Gaston Lachaise
by Lincoln Kirstein

The Sculpture of Elie Nadelman
by Lincoln Kirstein

The Sculpture of Jacques Lipchitz
by Henry R. Hope

The Museum of Modern Art, New York
Reprint Edition, 1969
Published for The Museum of Modern Art by Arno Press

730.92
F565

189815

Copyright © 1935, 1942, 1948, 1951 by
The Museum of Modern Art, New York
Reprint Edition, 1969 Arno Press
Library of Congress Catalog Card No. 71-86443

JAMES JOHNSON SWEENEY

ALEXANDER CALDER

THE MUSEUM OF MODERN ART, NEW YORK

TRUSTEES OF THE MUSEUM OF MODERN ART

Stephen C. Clark, *Chairman of the Board;* Mrs. John D. Rockefeller, Jr., *1st Vice-Chairman;* Samuel A. Lewisohn, *2nd Vice-Chairman;* John Hay Whitney*, *President;* John E. Abbott, *Vice-President;* Alfred H. Barr, Jr., *Vice-President;* Mrs. David M. Levy, *Treasurer;* Mrs. Robert Woods Bliss, Mrs. W. Murray Crane, Marshall Field, Philip L. Goodwin, A. Conger Goodyear, Mrs. Simon Guggenheim, Henry R. Luce, Archibald MacLeish, David H. McAlpin*, William S. Paley, Mrs. John Parkinson, Jr., Mrs. Charles S. Payson, Beardsley Ruml, Carleton Sprague Smith, James Thrall Soby, Edward M. M. Warburg*.

HONORARY TRUSTEES

Frederic Clay Bartlett, Frank Crowninshield, Duncan Phillips, Paul J. Sachs, Mrs. John S. Sheppard.

* On duty with the Armed Forces.

Copyright 1943 by The Museum of Modern Art, 11 West 53 Street, New York
Printed in the United States of America

4

CONTENTS

ACKNOWLEDGMENTS

The President and Trustees of the Museum of Modern Art and the Director of the Exhibition, James Johnson Sweeney, wish to thank those who have lent to the exhibition and, in addition, those who have generously rendered assistance: Herbert Matter, as consultant in the installation and for his invaluable assistance in making special photographs; and A. Stirling Calder; William F. Coles, Caracas, Venezuela; Stuart C. Henry, Berkshire Museum; Miss Laura Canadé, Weyhe Gallery; Mrs. Wallace K. Harrison; Pierre Matisse; Miss Marian Willard.

Miss Margaret Miller of the Museum staff assisted Mr. Sweeney in preparing the book and exhibition, and Bernard Karpel, Librarian of the Museum, arranged the bibliography.

The photographs reproduced on pages 10, 12, 13, 14, 15, 16, 17, 18, 19, 20, 28, 30, 31, 32, 34, 35, 36, 39, 40, 41, 43, 44, 45, 46, 47, 49, 51, 53, 54, 55, are by Herbert Matter.

LENDERS TO THE EXHIBITION

Mrs. Whitney Allen, Rochester, New York; A. Stirling Calder, Brooklyn, New York; Mr. and Mrs. Alexander Calder, Roxbury, Connecticut; Sandra Calder, Roxbury, Connecticut; The Columbia Broadcasting Company, New York, New York; Malcolm Cowley, Gaylordsville, Connecticut; Philip L. Goodwin, New York, New York; Miss Peggy Guggenheim, New York, New York; Mr. and Mrs. Wallace K. Harrison, New York, New York; Jean Hélion, Rockbridge Baths, Virginia; Mrs. Sidney Howard, New York, New York; Mr. and Mrs. C. Earle Miller, Downingtown, Pennsylvania; George L. K. Morris, New York, New York; Mrs. Paul Nelson, Washington, D. C.; Paul Nitze, Glen Cove, Long Island, New York; Amédée Ozenfant, New York, New York; Mrs. Ralph Delahaye Paine, New York, New York; Mr. and Mrs. George D. Pratt, Bridgewater, Connecticut; Baroness Hilla von Rebay, New York, New York; Miss Agnes Rindge, Poughkeepsie, New York; William Rogers, Springfield, Massachusetts; Mrs. José Luis Sert, New York, New York; Mr. and Mrs. James Thrall Soby, New York, New York; Mr. and Mrs. Richard Taylor, Bethel, Connecticut; Mrs. James di Tomasi, Cold Spring Harbor, New York; Mrs. Catherine White, New York, New York; Mrs. Beatrice K. Winston, New York, New York; Shepard Vogelgesang, New York, New York.

The Addison Gallery of American Art, Andover, Massachusetts; Art of this Century, New York, New York; The Arts Club, Chicago, Illinois; The Berkshire Museum, Pittsfield, Massachusetts; The Wadsworth Atheneum, Hartford, Connecticut.

Alexander Calder

ALEXANDER CALDER

Introduction

Exuberance, buoyancy, vigor are characteristics of a young art. Humor, when it is a vitalizing force not a surface distraction, adds a dimension to dignity. Dignity is the product of an artist's whole-hearted abandon to his work. All these are features of Alexander Calder's work, together with a sensibility to materials that induces new forms and an insatiable interest in fresh patterns of order.

Calder is an American. The most conspicuous characteristics of his art are those which have been attributed to America's frontier heritage — "that coarseness and strength combined with acuteness and inquisitiveness; that practical, inventive turn of mind, quick to find expedients; that masterful grasp of material things," . . . "that restless, nervous energy," . . . "that buoyancy and exuberance which come with freedom."* But Calder is a child of his own time. His vernacular is the vernacular of his age in America — an age in which the frontiers of science, engineering and mechanics have dominated the popular imagination in the same way that the national frontier dominated it a century ago.

On the side of tradition, two generations of sculptors — father and grandfather — gave him an intimate familiarity with the grammar and conventions of art. In Paris he came to know the researches of some of the most venturesome contemporary pioneers at a time when he himself was seeking a more radical departure. The result in Calder's mature work is the marriage of an internationally educated sensibility with a native American ingenuity. Through the individuality of his work he has an established place in contemporary art both here and abroad.

The last forty years have seen a profound reaction against the deliquescence of form which had marked Occidental sculpture since the Renaissance. Calder's art embodies this reaction.

From the time of Michelangelo until the opening of the twentieth century, nobility of style and simplicity of technique seemed usually incompatible. The sculptor apparently tried to disguise his materials rather than to demonstrate them. Along with this disrespect for the material, sculptors developed a facile virtuosity which during the Baroque period became a prime quality. Modeling in clay for reproduction in bronze or marble eventually came to replace direct carving. Fluidity of sculptural form reached its highest level with Bernini in the seventeenth century. But, in general, the relaxation of material restraints led to a decay of sculptural unity and force.

With the twentieth century a renewed desire for formal precision and integrity began to assert itself. In sculpture the shortest route to simplicity and direct expression lay through a re-establishment of the discipline of materials. The peculiarities of a raw material — the grain of the wood, the texture and hardness of a stone, the surface qualities of a metal — if respected, would exert a tonic restraint on the sculptor and his forms. African Negro sculpture was a clear illustration of the advantages of this discipline. It accepted and exploited the cylindrical shape of the tree-trunk as well as the incidental suggestions of its grain and knots.

* Frederick Jackson Turner: *The Frontier in American History*, p. 37.

With Brancusi, virtuosity of handling gave way to the barest simplicity and directness. The orthodox materials of sculpture — metal, wood and stone — were employed once again to display their individual properties, not to simulate those of one another. The lightness and apparent insubstantiality of a polished metal surface were exploited to suggest a *Bird in Flight* or the shimmer of a *Fish*. Among the younger men who followed Brancusi we find Calder, like Henry Moore, "always ready to share credit for his work with his material."*

Calder's characteristic material is metal. He has always avoided modeling in favor of direct handling — cutting, shaping with a hammer, or assembling piece by piece. Such an approach has fostered a simplicity of form and clarity of contour in his work. It allies him with Brancusi, Arp, Moore and Giacometti in their repudiation of virtuosity.

At the same time Calder's concern as an artist with mechanical forms and mechanical organizations, and his use of new or unconventional materials link him with the Russian constructivists of twenty-five years ago. Open composition was their interest, as opposed to the compressed unity of Brancusi. Their aim was to expand the conception of sculptural form, so long tied to nature and to conventional materials. Instead of advocating merely a reform in the use of the orthodox materials of sculpture, the constructivists explored new materials — steel, glass, celluloid, rhodoid and the like.

The Paris cubist painters had felt that a volume could be more truthfully rendered by making its form, or a section of it, transparent. In this way features on the other side, which would normally be masked, could be seen. The constructivist sculptors carried the theory a step further, employing such transparent materials as glass and celluloid for the same purpose. Transparent surfaces led to surfaces actually nonexistent, but indicated by lines — wires, strips of wood — or merely implied by other planes. These surfaces defined "empty," or more precisely, virtual volumes. Certain constructions organized enclosed volumes; others, by means of the implied projections of their lines and planes, were designed to organize the surrounding space; or the space within a volume was employed as a foil to a solid in a sculptural composition. Even movement was tentatively introduced by Gabo in 1920 to add a time element and to trace virtual forms in space.

This last problem is the one which Calder has explored more fully than any other artist, after coming to it quite independently of constructivism. But Calder's most original contribution is his unique enlivening of abstract art by humor. Through humor he satisfies the observer's appetite for feeling or emotion without recourse to direct representation. The appeal of representation had evidently been the culprit in upsetting the balance between form and subject in art. In the effort to readjust this balance the temptation had been to limit representational appeal drastically, even to expunge it. As a result the art produced by the extremists was often chilly to the point of torpor. Every living experience owes its richness to what Santayana calls "hushed reverberations." Even without direct representation, natural materials — wood and stone — all have their funded associations for us. The "machine age" emphasis in the constructivists' mate-

* Philip Hendy: "Henry Moore," *Horizon,* September, 1941, vol. IV, no. 21, pp. 200-26.

rials was a limitation. Where associations existed they were usually of an impersonal, scientific or industrial character. For their esthetic effects the constructivists could look only to formal relations of a geometrical, architectural character. Calder, however, with similar materials found a means to give a new vitality to his structures, without compromising the nonrepresentational approach. Toys pointed the way. If one can enjoy certain qualities that predominate in a toy, such as unfamiliar rhythms and provocative surprise, why should these features not be embodied in more ambitious esthetic expressions — provided, of course, they are held in proper balance with form and material?

The result in Calder's work is the replacement of representational interests by a humor that stirs up no specific associations and no emotional recollections to distract the observer's attention from the work of art itself. Through this conscious infusion of a playful element, Calder has maintained an independence of the doctrinaire school of abstract art as well as of orthodox surrealism. At the same time the humor in his work is a protest against false seriousness in art and the self-importance of the advance-guard painter, as well as of the academician. From this viewpoint it is a genial development of certain aspects of the dada movement.

The apparent spontaneity of Calder's work is no accident. It is rather what John Dewey describes as "complete absorption in subject matter that is fresh, the freshness of which holds and sustains emotion . . . Staleness of matter and obtrusion of calculation are the two enemies of spontaneity of expression. Reflection, even long and arduous reflection, may have been concerned in the generation of the material. But an expression will nevertheless manifest spontaneity if that matter has been vitally taken up into a present experience."*

* John Dewey: *Art as Experience,*
p. 70.

Studio of the artist. Roxbury, Connecticut.

Early Years

Alexander Calder was born in Philadelphia July 22, 1898. His parents are both artists. His mother is a painter; his father, A. Stirling Calder, a National Academician and one of the outstanding sculptors of the older generation. His grandfather, Alexander Milne Calder, born in Scotland, was also a sculptor, best known perhaps for his equestrian statue of General Meade in Fairmount Park, Philadelphia and for his figure of William Penn on the dome of the Philadelphia City Hall.

Calder's early years were spent in an atmosphere of art. His parents' friends were artists. He grew up in a studio. He became familiar with the procedures of painting and sculpture while posing as a model now for his mother, now for his father. Still, art as a calling had very little appeal for him at the outset. The precedent of two generations made it seem unenterprising. Tools were his main early interest, not brushes and clay (below).

Tools and an evident mechanical ingenuity suggested engineering. From 1915 to 1919 he studied at Stevens Institute of Technology. The four following years were given over to engineering. Then, in 1921, some drafting work in an engineer's office awakened a dormant interest. Shortly afterwards he began to draw regularly at a Public Night School on East 42nd Street, New York. The work was elementary drawing in charcoal, but he was enthusiastic and seldom missed a night.

The following summer he worked his way on a freighter through the Panama Canal to California. In the autumn he took a job in a logging camp in the state of Washington. Once again the old interest stirred and he wrote his mother for painting materials. He came east in the fall of 1923 and enrolled in the School of the Art Students' League.

Self-Portrait. 1907. Crayon drawing. 6 x 9".

Circus drawings from the *National Police Gazette*. May 23, 1925.

Art Student and Illustrator: New York 1923-1926

During his first year at the League School he studied two or three months with Luks, one month with Du Bois, a month or so with Robinson, and every evening with John Sloan. At the same time he tried his hand at various types of free-lance work. In 1924 a job doing regular half-page spreads for the *National Police Gazette* provided a congenial opening. The drawings were not distinguished. Throughout the series, however, we already see hints of that humor and observation which mark his mature work. This is especially true of the captions. And one of his assignments opened up an interest which was to play a major role in his future development.

In the spring of 1925 Calder was given a two-week pass to cover the Circus. One performance was enough to fill his half-page (above). But every evening saw him back sketching in the menagerie tent. He made the acquaintance of Dexter Fellows, Barnum and Bailey's famous publicity manager, and his pass was renewed for the following year.

The first product of this experience was a small book, *Animal Sketching*, published the following spring. But this interest in the Circus was to have much more important consequences. Out

Calder with his circus.

The Aerialists.

The Oriental Dancer.

The Acrobats.

(Left) Duck on Differential Wheels. 11″ long. (Right) Red Horse and Green Sulky. 23″ long. 1926. Toys. Wire and wood.

of it was to grow his miniature circus which brought him into touch with some of the leaders in Paris at a time when their stimulation was most valuable to him. Still more important, this miniature circus was to serve as a laboratory in which some of the most original features of his later work were to be developed.

The year 1926 saw the exhibition of his first oils in The Artists' Gallery, on East 61st Street, New York. This exhibition brought him his first critical notice, a line by Murdock Pemberton in *The New Yorker:* "A. Calder is also a good bet." Yet he was by no means certain that he had found his medium. He wanted to do something of his own. But he was a sculptor's son and a sculptor's grandson. And a piece of oak fence-rail picked up that spring in Connecticut reluctantly took the shape of his first wood carving — the *Flattest Cat.*

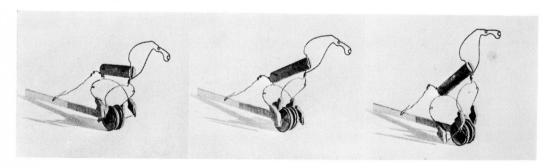

Galloping Horse. 1926. Toy. Wire, wood and leather. 21″ long.

14

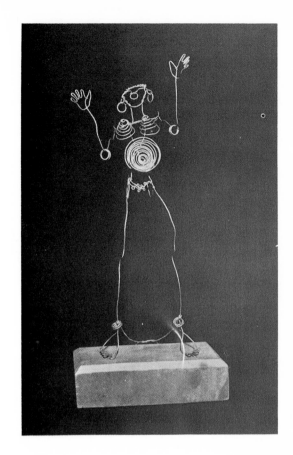

Josephine Baker. 1926. Brass wire. Ca. 28″ high. Private collection.

Calder's Circus: Paris 1926-1927

During his third year at the Art Students' League, the idea of Paris began to attract him. In late June he signed aboard the freighter, Galileo, for Hull, England. He spent three days in London; then, on to Paris. The father of a schoolmate from Stevens was practically his only acquaintance there. When he arrived he knew no older artists — only a fellow-student or two from the League. But in the autumn he met the English engraver, William Stanley Hayter. Hayter introduced him to the sculptor, José de Creeft. And Calder took up his experiments in carving again.

Spring and summer of 1927 also saw the beginning of his famous miniature circus and the production of several animated toys which de Creeft got him to exhibit that spring in the Paris Salon des Humoristes.

At the beginning the circus was merely a few ingenious figures which Calder had made for his own amusement. There was nothing elaborate about them: bits of articulated wire for arms and legs and a wooden body — a spool, or a cork (page 14). Still their creator could make them perform some most remarkable feats. Gradually the troupe increased. Word got round

15

Helen Wills. 1928. Wire. 14¾″ high.

Montparnasse. A casual turn or two to amuse a friend soon became a full-length performance.

The circus was given in Calder's narrow room; the guests would crowd onto the low studio bed; the performance would take place on the floor in front of them. A bit of green carpet was unrolled; a ring was laid out; poles were erected to support the trapeze for the aerial act and wing indicators of the "big top"; a spot-light was thrown on the ring; an appropriate record placed on a small portable phonograph; "Mesdames et Messieurs, je vous presente — ," and the performance began. There were acrobats, tumblers, trained dogs, slack-wire acts *à la japonaise;* a lion-tamer; a sword-swallower; Rigoulot, the strong-man; the Sultan of Senegambia who hurled knives and axes; Don Rodriguez Kolynos who risked a death-defying slide down a tight wire; "living statues"; a trapeze act; a chariot race: every classic feature of the tan-bark program (pages 12 and 13).

For the most part these toys were of a simplified marionette character. Yet they were astonishing in their condensed resemblance achieved almost entirely through movement. They were not mechanical. They had a living quality in their uncertainty. The dog might not succeed in jumping through the paper hoop. The bareback rider might not recover her balance. The aerialists might land in the net beneath, or might succeed in catching the swinging bars with their toes. The number of failures was uncertain; but an eventual success brought relief and restored equilibrium.

In turning to the circus Calder had adapted the time-honored tradition on which its performers based their routine. "Because the actual world, that in which we live, is a combination of movement and culmination, of breaks and reunions, the experience of a living creature is capable of esthetic quality. The live being recurrently loses and re-establishes equilibrium with his surroundings. The moment of passage from disturbance to harmony is that of intensest life . . .

16

Horse. 1928. Sheet brass. 10″ high.

Uncomfortable Face. 1928. Cocobolo wood. 21¼″ high.

17

Horse. 1928. Boxwood. 15½" high.

In a world made after the pattern of ours, moments of fulfillment punctuate experience with rhythmically enjoyed intervals . . . a world that is finished, ended, would have no traits of suspense and crisis, and would offer no opportunity for resolution. Where everything is already complete, there is no fulfillment."*

The circus had already taught Calder the esthetic of the unfinished, of suspense and surprise; it was on this he was to base all the most personal expressions of his later work.

In the spring of 1927 Marc Réal, a French artist, persuaded Legrand-Chabrier, one of the leading Paris critics of the circus, to visit Calder's room to view a performance. Legrand-Chabrier was amazed and charmed, and left to write an enthusiastic column on it in *Commoedia* conveying brilliantly the quality of Calder and his circus. Réal brought Gustave Fréjaville, another equally famous connoisseur of the circus. Word got to Hugier, the third of a great critical triumvirate. The news spread. Mary Butts, the English author of *Ashe of Rings,* brought Jean Cocteau over from the Champs Elysées to the Left Bank. Ramon Gomez de la Serna, the circus

* John Dewey: *Art as Experience,* p. 17.

authority of Madrid, and Sebastia Gasch, the Catalan art critic, caught up the story. Pascin and Hermine David urged Calder without success to hold a gallery exhibition of his *artistes*. Foujita arranged an elaborate performance of the circus in his atelier. Even Paul Fratellini, the eldest of the three famous clown brothers, came. He expressed such admiration for a rubber-hose dachshund whose legs, constructed of spokes of uneven lengths, made it wobble as it moved, that Calder presented him with a large scale model, "Miss Tamara," which Albert Fratellini led round on a leash in their act for several years.

The fame of Calder's circus spread quickly between the years 1927 and 1930. All the Paris art-world eventually came to know it. It brought him his first great personal success. But what was more important, the circus also provided the first steps in Calder's development as an original sculptor. Some of his tiny circus performers and animated toys had heads of wire as well as arms and legs. A friend, Clay Spohn, a painter, suggested that he make a whole figure of wire. The result was his first wire sculpture, *Josephine Baker* (page 15).

This was a new development. The tiny articulated circus-performers had taken a new scale and a new character. These figures were no longer merely toys wittily contrived from chance materials. They were now three-dimensional forms drawn in space by wire lines — much as if the background paper of a drawing had been cut away leaving only the lines. The same incisive grasp of essentials, the same nervous sensibility to form, and the same rhythmic organization of elements, which are virtues of a drawing, were virtues of this new medium.

Calder's earliest figures in wire still retained a certain flat frontality. In fact, the *Josephine Baker* suggests a decorative approach in which a promise of his later jewelry is already evident. But Calder's intuitive feeling for the possibilities of his medium quickly carried him into a convincing three-dimensionality. He began to mark essential planes by contour lines. He seemed to dissociate physical form from the completed mental concept of it. His figures were like peelings of form without weight or density. He made space intervene as a constructive factor (*Acrobats*, page 21). Through his naive approach he had hit upon a combination of draughtsmanship and metal construction that already had much in common with the open-form of the constructivists about 1920 and of individual researchers such as Lipchitz about 1927.

Double Cat. 1929. Wood. 4′ 3″ long.

19

Shark Sucker. 1930. Norwegian wood. 31½" long.

Wire and Wood: New York, Paris, Berlin 1927-1930

In April, 1928 Calder had his first one-man show, at the Weyhe Gallery in New York. This was made up principally of wire caricatures such as *Helen Wills* (page 16) or *The Hostess* and caricatural portraits of many well-known public figures of the day. His technical ability had increased remarkably. But such calligraphic humor in wire was still difficult to accept for those who were accustomed to regard sculpture as an interpretation of mass. His father was interested and only gently critical. His personal viewpoint did not lead him to discourage an independent one in his son, no matter how foreign to his own aims the latter's might seem to be. He liked to be able "to fondle sculpture." His only objection to this wiry kind was that it lacked the appeal to the sense of touch.

The three-dimensional character of Calder's wire sculptures, however, had developed steadily since his 1926 *Josephine Baker*. Possibly his experiments in wood carving, begun before leaving for Paris and now taken up with fresh enthusiasm, were a factor in this. In any case, the variety of woods, exotic and humble, which he has employed in his relatively limited wood sculpture production reveal his keen interest in materials. Both the texture and the form of a piece of wood appealed to him. They spoke to him and he followed their suggestions.

His first efforts at wood carving on his return to New York, in 1928, were mainly in low relief. But very quickly, as he allowed the natural form of a lump of wood to guide him, he developed a strong sense for three-dimensional conceptions as in *Uncomfortable Face* (page 17), *Camel*, or *Cow*. And the imagination with which he adapted the peculiarities of his materials was to provide an increasingly richer source of form from his austere *Horse* in weathered boxwood of 1928 (page 18) through *Shark Sucker* (above) down to his Martian phantasy, *Apple Monster*, in the late thirties (page 41).

20

Acrobats. 1929. Wire. Ca. 27″ high. Private collection.

Portrait of Shepard Vogelgesang. 1930. Wire. Ca. 15″ high. Collection Shepard Vogelgesang, New York.

21

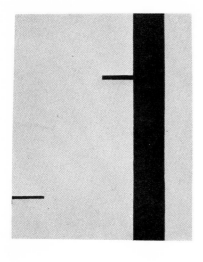

(Left) Composition. 1930. Oil on canvas. 22 x 19″. (Right) Composition. 1930. Oil on canvas. 18 x 27″.

A few weeks after the opening of his exhibition at Weyhe's, Calder again caught public attention at the Independents in New York with his *Romulus and Remus* group, a fantastic ten-foot long, copper-wire she-wolf nursing a pair of wire youngsters from a row of pendent door-stops. In November Calder left once more for Paris, to remain there until June of the following year.

Calder had now achieved a certain recognition, but primarily as a humorist. He had left painting for a form of wire-drawing in space. He had come to an easy mastery of this medium and in doing so had broken away to some degree from the conventional path. But he realized that wire sculpture had its limitations as an expression.

Up to this time his associations in Paris had been mainly among the less serious members of the Paris art world. He had arrived there knowing none of the leaders. Neither the *croquis* sessions of the Grand Chaumière nor the terrace of the Dôme had brought him much closer. The success of his circus and his wire sculpture in New York had come easily out of something natural to him. But in facing the problems of three-dimensional composition and the discipline of harder materials he had taken the first step in a new direction. The results, however, were not to appear until considerably later. Certain other factors had still to make their contribution; notably, a new group of associations in Paris among fellow-artists who were also searching for fresh ways to give the inherited traditions new life.

22

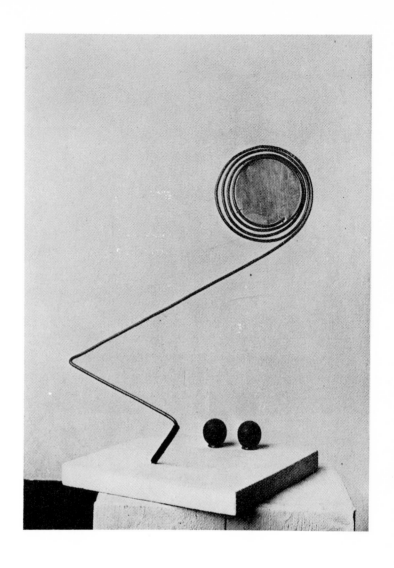

Kiki's Nose. 1931. Stabile. Brass wire, tin. Ca. 18″ high. Private collection, Paris.

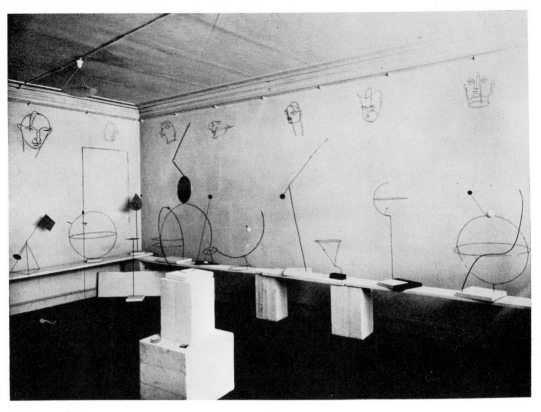

Calder exhibition. Galerie Percier. Paris, April, 1931.

Before Calder's return to Paris in November, 1928 a friend suggested that he should make the acquaintance there of the Catalan painter, Joan Miro, and promised to write him. One evening about New Year's, when Calder was showing the circus to some American friends in his studio, Miro dropped in. Calder decided to repay the call and eventually found his way over to Miro's studio in Montmartre. Most of Miro's pictures were away at the time on exhibit in Brussels. There were only a few of his constructions in the studio — such as his 1928 *Spanish Dancer,* a feather fixed with a large colored pin to a bare cardboard ground. Calder "didn't understand his stuff"; nevertheless out of this meeting grew a friendship that was to be very valuable to Calder during the next ten years.

Another afternoon Calder was sitting on the terrace of the Dôme with Kuniyoshi. Pascin happened by. Kuniyoshi introduced them. Pascin had seen Calder's exhibition at Weyhe's in New York and had liked it. The sensibility of the wire forms had appealed to him as a draughtsman. Calder arranged a small party shortly afterwards and invited Pascin. Hermine David was having a *vernissage* the same day. Pascin arrived from the *vernissage* bringing all present — about forty.

24

In January Calder had an exhibition at the Galerie Billiet. Pascin wrote the preface. The same month, in the Salon des Indépendants, he exhibited a new, over life-size figure, *Spring,* described by Paul Fierens as *sculpture à claire-voie,* or "openwork" sculpture. The Billiet exhibition proved Calder to be already an accomplished technician in a limited field. His ability to handle wire had brought him to an advanced point in open sculptural composition. His only serious fault was the frequency with which he still allowed the illustrator's spirit and two-dimensional technique to dominate his work. But in portrait heads, such as that of *Shepard Vogelgesang* (page 21) finished shortly before he left New York, a better balance between representation and structure had already begun to appear. And this newly acquired grasp of three-dimensional form becomes increasingly evident in similar portraits of Fernand Léger, Amédée Ozenfant, Kiki, the famous model, and others completed on returning to France.

In April, 1929 Calder exhibited some wood sculptures and wire caricatures in Berlin at the Neumann-Nierendorf Gallery. And during his stay in Berlin he made his first piece of jewelry for a woman painter, Chantal Quenneville: a collar with a projecting horizontal wire-beam from which a wire fly dangled.

On his return to New York Calder had an exhibition of wood and wire sculpture, paintings and textile designs at the Fifty-sixth Street Galleries. At the same time in an adjoining room was exhibited a private collection of eighteenth century caged mechanical-birds that twit-

Illustrations for *Fables of Aesop,* according to Sir Roger L'Estrange, Paris, 1931.

Dancing Torpedo Shape. 1932. Motorized mobile. Wood, iron
wire, aluminum. 32½″ high. Berkshire Museum, Pittsfield,
Massachusetts.

tered. That year Calder designed his first wire goldfish bowls, through which wire fish were
made to swim back and forth by the turning of a tiny crank. Once again an animal rhythm
had caught his eye. This time it was composed within a framed three-dimensional space.
The result was a sort of music-box with visual rhythms. Its structure was still based on his
articulated toys and circus devices. But now for the first time in his work we have a composition of movements bound to an immobile base, its primary purpose to satisfy an esthetic sense
through rhythm. This was to be the basic principle of his mobiles three years later.

Since the spring of 1927 when Legrand-Chabrier first described Calder's circus in *Commoedia*
its reputation had constantly spread. Just before his return to New York he had given several
farewell performances in his studio. Legrand-Chabrier again attended and again wrote it up
even more enthusiastically. The troupe had practically doubled since he had last seen it. Fréjaville came, and Fuzier. And when Calder returned to Paris in March of 1930 all those painters
who had not seen the circus, had heard of it and were at any rate inquisitive. Varèse brought
Kiesler and Jean Painlevé to a performance one evening. Another evening, Kiesler brought
Léger, the critic Carl Einstein, Théo van Doesburg and Mondrian. In those days Calder was
still unfamiliar with such names. But a neighbor, an American abstract painter, William Einstein,
was well acquainted with the researches and personalities of contemporary art. The evening
Kiesler brought Mondrian, Einstein was in charge of the phonograph. He recognized Mondrian
and afterward explained to Calder who he was. His enthusiasm warmed Calder to a visit to
Mondrian's studio.

26

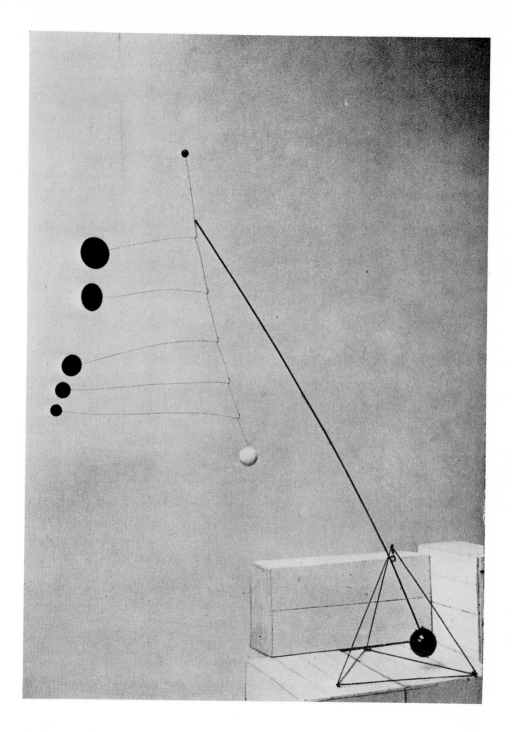

Calderberry Bush. 1932. Mobile. Steel wire and rod, sheet aluminum and wood. 7′ high. Private collection, New York.

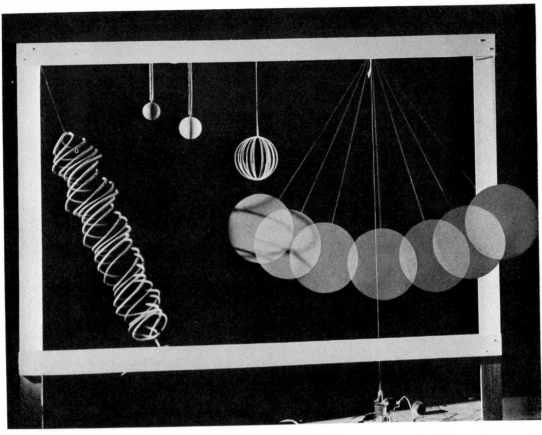

White Frame. 1934. Motorized mobile. Wood panel, wire and sheet metal. 7′ 6″ x 9″.

Abstract Stabiles: The Influence of Mondrian, 1920

The visit to Mondrian was to mark the turning which led to all Calder's most characteristic future developments. It was what gave him, as he described it, "the necessary shock." Mondrian's large, light, irregular studio was like one of his own pictures — or a spatial translation of one. The immaculate white walls were composed by removable rectangles of red, blue and yellow; the red cube of a phonograph accented the spacious calm of the central room. Calder afterwards recalled how exciting the first view was to him, "with a cross light (there were windows on both sides), and I thought at the time how fine it would be if everything there moved; though Mondrian himself did not approve of this idea at all. I went home and tried to paint. But wire, or something to twist or tear, or bend is an easier medium for me to think in."*

* "Mobiles," *The Painter's Object,* edited by Myfanwy Evans, see Bibl. 3.

This revived interest in painting lasted barely three weeks. But from the character it took (page 22) one sees at once the consequence of his encounter with Mondrian's work, not a return to painting but a very evident turn from representational interests to abstract composition. And the step taken after this visit to Mondrian's studio was never to be retraced. When Calder returned to Paris after his marriage in January, 1931, he began to broaden his acquaintances among the admirers of Mondrian. Through his compatriot, William Einstein, he met Hans Arp and Jean Hélion. Théo van Doesburg, the founder of the de Stijl group, had come with Kiesler the year before to a presentation of the circus. Now Hélion and Arp prevailed on Calder to join van Doesburg's newly founded Paris group of nonrepresentational artists, Abstraction-Création. The interests of his new associates were quite different from those of his earlier Paris days. And when his exhibition at the Galerie Percier took place, we find him self-consciously apologizing for the inclusion of a row of some of his finest wire portraits which Mendes-France, the director of the gallery, urged him to show (page 24). On the back of a photograph of the exhibition Calder wrote: "Pay no attention to the portraits, the gallery insisted that I include them."

The paintings Calder undertook after his visit with Mondrian were exercises. But the sculpture which was exhibited at the Galerie Percier shows a full assimilation of his experiences; "Simple things," as Calder described them, "ranged on a plank against a wall." But he is perfectly justified in stating: "In a way, some of those things were as plastic as anything I have done."*

* Bibl. 3.

A Universe. 1934. Motorized mobile. Pipe, wire and wood. 40½" high. The Museum of Modern Art, New York.

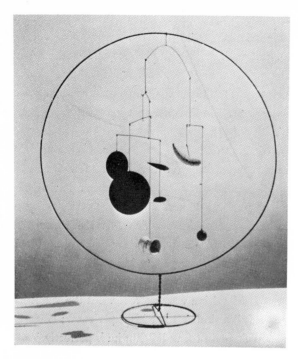

Agnes' Circle. 1934. Mobile. Steel wire, rod and sheet aluminum. 36″ high. Collection Miss Agnes Rindge, Poughkeepsie, New York.

It was to this type of stationary abstract sculpture that Arp, a few months later, gave the name "stabiles."

Another consequence of Calder's visit to Mondrian was the introduction of color into his sculpture. While draughtsmanship was an essential feature of his early wire sculpture, his new work had been obviously affected by painting. The tiny spheres and disks of the "volumes, vectors and densities," as Calder described the objects in the Percier exhibition, were painted strong blues, reds and blacks. These showed up strikingly against the whitened wires and the dead white bases of the constructions.

To take such a step into the abstract field was an extremely serious departure for an artist in Calder's position at the time. He had already established himself in the public mind as a humorist — a talented and witty one. He had built up a reputation and a certain patronage. Now those who had enjoyed what he had previously done so well were left completely at a loss. Fernand Léger wrote the preface to the Percier exhibition catalog. He opened his introduction with the question: "Eric Satie illustrated by Calder, why not? He is serious without seeming to be." and closed with the statement: "Before these new works, transparent, objective, exact, I think of Satie, Mondrian, Marcel Duchamp, Brancusi, Arp; those incontestable masters of reticent and silent beauty. Calder is of that line. He is an American 100%. Satie and Duchamp

Steel Fish. 1934. Mobile. Iron, sheet steel, steel rod, sheet aluminum. 10' high. Collection Philip L. Goodwin, New York.

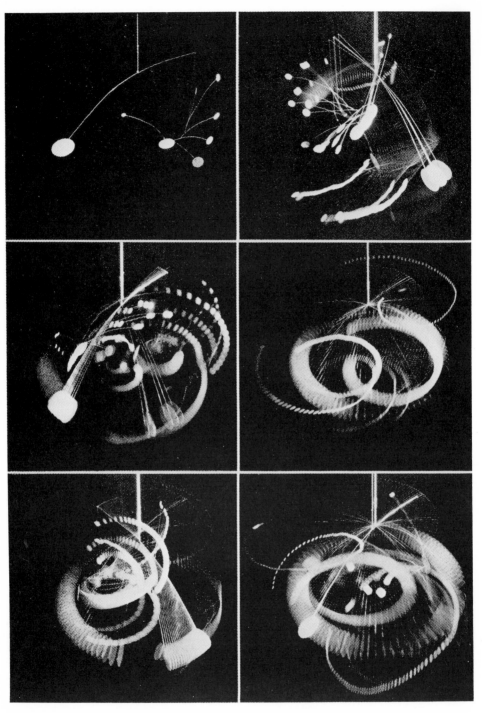

Hanging Mobile. 1936. Aluminum, steel wire. Ca. 28″ wide. Collection Mrs. Meric Callery, Paris. Still (upper left) and in motion.

32

are 100% French. Yet we meet." Some critics picked up Léger's line in the catalog introduction, "he is serious without seeming to be." They asked, why be serious if this is the result when it is so easy for Calder to be gracefully amusing? Others who knew him only as a humorist, felt this was merely some elaborate joke. But the effect of Mondrian's work had made up Calder's mind. He had half-consciously felt that his representational work in wire had its limitations. When he saw what Mondrian had achieved, he realized how close to convention his naturalistic and caricatural drawings remained even when translated into wire. Abstract composition was the field he had been looking for. To enter it he would have to leave the other behind. Those who enjoyed his earlier work might follow him if they cared to. It was not for him to stay with them.

Still the naturalistic draughtsman in Calder was by no means superseded by the abstract constructor. In the summer of 1931, he produced some of his finest graphic work and a masterpiece of American book illustration, the *Fables of Aesop* for Harrison of Paris (page 25).

The First Mobiles: Manual and Motor, 1930-31

In the Galerie Percier exhibition Calder had not yet undertaken to incorporate movement into abstract design. But to realize his original idea, that Mondrian's rectangles ought to be made to oscillate or vibrate, Calder had available all the technical experience of his animated toys and circus devices. His 1929 mechanical goldfish bowl had since led to several other variations of the original. For them he had worked out a technique of simple mechanical devices for controlling a patterned rhythm of moving objects within a fixed frame. Now he again took up the problem of motion. At first he limited himself to a slight rhythmic movement in a single object fixed to a base. Then the idea struck him of making "two or more objects find actual relations in space" (*Dancing Torpedo Shape,* page 26).

This was the first feature of his new approach: the organization of contrasting movements and changing relations of form in space. This was also the point at which Calder went beyond anything the Russian constructivists had realized in mobile sculpture. For Gabo's *Kinetic Sculpture* of 1920 offered only the rhythmic swing of a single erect element — a weighted flexible perpendicular, fixed to a base. In Calder's mobile sculptures of 1931, small spheres of different sizes painted in contrasting primary colors were moved up and down thin curved wires at contrasting rates of speed, as in *A Universe,* 1934 (page 29). Various geometrical shapes were made to turn rhythmically about creating constantly changing relations of forms. Some of the constructions were driven by small electric motors, others were moved by tiny hand cranks.

The shapes employed were still strictly geometrical, like those of his stationary abstract arrangements of the Galerie Percier exhibition. In his work of this period he had put aside organic forms as completely as the constructivists had. But for all their geometrical forms and mechanical movements these new constructions had a living quality and spirit of humor about them that went back to the wit and observation of his wire sculptures and the gaiety of his circus and animated toys.

33

Gibraltar. 1937. Stabile. Lignum vitae, plank walnut and steel rod. 28⅝" high.

In these new constructions Calder had managed to give abstract forms the movements which he had mimicked from nature in his toys. The surprise and charm of his circus performers and toys lay in their striking truth to characteristic human and animal movements. This was the source of life and variety in their rhythms. In the toys he had parodied a duck dragging a recalcitrant worm out of the ground: now in the mobiles the hammer motion of the duck's head and beak was reduced to the simplest form of mechanical movement. He had begun with natural movements — the galloping of a horse (page 14), the seductive wriggles of his Oriental dancer (page 13), the frenzied trot of the circus stretcher-bearers — now he was dealing with motion not in any representational frame of reference, but for its own sake. Form had been reduced to its geometrical bases, motion had followed suit. Calder felt that to combine two or more simple movements with contrasting rates of speed gave the best effect because, while simple, they are capable of infinite combinations. He had left synthesis for essence; he had come from the naturalistic to the abstract. Still these movements had kept a liveliness and variety, perhaps due to the fact that their indirect inspiration was a caricature of nature not the bare rhythms of a machine.

Whale. 1937. Stabile. Sheet steel. 6' 6" high. On extended loan by the artist to The Museum of Modern Art, New York.

And, as a consequence of this underlying parody of human and animal movements, these machines had, perhaps, a closer relationship with dada and futurism than with constructivism. The resemblance between Calder's Galerie Percier "volumes, vectors and densities" and early constructivist work was evident. But while constructivism was a calculated, unemotional expression, dada was a laughing iconoclasm based on the belief that a healthy art could only flourish if the conventional trappings and false seriousness of art were stripped away. Dada was an outgrowth of Italian futurism. The futurists had preached the importance of incorporating movement as an esthetic factor. Art had too long been static. The modern world was a world of movement. Modern art should embody it. Duchamp and Picabia, in their interest in the representation of movement and the satirical use of machine forms, effected a link between futurism and dada in such work as Duchamp's *The King and Queen Crossed by Swift Nudes* and Picabia's *The Infant Carburetor*. The spirit of Calder's new machines was certainly closer to such work than to that of the Russians. His humor was more genial. But humor took the place of subject matter with Calder, just as a less innocent type of humor was that of the dadaists. The link becomes even closer in the term, "mobile," which had perhaps its first esthetic application about 1917 in Duchamp's notes for *La Mariée mise à nue par ses célibataires, même*. And when Calder, shortly before the Galerie Vignon exhibition, asked Duchamp to suggest a name for the new constructions Duchamp without hesitation proposed "mobiles."

Dancers and Sphere. 1936. Motorized mobile. Wood, steel wire, sheet aluminum. 17¾" high.

36

Swizzle Sticks. 1936. Mobile. Plywood panel, wire, wood, lead. 48 x 33″. Collection Mr. and Mrs. James Thrall Soby, New York.

Wind Mobiles, 1932

Such motor-driven or hand-cranked mobiles had the advantage of a power to control their performance and superimpose movements in the fashion of a ballet's choreography (*Dancing Torpedo Shape,* page 26). This, however, meant a set pattern. And Calder soon began to feel it a restriction: without complicated mechanisms, such controlled patterns ran the risk of becoming monotonous in their repetitions. A free natural movement would be more desirable in many ways. What might be sacrificed in formal patterns, would be made up for in rhythmic variety. Unpredictability of movement would give a greater sense of life. Chinese wind bells were made to please the ear with their tinkling tunes by a gust of air. Why should the wind not be enlisted to please the eye with rhythmically swinging sculptural forms — and for that matter to entertain the ear with their jangling?

The result was Calder's first wind-mobile, begun shortly after his Galerie Vignon exhibition. And this was the principle on which most of his future mobiles were to be based. It is true that some of his most ambitious motorized mobiles, the *White Frame* (page 28) and the *Black Box,* were produced in 1934 and 1935. Still his motorized production after 1933 was principally limited to colored wall panels against which various forms were made to describe rhythmic patterns (*Little Blue Panel* and *Orange Panel*). With his wind-mobiles movements and rhythms became more relaxed, more free — took an air of spontaneity. Little by little, chance began to play a larger part in their rhythms — eventually even in their constituent elements.

Free Forms in Free Movement: Friendship with Miro

Perhaps this reawakening of fantasy came out of a closer intimacy with Miro. Their friendship had grown steadily since their first meeting; and Calder's difficulty in responding to Miro's painting had long since disappeared. Miro at the same time had become an enthusiastic admirer of Calder's work. In August, 1932 Calder returned to Paris by way of Spain and visited Miro on his farm at Montroig, near Barcelona. The following January at Miro's suggestion Gomez de la Serna, Spain's leading circus critic, invited Calder to Madrid to present his circus during an exhibition of his work at the Residencia de Estudiantes; and Miro arranged an exhibition for him through the Amics de l'Art Nou in Barcelona. Later that spring Calder exhibited with Miro, Hélion, Pevsner, Seligmann and Arp at the Galerie Pierre in Paris. Miro's work at that time had probably touched its most abstract point. And we can recognize a definite affinity between the forms in Miro's and Arp's work of this period and Calder's which has had persistent echoes in his work even to the present day. Miro had long ago broken with the surrealist group. His fantasy, however, had by no means dried up at the separation. And Miro's fantasy as well as his sly, gnomish, yet robust humor had come to appeal very deeply to Calder.

It is likely that this new interest in chance rhythms and chance forms on Calder's part owed much to Miro. However, it is obvious from Calder's earlier approach to wood carving that he could scarcely hold happily with Mondrian's creed: "In the new art, forms are neutral . . . The

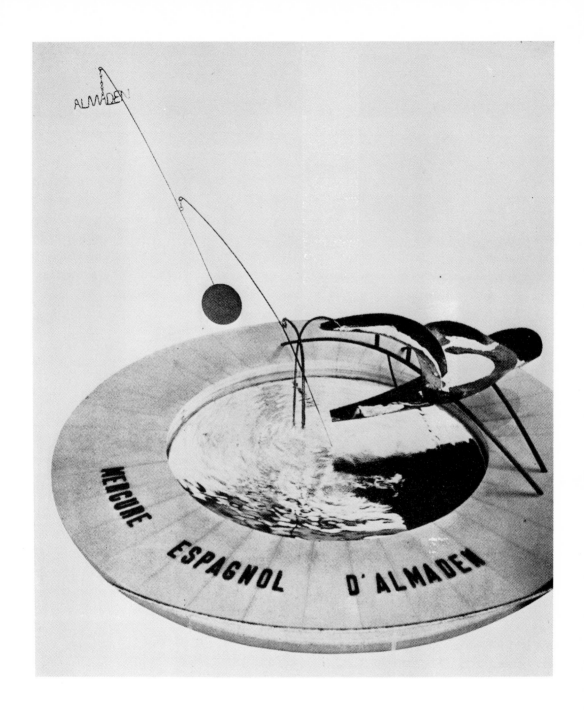

Mercury Fountain. Spanish Pavilion, Paris Exposition, 1937. Steel rod and sheet steel surfaced with pitch. 8′ 6″ high.

new art effort suppresses the subject and the particularized form."* The richness of natural forms meant too much to him. His late severely geometrical forms had taken first a freer modeling; then little by little calculated forms gave way to forms suggested by the material — a lump of wood, a piece of bone — till finally the materials employed seemed scarcely touched by tools. At the same time, chance rhythms had come to supplant patterned rhythms. By 1934, the novice stage of his work was over. The geometrical cycle opened by the shock of Mondrian's studio was completed. The organic cycle was now beginning; and with it a search for new suggestions from new materials for both static and mobile sculpture, and for a new sculpture in space.

Return to America, 1933

Up to this time Calder's work had been intimate studio expressions. With the return to the United States in the summer of 1933 there began to develop a feeling for increased scale. The confined studio quarters of Montparnasse had given place to the open countryside of Connecticut. The dimensions of his sculpture seemed to respond to the scale of his new environment.

* Piet Mondrian, *L'Art nouveau de la vie nouvelle*, 1931. See bibl. 26. p. 13.

Tight Rope. 1937. Mobile. Ebony, steel rods and wire, lead weights. 9′ 3½″ long.

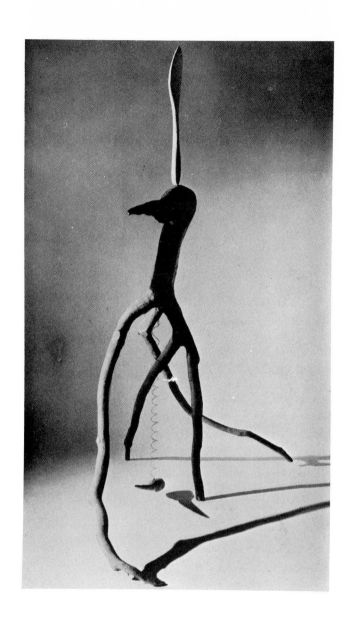

Apple Monster. 1938. Stabile. Apple branch, wire spring. 5′ 7″ high.

Lobster Trap and Fish Tail. Mobile. 1939. Steel wire and sheet aluminum. Ca. 15′ long. The Museum of Modern Art, New York.

Before leaving Paris Calder had produced a large motorized composition entitled the *Red Frame*. Its size and construction made it difficult to ship. But shortly after settling in Roxbury he produced another composition along the same lines, *White Frame,* the largest motorized mobile he had yet realized (page 28). And the same year, 1934, saw his first outdoor mobile, *Steel Fish* (page 31), set up on the hill behind his farmhouse at Roxbury.

On first abandoning mechanical rhythms for free rhythms he had tended to see his forms as two dimensional compositions, for example, the *Calderberry Bush,* 1932 (page 27). But just as Calder's wire sculpture, predominantly two-dimensional at the outset, came to suggest transparent volumes, such large-scale, free-swinging mobiles as the *Steel Fish* now began to describe, with gestures

42

Spherical Triangle. 1939. Mobile. Sheet steel and steel rods. 8' high.

Thirteen Spines. 1940. Mobile. Steel sheet, rods, wire and aluminum. 7′ high.

44

Black Beast. 1940. Stabile. Sheet steel. 8′ 9″ high.

like a dancer, volumes in space. These are most graphically recorded for us by multiflash photography (page 32).

In realizing these gesture compositions of virtual volumes through his mobiles, Calder had carried the transparency of his early wire sculpture beyond the transparency of the constructivists' work. And in hanging his mobile elements free, he had given them a far greater opportunity "to find actual relationships in space" than he had provided in his most ingenious motorized mobiles of the Galerie Vignon.

Calder's love of the spectacular had always been keen. This was evident from certain features of his circus and such a tour de force as *Romulus and Remus*. In 1935 and 1936 Miss Martha Graham recognized the dramatic possibilities of his mobile panels and had several enlarged to serve as "plastic interludes" during the performances by her dance group at Bennington and in

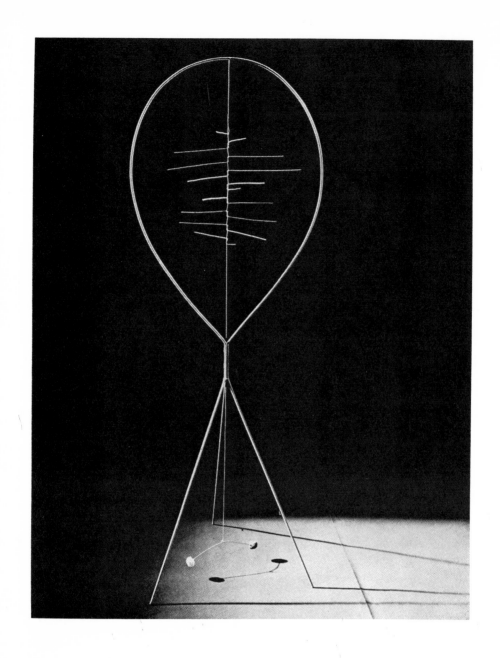

Hour Glass. 1941. Mobile. Steel rod and wire. 5′ high.

46

New York. In 1936 he also fulfilled Fernand Léger's query of 1931 "Eric Satie illustrated by Calder, why not?" by designing a setting for a production of Satie's *Socrate* at the Wadsworth Atheneum in Hartford.

At the same time, during these years, 1933 to 1937, Calder was consistently extending his interests in unconventional materials and unusual uses of familiar ones. The contrasts of porcelain, wood and metal in *Agnes' Circle* (page 30) had led to similar oppositions of material in free-swinging mobiles. String, though perishable, allowed a greater freedom of movement than wire (*Swizzle Sticks,* page 37). Rough wood was contrasted with carefully planed wood forms, dainty spheres and disks of metal (*Gibraltar,* page 34). Heavy crudely-cut blocks were contrasted with light wire figures that danced at the slightest breath of air (*Tight Rope,* page 40). Glass and polished metal were exploited for their luminous effects.

The conscious avoidance of technical "finish" in Calder's work was always one of its qualities. In his sculpture it offers an equivalence to the nervous quality of a line in drawing. The larger lines of the total form provide the discipline or framework. This is always carefully worked out and respected. Within it the rough, unfinished elements provide a detail interest — a subordinate textural variety which gives a living quality to many of the materials he employs which, if "finished," would have no life. This "unfinished" quality within a dominant structural unity is

Cockatoo. 1941. Mobile. Sheet steel and wire. 36¼″ high. Collection Mr. and Mrs. C. Earle Miller, Downingtown, Pennsylvania.

Red Petals. 1942. Mobile. Sheet steel and wire, sheet aluminum. 9′ 2″ high. The Arts Club, Chicago.

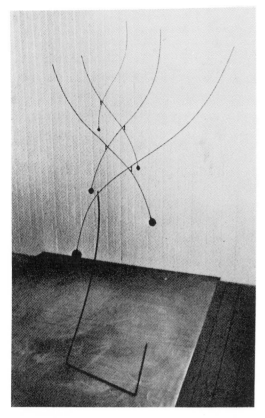

Little Tree. 1942. Mobile. Steel wire, rods
and disks. Ca. 27″ high. Collection Edgar
Kaufmann, Jr. Pittsburgh, Pennsylvania.

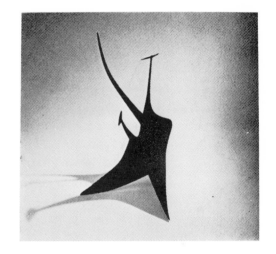

Black Thing. 1942. Stabile. Sheet steel. 31¼″
high. Private collection, New York.

189815

the formal equivalent of the recurrent failure of his circus performers to achieve their feats — the
equestrienne to recover her balance on the horse's back or the aerialist to catch the swinging bar.
But these rough effects, like the circus performers' failures, must eventually be tied together by
the satisfaction of the main form. They provide the features of "disturbance" out of which
harmony is resolved in the main design.

There was, however, some danger that his often casual technique and lack of "finish" might
be carried too far. But now Calder's new work at larger pieces after his return to the United
States required greater technical care. This in no way conflicted with his maintenance of a lack
of "finish," where such a lack was a quality. The increase in scale merely made it necessary to
pay greater heed to structural problems (*Whale,* page 35).

The Mercury Fountain, 1937

In April, 1937 Calder returned to France for a visit. Paris, at the time, was in the midst of preparations for its Exposition of that year. An opportunity on the Exposition grounds gave Calder a chance to draw full advantage from his three years research in large-scale sculpture in the United States and his increased knowledge of showmanship.

Miro and Picasso were preparing mural decorations for the Spanish Pavilion. Miro had introduced Calder to the architects of the Pavilion, José Luis Sert and Luis Lacasa. One of the principal Spanish exhibits was to be mercury from the mines of Almaden in the southwest of Spain, one of the important objectives of Rebel attacks at the time. A fountain which would spout mercury was being constructed in Barcelona. But from photographs sent from Spain the architects felt it would neither harmonize with the Miro and Picasso murals, nor with the architecture of the Pavilion. Sert who knew Calder's work and admired it suggested that he design another to be used in its stead.

The result was one of the most outstanding successes of the Exposition (page 39). Unaware of the artist's nationality, André Beucler, the author of a comprehensive review of the Fair in the *Arts et Métiers Graphiques* wrote:

In this field of plastic expression, Spain has realized a masterpiece: the mercury fountain. The exploitation of the mercury of Almaden is an important industry for Spain. There would have been many ways to make this theme tedious. They could have explained the nature of this metal, its properties, they could have exhibited it with all the trappings apparently due to precious things (as was done for the Belgian diamonds) but, true artists, the Spaniards concentrated on one thing only: on the beauty of the mercury in its mysterious fluidity. The architects of the Spanish Pavilion, L. Lacasa and José Luis Sert therefore designed a fountain, a simple basin, in the center of which a strange construction of black iron, graceful and precise like a great insect, allowed the mercury to flow slowly, to collect itself into a mass, to scatter, to roll from time to time in melting pearls, to play perpetually by itself, to the delight of the public which was present for the first time at the delicate spectacle of mercury moving in a fountain. *

In concluding the writer adds, "It should be observed in this connection the powerful attraction which every animated presentation exercises on the public."

Glass and polished steel, Calder was told, were the only materials which would withstand the corrosive effects of mercury. Neither satisfied him. Neither afforded sufficient color-contrast to the mercury. But the concrete basin for the fountain was lined with pitch. Pitch, then, would resist corrosion. And pitch afforded the greatest possible color contrast to the mercury: the metal structure was painted black and lined with pitch.

Due to the weight of the mercury and the loss in splashing, Calder was allowed to spill it only from a height of little more than a yard. To give the whole design more height and to introduce a further element of mobility Calder hung a rod vertically from the top of the structure by a ring at its center of balance. The lower end of this rod was widened into a plate of irregular

* Bibl. 11.

50

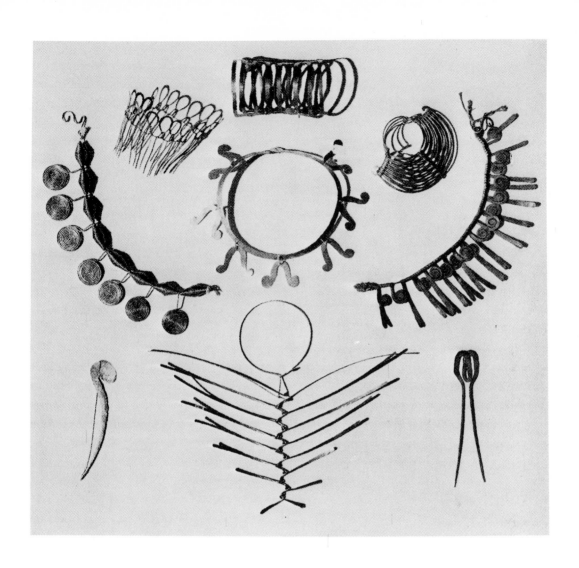

Jewelry. 1940-41. Brass wire, silver wire.

Horizontal Spines. 1942. Mobile. Steel sheet, wire and rods, and sheet aluminum. 4′ 5″ high. Collection Addison Gallery, Phillips Academy, Andover, Massachusetts.

form and was set so that the stream of mercury leaving the chute would strike it and cause the rod to sway. From the upper end of this rod a lighter, free-swinging rod was hung; at its tip was suspended the name of the mines, Almaden, in brass wire.

The *Mercury Fountain* was a key-point in the evolution of Calder's art. Here all the important threads of his work up to this point were drawn together. The spirit of play won the public to it as to a glorified mechanical toy. It had a technician's structure, in which both the engineer and the artist in Calder collaborated. Movement and the changing relations of form in space were there; new effects through new materials; an outdoor scale; a fixed construction to which a mobile arm related the lines and forms it described by its movements. All were bound together in a three-dimensional unity of open form over the circular, concrete basin: an ambitious and deeply personal realization. With it Calder achieved the first full mastery of his new idiom. He now had the assurance to speak out boldly in the future.

New Ventures: 1937-43

The winter of 1937 Calder spent in England. An exhibition of his work was held at the Mayor Gallery in London. But the spring of 1938, in Roxbury, already saw the fruits of this new-won confidence. His large *Apple Monster* (page 41) shows greater freedom in following the suggestions of his material on an increased scale. His motorized panels now took a frank ballet character in several instances, with even a proscenium arrangement in one on which chunky wooden forms were fixed. In the *Spherical Triangle* (page 43) he carried the relationship of large black sheet-iron forms from the static character of *Whale* into the mobile field.

In November, 1938 a retrospective exhibition of his work was held at the George Walter Vincent Smith Art Gallery of Springfield, Massachusetts. Eighty-four items were included, from his earliest wire and wood sculpture, water-colors and drawings to several large mobiles and stabiles of that autumn.

Spiny. 1942. Stabile. Sheet aluminum. 26″ high.

53

Vertical Constellation with Yellow Bone.
1943. Stabile. Steel wire and wood. 23¼"
high.

Wall Constellation with Red Object. 1943. Stabile.
Steel wire and wood. 25¾" high.

The following spring, for the 1939 New York World's Fair, he designed a fountain display which he described as a "water ballet."* The dance was to be performed by fourteen forty-foot jets of water thrown up by revolving nozzles. It was punctuated by "water bombs" or isolated bursts of water which fell back into the basin of the fountain with an explosive sound. The entire performance, which should have lasted five minutes, was patterned on a complex choreographic schedule. Unfortunately, he did not receive the same sympathetic cooperation from the New York engineers in charge that he had in Paris. Although the necessary equipment was installed, a failure to follow the stipulated timing destroyed the possibilities of rhythmic variation and defeated the ballet effect.

Throughout this period, however, his mobiles lost none of their rhythmical freedom as is evidenced by the inexhaustible shadow-play of the large *Lobster Trap and Fish Tail* (page 42)

* Bibl. 62.

54

Morning Star. 1943. Stabile. Sheet steel, steel wire and wood. 6′ 7″ high.

which revolves in the Museum of Modern Art stair-well. Nor did the scale of his stabiles cease to grow. The dull black, riveted sheet-steel structures initiated with the *Whale* now lost their curvilinear contours for the predominantly sharp-angle forms of the *Black Beast* (page 45). Even the free-swinging elements moved with a slow, menacing heaviness in pieces like his 1940 *Black Petals*.

In December, 1940 the first exhibition solely devoted to his jewelry was held at the Willard Gallery, New York. For years he had been making occasional pieces as gifts for his friends. At first they were mainly designed in brass wire. This was either twisted into patterns somewhat reminiscent of Bronze Age ornaments in their simplicity and directness of technique, or into humorous naturalistic forms, or stylized monograms. The technique at the outset was clearly related to that of his first wire sculpture, *Josephine Baker*. But soon the twisted wire was hammered into flat strips which allowed a greater variety of effects and uses. The humorous and naturalistic treatment became less frequent. Pebbles, bits of colored glass or weathered bones were incorporated, cabochon fashion. Silver and gold wire came to be used more commonly than brass (page 51).

The beauty of his jewelry lies primarily in its decorative linear qualities. Nevertheless just as its technique and its linearism had roots in Calder's early wire sculptures, the grace of its lines and the fantasy of its forms had their echo in a new departure in Calder's constructions of 1941 and 1942. Perhaps this was in part a reaction from the overpowering, grim, black, sharp-angle forms of the previous year. But in any case, with the year 1941 we see a distinct turn from the more massive phase which Calder had just gone through, to one of gay colors and slender forms as in *Yucca*. Where the dull black tone is still retained we have a delicacy of formal elements closely reminiscent of jewelry forms. And the fantasy of some of the finest jewelry has its larger realization in mobiles such as the *Cockatoo* (page 47), or the delicate mobile bars of the *Hour Glass* (page 46).

Then, in 1942, we see in the stabiles a return to the more solid curvilinear forms of 1937 and 1940 (*Spiny*, page 53), but with a new grace inherited from the preceding season. At the same time his mobiles reveal an even fresher fantasy, echoing evident features of his jewelry (*Horizontal Spines*, page 52).

Compositional organization of three-dimensional space through new means, was the problem to which Calder as a sculptor was always returning. The scarcity of materials due to the war possibly caused him in 1943 to look in a new direction. A new type of stabile, "constellations," began to appear. These were structures of small pieces of polychromed and unpainted wood fixed together by heavy wire, and intended to stand on a base in the conventional manner (*Vertical Constellation with Yellow Bone*, page 54). These led to similar constellations, somewhat lighter in character, made to hang from the wall without obvious means of support (*Hanging Constellation with Red Object*, page 54). Finally we have the constellation translated into a stabile, free-standing in space, *Morning Star* (page 55), quite different in character from any of its immediate predecessors. And with it Calder has opened up a new avenue to explore.

56

CATALOG OF THE EXHIBITION

An asterisk (*) preceding the catalog number indicates that the work is illustrated in the text. When no lender is listed, the work has been lent by the artist.

*1. SELF-PORTRAIT. 1907.
Crayon drawing. 6 x 9".
Lent by Mr. A. Stirling Calder, Brooklyn, New York.

2. DOG. 1909.
Sheet brass, 4½" long.
Lent by Mr. A. Stirling Calder, Brooklyn, New York.

*3. RED HORSE AND GREEN SULKY. 1926. Toy.
Wire and wood, 23" long.

4. DUCK AND SNAKE. 1926. Toy.
Wire, cloth and wood, 25½" long.

5. MAGPIE. 1926. Toy.
Wire and wood, 8" high.

6. DUCK PULLING UP WORMS. 1926. Toy.
Wood and wire, 4¼" high.

*7. GALLOPING HORSE. 1926. Toy.
Wire, wood and leather, 21" long.

*8. DUCK ON DIFFERENTIAL WHEELS. 1926. Toy.
Wire and wood, 11" long.

9. FROG. 1926. Toy.
Wood, cardboard, leather, 21" long.

10. PIEBALD HORSE. 1926. Toy.
Wire and cloth, 9½" long.

*11. JOSEPHINE BAKER. 1926.
Brass wire, 18" high.
Lent by Mrs. James di Tomasi, Cold Spring Harbor, Long Island.

12. THE HOSTESS. 1928.
Wire, 11½" high.
The Museum of Modern Art, New York.

13. CALVIN COOLIDGE. 1928.
Wire, 12¼" high.

14. SEA GULL. 1928.
Wire, 9" high.

*15. HELEN WILLS. 1928.
Wire, 14¾" high.

*16. HORSE. 1928.
Boxwood, 15½" high.

*17. UNCOMFORTABLE FACE. 1928.
Cocobolo wood, 21¼" high.

18. CAMEL. 1928.
Tulipwood, 17" high.
Lent by Mrs. Sidney Howard, New York.

19. WOMAN WITH SQUARE UMBRELLA. 1928.
Wood, 19" high.
Lent by Mr. Paul Nitze, Glen Cove, Long Island, New York.

20. LICORICE. 1928.
Ebony, 29" high.
Lent by Mrs. Beatrice K. Winston, New York.

*21. HORSE. 1928.
Sheet brass, 10" high.

22. COW. 1928.
Wood, 17" high.
Lent by Mr. and Mrs. George D. Pratt, Bridgewater, Connecticut.

*23. DOUBLE CAT. 1929.
Wood, 4'3" long.

24. FISH. 1929.
Wire, 16" long.
Lent by Mr. A. Stirling Calder, Brooklyn, New York.

25. GOLDFISH BOWL. 1929.
Brass wire, 15¾" high.
Lent by Mr. A. Stirling Calder, Brooklyn, New York.

26. ACROBATS. 1929.
Wire, 33" high.

*27. PORTRAIT OF SHEPARD VOGELGESANG. 1930.
Wire, 15" high.
Lent by Mr. Shepard Vogelgesang, New York.

28. PORTRAIT OF AMÉDÉE OZENFANT. 1930.
Wire, 13" high.
Lent by Mr. Amédée Ozenfant, New York.

*29. SHARK SUCKER. 1930.
Norwegian wood, 31½" long.

30. EXTENDED SPHERES. 1931. Stabile.
Steel rods and wood, 23" high.
Lent by Mr. William Rogers, Springfield, Massachusetts.

31. TWO SPHERES. 1931. Motorized mobile.
Wood and wire, 21½" x 11".

32. DOUBLE ARC AND SPHERE. 1932. Motorized mobile.
Wood and wire, 24" high.
Lent by the Berkshire Museum, Pittsfield, Massachusetts.

*33. DANCING TORPEDO SHAPE. 1932. Motorized mobile.
Wood, iron wire, aluminum, 32½" high.
Lent by the Berkshire Museum, Pittsfield, Massachusetts.

*34. CALDERBERRY BUSH. 1932. Mobile.
Steel wire and rod, sheet aluminum and wood, 7' high.
Lent anonymously.

35. CIRCLE WITH BALL AND DISK. 1933. Mobile.
Metal, wood and wire, 5'1¼" high.

*36. AGNES' CIRCLE. 1934. Mobile.
Steel wire, rod and sheet aluminum, 36" high.
Lent by Miss Agnes Rindge, Poughkeepsie, New York.

*37. STEEL FISH. 1934. Mobile.
Iron, sheet steel and rod, sheet aluminum, 10' high.
Lent by Mr. Philip Goodwin, New York.

*38. WHITE FRAME. 1934. Motorized mobile.
Wood panel, wire and sheet metal, 7'6" x 9'.

*39. A UNIVERSE. 1934. Motorized mobile.
Steel rod, wire and wood, 40½" high.
The Museum of Modern Art, New York.

40. DOUBLE FACE. 1935. Toy.
Sheet aluminum, 12" high.
Lent by Sandra Calder, Roxbury, Connecticut.

41. LITTLE BLUE PANEL. 1935. Motorized mobile.
Wood and iron wire, 19¾ x 15¾".
Lent by the Wadsworth Atheneum, Hartford, Connecticut.

42. MOBILE. 1935.
Colored metal, 17" long.
Lent by Mr. George L. K. Morris, New York.

43. VERTICAL WHITE FRAME. 1936. Mobile.
Sheet steel and wood, 8' x 6'.
Lent by Mrs. Whitney Allen, Rochester, New York.

44. ORANGE PANEL. 1936. Motorized mobile.
Wood, wire, sheet steel, 3' x 4'.

*45. GIBRALTAR. 1936. Stabile.
Lignum vitæ, plank walnut, and steel rod, 28⅝" high.

*46. DANCERS AND SPHERE. 1936. Motorized mobile.
Wood, steel wire, sheet aluminum, 17¾" high.

47. NINE DISKS. 1936. Mobile.
Sheet steel, steel rod, 15' high.

48. PRAYING MANTIS. 1936. Mobile.
Steel rod and wood, 6'6" high.
Lent by The Wadsworth Atheneum, Hartford, Connecticut.

*49. SWIZZLE STICKS. 1936. Mobile.
Plywood panel, wire, wood, and lead, 48" x 33".
Lent by Mr. and Mrs. James Thrall Soby, New York.

50. STARFISH. 1937. Mobile.
Wood and string, 37" wide.

51. WHITE PANEL. 1934. Mobile.
Wood panel, steel rods, sheet aluminum, 7'6" x 9'.

52. BIG BIRD. 1937. Stabile.
Sheet steel, 8'5" high.

53. WILLIAM S. PALEY TROPHY. 1937.
Nickel steel, 37" to sphere.
Lent by The Columbia Broadcasting System.

*54. WHALE. 1937. Stabile.
Sheet steel, 6'6" high.
On extended loan by the artist to The Museum of Modern Art.

55. MERCURY FOUNTAIN. 1937. (model)
Plywood, iron, tin and steel rod. 13'6" high.

*56. TIGHT ROPE. 1937. Mobile.
Ebony, steel rods, wire and lead, 9'3½" long.

*58. APPLE MONSTER. 1938. Stabile.
Apple branch, wire spring, 5'7" high.

*59. SPHERICAL TRIANGLE. 1939. Mobile.
Sheet steel and steel rods. 8' high.

60. CAGE WITHIN A CAGE. 1939. Stabile.
Steel rods, wire thread, ca. 3'4" high.

61. BLACK AREAS. 1939. Mobile.
Sheet steel and wire, ca. 40" wide.
Lent by Mr. Jean Hélion, Rockbridge Baths, Virginia.

*62. LOBSTER TRAP AND FISH TAIL. 1939. Mobile.
Steel wire and sheet aluminum, ca. 15' wide.
The Museum of Modern Art, New York.

63. TRIPOD. 1939. Mobile.
Metal with colored disks. 7'6" wide.
On extended loan by the artist to The Museum of Modern Art.

64. BLACK, BRASS, RED AND WHITE. 1940. Mobile.
Sheet steel, brass and aluminum, ca. 6'6" wide.

*65. BLACK BEAST. 1940. Stabile.
Sheet steel, 8'9" high.

66. EUCALYPTUS. 1940. Mobile.
Steel rod, sheet steel, 7'10" high.
Lent by Mr. and Mrs. Wallace K. Harrison,
New York.

67. HOLLOW EGG. 1940. Stabile.
Steel rod, steel wire, 4'6" high.

*68. THIRTEEN SPINES. 1940. Mobile.
Sheet steel, steel rods and wire, aluminum, 7'
high.

68a. BLACK PETALS. 1940. Mobile.
Sheet steel, 7'4" high.

69. ARC OF PETALS. 1941. Mobile.
Steel wire and sheet aluminum, ca. 7½' wide.
Lent by Art of This Century, New York.

70. YUCCA. 1941. Mobile.
Sheet steel, sheet aluminum, steel wire, ca. 5'
high.
Lent by Baroness Hilla von Rebay, New York.

71. LITTLE LEAVES. 1941. Mobile.
Sheet steel, steel rods, 31" high.
Lent by Mrs. Ralph Delahaye Paine, New
York.

*72. BLACK DOTS. 1941. Mobile.
Sheet steel and string, ca. 35" wide.
Lent by Mrs. Charles B. Goodspeed, Chicago.

73. CLANGER. 1941. Mobile.
Sheet steel, steel wire and sheet aluminum, 9'
high.
Lent by Mr. Malcolm Cowley, Gaylordsville,
Connecticut.

*74. HOUR GLASS. 1941. Mobile.
Steel rod and wire, 5' high.

*75. COCKATOO. 1941. Mobile.
Sheet steel and wire, 36¼" high.
Lent by Mr. and Mrs. C. Earle Miller, Down-
ingtown, Pennsylvania.

76. ELEPHANT. 1942. Stabile.
Sheet steel, 20¾" high.

77. HANGING SPHERES. 1942. Mobile.
Wood, steel rod, and string, 27" wide.
Lent by Mr. and Mrs. Richard Taylor, Bethel,
Connecticut.

*78. HORIZONTAL SPINES. 1942. Mobile.
Sheet steel, steel wire and rods, and sheet
aluminum, 4'5" high.
Lent by the Addison Gallery, Phillips Academy,
Andover, Massachusetts.

*79. SPINY. 1942. Stabile.
Sheet aluminum, 26" long.

*80. BLACK THING. 1942. Stabile.
Sheet steel, 31¼".
Lent anonymously.

*81. RED PETALS. 1942. Mobile.
Sheet steel, steel wire, sheet aluminum, 9'2"
high.
Lent by The Arts Club, Chicago.

*82. VERTICAL CONSTELLATION WITH YELLOW
BONE. 1943. Stabile.
Wood and steel rod, 23¼" high.

83. VERTICAL CONSTELLATION WITH BOMB. 1943.
Stabile.
Wood and steel rod, 31¼" high.

*84. WALL CONSTELLATION WITH RED OBJECT.
1943. Stabile.
Wood and steel rod, 25¾" high.

85. WALL CONSTELLATION WITH ROW OF OB-
JECTS. 1943. Stabile.
Wood and steel rod, 33" high.

86. MORNING STAR. 1943. Stabile.
Sheet steel, wire and wood, 6'7" high.

Jewelry 1933-43

87. BOOMERANG NECKLACE. Hammered brass.

88. SPIRAL PIN. Galvanized iron, blue glass.

89. LEAF PIN. Silver.

90. PENDANT. Bone and gold.

91. BRACELET. Silver.

92. EARRINGS. Silver.

93. NECKLACE. Silver.

94. BRACELET (Small). Silver.

95. NECKLACE OF CONES. Brass Wire.

96. FISH PIN. Silver.
Above pieces lent by Mrs. Alexander Calder,
Roxbury, Connecticut.

97. SPIRAL AND STAR PIN. Brass.
Lent by Mrs. José Luis Sert, New York.

98. BROOCH. Silver.
Lent by Mrs. Catherine White, New York.

BRIEF CHRONOLOGY

1898   Born July 22, Philadelphia, Pennsylvania.

1919   Graduated as mechanical engineer, Stevens Institute of Technology.

1919-   Various apprentice engineering jobs.
1922

1922   Began to draw evenings in public night school, East 42 Street, New York, under Clinton Balmer.

1923   Interest in landscape painting awakened while on West Coast. Studied Art Students' League, New York, until 1926.

1924   Free-lance work for *National Police Gazette* until 1926.

1925   Winter: drawings for *Animal Sketching*.

1926   First paintings exhibited. *Animal Sketching* published. Began wood carving. To England by freighter. Paris: began circus; made first animated toys; first wire sculpture, *Josephine Baker*.

1927   Paris: toys exhibited, Salon des Humoristes. Returned to New York in August. Autumn: Oshkosh, Wisconsin, to supervise manufacture of toys from his models. Wood sculpture.

1928   New York, April: first one-man exhibition, Weyhe Gallery (wire sculpture). *Romulus and Remus* exhibited at Independents, New York. To Paris, November; met Miro, Pascin.

1929   Paris, February: exhibition of wire and wood sculptures, Galerie Billiet. Catalog preface by Pascin. Berlin, April: exhibition Neumann-Nierendorf Gallery. First jewelry. Returned New York, June. Wire goldfish bowls with moving fish.

1930   Paris, March to December: exhibited at XIe Salon de l'araignée. Met Léger, van Doesburg, Mondrian. Experimented briefly with abstract painting. Exhibited wood and wire sculpture, Museum of Modern Art, New York: *Paintings and Sculptures by Living Americans*. First showing in Salon des Sur-Indépendents, Paris.

1931   Married Louisa James. Returned to Paris. Met Arp, Hélion, van Doesburg. Became member of Abstraction-Création group. April: First abstract constructions at Galerie Per-

cier; catalog preface by Léger. Illustrations for *The Fables of Aesop*.

1932   Paris, February: first exhibition of "mobiles," Galerie Vignon. Exhibited at Association Artistique "1940." New York, June: exhibition, Julien Levy Gallery.

1933   Madrid, Barcelona, January: circus; exhibitions of objects and drawings. Paris: group show, Galerie Pierre, with Arp, Hélion, Pevsner, Seligmann, Miro. July: returned to U.S.A. Purchased farm, Roxbury, Connecticut.

1934   Roxbury. First exhibition, Pierre Matisse Gallery, New York.

1935   Chicago: setting for Martha Graham's *Panorama*, Bennington, Vermont.

1936   Setting for Eric Satie's *Socrate*, Wadsworth Atheneum, Hartford, Connecticut; "Plastic interludes" for Martha Graham's *Four Movements*, New York.

1937   April: visit to France; *Mercury Fountain*, Spanish Pavilion, Paris Exposition. October to London. Exhibition Mayor Gallery.

1938   February: returned to U.S.A. Retrospective exhibition, Springfield, Massachusetts.

1939   *Water Ballet*, New York World's Fair. First prize, Plexiglas sculpture competition, Museum of Modern Art.

1940   First jewelry exhibition, Willard Gallery, December, New York.

1941   Decoration for ballroom, Hotel Avila, Caracas, Venezuela.

1943   Constellations.

EXHIBITIONS OF CALDER'S WORK

1928   NEW YORK. *Weyhe Gallery*
        Feb. 20-Mar. 3

1929   PARIS. *Galerie Billiet*
        Jan. 25-Feb. 7

1929   NEW YORK. *Weyhe Gallery*
        Feb. 4-23

1929   BERLIN. *Neumann & Nierendorf*
        April

1929   NEW YORK. *Fifty-sixth Street Galleries*
        Dec. 2-14

1930 CAMBRIDGE. *Harvard Society for Contemporary Art*
Jan. 27-Feb. 4

1931 PARIS. *Galerie Percier*
Apr. 27-May 9

1932 PARIS. *Galerie Vignon*
Feb. 12-29

1932 NEW YORK. *Julien Levy Gallery*
May 12-June 11

1933 PARIS. *Galerie Pierre Colle*
May 16-18

1933 MADRID. *Sociedad de Cursos y Conferencias, Residencia of the University of Madrid.*
January

1933 BARCELONA. *Amics de l'Art Nou, Galeries Syra*
January

1934 NEW YORK. *Pierre Matisse Gallery*
Apr. 6-28

1935 CHICAGO. *Renaissance Society, University of Chicago*
Jan. 14-31

1935 CHICAGO. *Arts Club*
Feb. 1-26

1937 HOLLYWOOD. *Antheil Gallery.*

1937 HONOLULU. *Honolulu Museum.*

1937 LONDON. *Mayor Gallery*
December

1938 SPRINGFIELD. *George Walter Vincent Smith Art Gallery*
Nov. 8-27

1939 NEW YORK. *Pierre Matisse Gallery*
May 9-27

1940 NEW YORK. *Willard Gallery*
Dec. 8-25

1941 NEW ORLEANS. *Arts and Crafts Club*
Mar. 28-Apr. 11

1941 NEW YORK. *Pierre Matisse Gallery*
May 27-June 14

1941 NEW YORK. *Willard Gallery*
Dec. 3-25

1942 CINCINNATI. *Cincinnati Art Museum*
Apr. 7-May 3

1942 NEW YORK. *Pierre Matisse Gallery*
May 19-June 6

1942 LOS ANGELES. *Design Project.*
Sept. 27-Oct. 27

1942 SAN FRANCISCO. *San Francisco Museum.*

1942 NEW YORK. *Willard Gallery*
Dec. 1-24

1943 NEW YORK. *Pierre Matisse Gallery*
May 18-June 12

1943 ANDOVER. *Addison Gallery of American Art*
June 5-July 6

1943 NEW YORK. *Museum of Modern Art*
Sept. 29-Nov. 28

WORK BY CALDER IN AMERICAN MUSEUMS

ANDOVER, MASSACHUSETTS. ADDISON GALLERY, PHILLIPS ACADEMY.
1 standing mobile.

CHICAGO. THE ARTS CLUB.
1 standing mobile.

HARTFORD, CONNECTICUT. THE WADSWORTH ATHENEUM.
1 motorized panel mobile.
1 standing mobile.

HONOLULU. HONOLULU ACADEMY OF ART.
1 wire sculpture.
1 motorized panel mobile.

NEW YORK. ART OF THIS CENTURY.
1 suspended mobile.

NEW YORK. ART OF TOMORROW.
1 motorized panel mobile.

NEW YORK. THE METROPOLITAN MUSEUM OF ART.
1 suspended mobile.

NEW YORK. THE MUSEUM OF MODERN ART.
2 wire sculptures.
1 motorized mobile.
1 suspended mobile.

NORTHAMPTON, MASSACHUSETTS. SMITH COLLEGE MUSEUM.
1 mobile.

PITTSFIELD, MASSACHUSETTS. BERKSHIRE MUSEUM.
2 motorized mobiles.
2 mobiles installed in auditorium ventilators.

PHILADELPHIA. THE PENNSYLVANIA MUSEUM OF ART.
1 wall mobile.

ST. LOUIS. CITY ART MUSEUM.
1 suspended mobile.

WASHINGTON, D. C. THE PHILLIPS MEMORIAL GALLERY.
2 drawings.

ETCHINGS

1935 One etching in *23 Engravings,* a portfolio edited by Anatole Jakovski, G. Orobitz et cie., Paris.

1940 *Sunday.* Line etching submitted for *PM Competition: The Artist as Reporter* at the Museum of Modern Art, New York.

1942 One etching in *Portfolio of Eleven Original Works,* published by VVV, New York. Limited edition of 50, containing etching-frottage objects by Breton, Chagall, Ernst et al.

ILLUSTRATIONS

Books

1926 *Animal Sketching,* Pelham, New York. Bridgman Publishers.

1931 *Fables of Aesop* with fifty drawings, Paris. Harrison of Paris.

Magazines

1924- *National Police Gazette:* drawings in May 3,
1926 Aug. 2, 1924; Feb. 21, March 21, April 4, May 23, June 27, Aug. 1, Aug. 22, Oct. 31, Nov. 14, 1925; May 1, July 3, 1926.

1937 *Transition* Winter no 26, pp. 135-7. Decor for *OH to AA,* a playlet by Charles Tracy.

1941 *Vertical* Cover design and title page.

1942 *Dyn* 1 no 3, pp. 4b, 9, 16, 20 a-b-c, 26. Fall 1942.

1943 *View* 3 no 1: pp. 20-1. Children's page.

POSTERS

1925 *The Glass Slipper,* a Theatre Guild production, New York.

1926 Holland-American Line.

THEATRICAL WORK

1929 *Miss Tamara,* rubber hose and wire dachshund for the clown, Paul Fratellini, Paris.

1935 *Panorama,* for Martha Graham. Mobiles for First Workshop production at the Bennington School of the Dance, Vermont.

1936 *Horizons,* for Martha Graham. Mobile settings for 33rd concert, New York.

1936 *Socrate,* by Erik Satie. Mobile settings for production at the First Hartford Festival, Connecticut.

BIBLIOGRAPHY

The arrangement of this bibliography is alphabetical, under the author's name wherever possible. Catalogs of exhibitions in public museums are listed under the name of the city where the museum is located, while private exhibition galleries are listed under the name of the gallery. The bibliographical form is modelled upon that used in the Art Index.

SAMPLE ENTRY for magazine article: SWEENEY, JAMES JOHNSON. Alexander Calder. 4il Axis 1no 3: 19-21 Jy 1935.

EXPLANATION: An article by James Johnson Sweeney, entitled "Alexander Calder," with 4 illustrations, will be found in Axis, volume 1, number 3, pages 19 through 21, issue dated July 1935.

ABBREVIATIONS: Ag *August,* Ap *April,* c *copyright,* ed *editor,* F *February,* il *illustration (s),* Ja *January,* Je *June,* Jy *July,* Mr *March,* My *May,* N *November,* no *number(s),* O *October,* p *page(s),* pl *plate(s),* S *September,* sup *supplement.*
* Entries so marked are in the Museum library.

Statements by Calder

*1. ABSTRACTION-CRÉATION, ART NON FIGURATIF 1:6 1932. Translated in *Art of this century* (See 7).

*2. ANDOVER, MASS. ADDISON GALLERY OF AMERICAN ART. Mobiles by Calder. Je 5-Jy 6 1943. Exhibition catalog.

*3. EVANS, MYFANWY, ed. The painter's object. il. London, Gerald Howe, ltd., 1937. Alexander Calder: *Mobiles,* p62-7.

4. PITTSFIELD, MASS. BERKSHIRE MUSEUM. Modern painting and sculpture. Ag. 12-25 1933? Exhibition catalog.

5. Mercury fountain. Stevens Indicator 55no3:2-3,7 My 1938.

6. Mercury fountain. Technology Review 40:202 Mr. 1938. Illustration, p25 N 1937.

*7. ART OF THIS CENTURY. Edited by Peggy Guggenheim. il New York, Art of this century, 1942.
Brief biographical note. Translation of Calder's statement in *Abstraction.*

Books and Articles

*8. ARTS CLUB, CHICAGO. "Mobiles" by Alexander Calder. F 1-26 1935. Catalog, with introduction by James Johnson Sweeney.

BARR, ALFRED H., JR. See 47,48,49.

9. BELLONI, LA COMTESSE. Staltrad. Göteborgs Handels och Sjöfarts-Tidning. F 20. p.5 1932 Ill.

*10. BENSON, EMANUEL MERWIN. Seven sculptors: Calder, Gargallo, Lehmbruck, Lipchitz, Manolo, Moore, Wolff. il American Magazine of Art 28:454-69 Ag 1935. Calder, p468-9.

*11. BEUCLER, ANDRÉ. Les moyens d'expression. il Arts et Métiers Graphiques 62:15-36 Mr 1938.

*12. BIRD, PAUL. Calder and nature. il Art Digest 13:22-3 My 15 1939. Exhibition at Pierre Matisse Gallery.

*13. BREUNING, MARGARET. Calder mobiles and stabiles. Magazine of Art 32:361 Je 1939. Exhibition at Pierre Matisse Gallery.

14. BUFFET-PICABIA, GABRIÈLLE. Alexander Calder, ou le roi du fil de fer. Vertigral 1no1: 1 1932.

*15. CIRCLE, INTERNATIONAL SURVEY OF CONSTRUCTIVE ART. Editors: J. L. Martin, Ben Nicholson, N. Gabo. il London, Faber and Faber, 1937.
Sculpture, pl 19-20. Exhibitions, p279-81.

*16. COAN, ELLEN STONE. The mobiles of Alexander Calder. Vassar Journal of Undergraduate Studies il 15:1-18 My 1942.

*17. DESIGN PROJECT, LOS ANGELES. Calder exhibition. S 27-O 27 1941. Catalog, with introduction by René Lefevbre-Foinet.

*18. F., R. (FRANKEL, ROBERT ?) Calder, a humorous and inventive artist. Art News 35:14,22 Mr 13 1937.
Exhibition at the Pierre Matisse Gallery.

19. FRÉJAVILLE, GUSTAVE. Les poupées acrobats du cirque Calder. Commoedia Ap 24 1929.

*20. GALERIE BILLIET, PARIS. (Exposition Calder) Ja 25-F 7 1929. Catalog, with introduction by Jules Pascin.

*21. GALERIE PERCIER, PARIS. Alexander Calder. Ap 27-My 9 1931. Catalog, with introduction by Fernand Léger.

22. GASCH, SEBASTIÀ. Il circ Calder. Mirador Ja 1933.

*23. ————————El escultor americano Calder. 2 il AC no7:43 1932.

24. GAUSSIN, YVAN. On remplace le crayon et la couleur par—du fil de fer. La Rumeur Ja 30 1929.

25. GEORGE, WALDEMAR. Sculptures de Calder. La Presse (Paris) F 14 1929.

*26. GIEDION-WELCKER, CAROLA. Modern plastic art. 166p il Zurich, H. Girsberger, 1937. English version by P. Morton Shand.

27. GLASER, CURT. Porträts, drahtkunst, u.a. Berliner Börsen-Courier Ap 5 1929.

*28. GRIGSON, GEOFFREY, ed. The arts to-day. il London, John Lane, 1935. Painting and sculpture to-day, p71-109.

*29. HASKELL, DOUGLAS. Design in industry, or Art as a toy. 14il Creative Art 4:sup56-7 F 1929.

*30. HAWES, ELIZABETH. More than modern—wiry art. Charm Ap 1928.

*31. HELLMAN, GEOFFREY T. Profiles: Everything is mobile. il New Yorker 17:25-30,33 O 4 1941.

*32. HILDEBRANDT, HANS. Die kunst des 19. und 20. jahrhunderts. 458p il Wildpark-Potsdam, Akademische Verlagsgesellschaft Athenaion m.-b.H,c1924. (postscript 1931).

*33. JAKOVSKI, ANATOLE. Alexandre Calder. 4il Cahiers d'Art 3no5-6:244-46 1933.

*34. ————————Six essais. Arp, Calder, Hélion, Miro, Pevsner, Seligmann. 47p il Paris, Chez Jacques Povolozky (1933?)

35. Les jouets de Calder. Les Echoes des Industries d'Art p23 Ag 1927.

*36. L., J. (LANE, JAMES ?) Alexander Calder as jewelry designer. Art News. 39:10-11 D 14 1940. Exhibition at the Willard Gallery.

37. LEGRAND-CHABRIER. Alexandre Calder et son cirque automatique. La Volonté My 19 1929.

38. ————————Un petit cirque à domicile. Candide Je 23 1927.

*39. LUCERNE. KUNSTMUSEUM. Thèse, antithèse, synthèse. F 24-Mr 31 1935. Catalog of an exhibition. Calder, p32,40.

40. MARKSTROM, INGEBORG. Staltradskulptur. Svenska Dagbladet Mr 10 1929.

*41. MATISSE, PIERRE, GALLERY. Calder mobiles. Ap 6-28 1934. Catalog, with introduction by James Johnson Sweeney.

*42. "Mobile" en mouvement. 2il Cahiers d'Art 14no1-4:74 1939.

*43. Morris, George L. K. Relations of painting and sculpture. il Partisan Review 1no1:63-71 Ja-F 1943.

44. Mouvement. Je 1 1933.

*45. Museums acquire Calder's "Art in motion." il Art Digest 9:16 N 1 1934.

*46. New York. Museum of Modern Art. (Alexander Calder, miscellaneous uncatalogued material.) A folder of bibliographies, catalogs, clippings and reproductions.

*47. ——————Fantastic art, dada, surrealism. 246 p il New York (The Museum) 1936. Edited by Alfred H. Barr, Jr.

*48. —————Cubism and abstract art. 249p il New York (The Museum) 1936. Text by Alfred H. Barr, Jr.

*49. Paris. Musée de Jeu de Paume. Trois siècles d'art aux Etats-Unis. Exposition organisée en collaboration avec le Museum of Modern Art, New York, il Paris, Editions des musées nationaux, 1938.
A. H. Barr, Jr.: Sculpture in the United States, p32-3.

*50. Plexiglas sculpture prizes are awarded. 5il Pencil Points 20no6:sup56-7 Je 1939. Competition sponsored by the Museum of Modern Art and Röhm & Haas.

51. Powell, Hickman. His elephants don't drink. New York World My 18 1931.

52. Ramond, Edouard. Sandy Calder ou le fil de fer devient statue. Paris-Montparnasse Je 15 1929.

53. Read, Herbert Edward. Unit 1, the modern movement in English architecture, painting, sculpture. il 124p London, Cassell & Co., 1934.

*54. Renaissance Society of the University of Chicago. Calder mobiles. Ja 14-31 1935. Catalog, with introduction by James Johnson Sweeney.

*55. S., J. Alexander Calder, Pierre Matisse Gallery. Art News 32-11 Ap 14 1934.

*56. San Francisco. Golden Gate International Exposition, 1939-40. Decorative arts, official catalog. San Francisco, San Francisco Bay Exposition company, c1939. Calder mobile, p88, with comment by James Johnson Sweeney.

*57. Sayre, Ann H. Mobiles and objects in the abstract language. Art News 34:8 F 22 1936. Exhibition at Pierre Matisse Gallery.

*58. Springfield, a Calder show. Art News 37:18 N 18 1938.

*59. Springfield, Mass. George Walter Vincent Smith Museum. Calder mobiles. N 8-27 1938. Catalog, with introduction by James Johnson Sweeney, and biographical note by C. S. Pond.

*60. Stabiles and mobiles. il Time p46-7 Mr 1 1937.

*61. Sweeney, James Johnson. Alexander Calder. 4il Axis 1no3:19-21 Jy 1935.

*62. —————Alexander Calder: Movement as a plastic element. 12il Architectural Forum 70:144-9 (Plus 24-9) F 1939.
Plus supplement, number 2.

*63. —————L'art contemporain aux Etats-Unis. il Cahiers d'Art. 13no1-2:45-68 1938. Calder, p52. Illustration, p67.
—————See 8,41,54,56.

64. Szittya, W. Alexander Calder. Kunstblatt 13:185-6 Je 1929.

*65. Tinkling metal. Art Digest 16:12 Je 1942. Exhibition at the Pierre Matisse Gallery.

66. Vanity Fair. (Hall of Fame nomination) Mr 1930.
Waldemar, George. See 25.

67. Werner, B. E. Porträts, skulpturen, drahtplastiken. Deutsche Allgemeine Zeitung Ap 12 1929.

68. Westheim, Paul. Legenden aus dem künstlerleben. Kunstblatt 15:246-8 1931.

Film on Calder

1929 *Alexander Calder*, Berlin Institut für Kulturforschung. Directed by Dr. Hans Cürlis; photographed by Walter Türck. Part of an instructional series called *Artists at Work*.

Six thousand five hundred copies of this book have been printed in October, 1943 for the Trustees of the Museum of Modern Art by the Carey Press Corporation, New York.

THE SCULPTURE OF
JOHN B. FLANNAGAN

Triumph of the Egg I. Granite, 1937. The Museum of Modern Art.

THE SCULPTURE OF JOHN B. FLANNAGAN

EDITED BY DOROTHY C. MILLER

INTRODUCTION BY CARL ZIGROSSER

AND A STATEMENT BY THE ARTIST

THE MUSEUM OF MODERN ART · NEW YORK

ACKNOWLEDGMENTS

The President and Trustees of the Museum of Modern Art and the Director of the Exhibition, Dorothy C. Miller, wish to thank those who have lent works of art from their collections to the exhibition. Invaluable assistance has been given by Mr. Carl Zigrosser, who has generously contributed the introduction to the catalog and has supplied important information about the sculpture. Mrs. John B. Flannagan, Miss Laura Canadé and Mr. Curt Valentin have also been of great assistance in assembling the exhibition and the catalog. In addition, the Museum is indebted to the following: Edward W. Forbes, Mrs. Juliana R. Force, Bartlett H. Hayes, Jr., Horace H. F. Jayne, Miss Agnes Rindge, and Dr. W. R. Valentiner. The American Federation of Arts has permitted the use in the catalog of *The Image in the Rock*, first published in the *Magazine of Art*.

TRUSTEES OF THE MUSEUM

Stephen C. Clark, *Chairman of the Board*; Mrs. John D. Rockefeller, Jr., *1st Vice-Chairman*; Samuel A. Lewisohn, *2nd Vice-Chairman*; John Hay Whitney, *President**; David H. McAlpin, *Treasurer**; Alfred H. Barr, Jr., *Vice-President and Director*; John E. Abbott, *Executive Vice-President*; Mrs. Robert Woods Bliss, Mrs. W. Murray Crane, Marshall Field, Edsel B. Ford, Philip L. Goodwin, A. Conger Goodyear, Mrs. Simon Guggenheim, Mrs. David M. Levy, Henry R. Luce, Archibald MacLeish, William S. Paley, Mrs. John Parkinson, Jr., Mrs. Charles S. Payson, Beardsley Ruml, Carleton Sprague Smith, James Thrall Soby, Edward M. M. Warburg*.

*On duty with the Armed Services.

HONORARY TRUSTEES

Frederic Clay Bartlett, Frank Crowninshield, Duncan Phillips, Mrs. Rainey Rogers, Paul J. Sachs, Mrs. John S. Sheppard.

STAFF OF THE MUSEUM

Alfred H. Barr, Jr., *Director*; John E. Abbott, *Executive Vice-President*; Monroe Wheeler, *Director of Exhibitions and Publications*; Frances Hawkins, *Secretary*; Ione Ulrich, *Assistant Treasurer and Comptroller*.

Department of Painting and Sculpture: Alfred H. Barr, Jr., *Curator*; Dorothy C. Miller, *Associate Curator*; Elise Van Hook, *Assistant*.

Department of Architecture: Alice M. Carson, *Acting Curator*.

Film Library: John E. Abbott, *Director*; Iris Barry, *Curator*; Edward F. Kerns, *Technical Director*; Allen Porter, *Circulation and Exhibition Director**.

Department of Industrial Design: Eliot F. Noyes, *Director**; Alice M. Carson, *Acting Director*.

Department of Photography: Beaumont Newhall, *Curator**; Nancy Newhall, *Assistant in Charge*.

Department of Exhibitions: Monroe Wheeler, *Director*; Carlos Dyer, *Technical Assistant*.

Department of Circulating Exhibitions: Elodie Courter, *Director*.

Department of Publications: Monroe Wheeler, *Director*; Holger E. Hagen, *Manager**; Frances Pernas, *Assistant Manager*.

Library: Beaumont Newhall, *Librarian**; Bernard Karpel, *Acting Librarian*.

Dance Archives: Paul Magriel, *Librarian**; Sidney Edison, *Acting Librarian*.

Publicity Department: Sarah Newmeyer, *Director*.

Department of Registration: Dorothy H. Dudley, *Registrar*.

Educational Project: Victor D'Amico, *Director*.

Armed Services Program: James Thrall Soby, *Director*.

Production Manager: Rand Warren.

Information Desk: Lillian W. Clark.

*On leave of absence with the Armed Services.

COPYRIGHT 1942 THE MUSEUM OF MODERN ART · NEW YORK
PRINTED IN THE UNITED STATES OF AMERICA

CONTENTS

Illustration on cover and title page: Crayon
study for granite *Dog,* 1932-33 (No. 53)

Jonah and the Whale: Rebirth Motif. 1937. Bluestone, 30½″ high.
Lent by the Weyhe Gallery.

THE IMAGE IN THE ROCK

OFTEN THERE IS an occult attraction in the very shape of a rock as sheer abstract form. It fascinates with a queer atavistic nostalgia, as either a remote memory or a stirring impulse from the depth of the unconscious.

That's the simple sculptural intention. As design, the eventual carving involuntarily evolves from the eternal nature of the stone itself, an abstract linear and cubical fantasy out of the fluctuating sequence of consciousness, expressing a vague general memory of many creatures, of human and animal life in its various forms.

It partakes of the deep pantheistic urge of kinship with all living things and fundamental unity of all life, a unity so complete it can see a figure of dignity even in the form of a goat. Many of the humbler life forms are often more useful as design than the narcissistic human figure, because, humanly, we project ourselves into all art works using the human figure, identifying ourselves with the beauty, grace, or strength of the image as intense wish fulfillment; and any variant, even when necessitated by design, shocks as maimed, and produces some psychological pain. With an animal form, on the contrary, any liberty taken with the familiar forms is felt as amusing—strange cruelty.

To that instrument of the subconscious, the hand of a sculptor, there exists an image within every rock. The creative act of realization merely frees it.

The stone cutter, worker of metal, painter, those who think and feel by hand, are timeless, haunted by all the old dreams. The artist remembers, or else is fated by cosmic destiny to serve as the instrument for realizing in visible form the profound subterranean urges of the human spirit in the whole dynamic life process—birth, growth, decay, death.

The stone carving of an alligator called *Dragon Motif* was simply chiseled with primary interest in the abstract circular design. Yet in so doing fascinated by something of the wonder and terror that must have made the fearsome monster fantasy—an old dream. Vitalized by that perfect design pattern, the circle, fitting symbol of eternity, the movement is both peripheral and centrifugal. Restless, it moves ever onward, finally to turn back into itself, an endless movement.

With such abstract purpose, instead of classic poise, there is more of the dynamic tension that is movement, even accentuated by devices that are restless such as a deliberate lack of obvious balance in design and the use of repetition to heighten the occult activity with velocity, as in the psyche of our time—speed without pauses or accents.

Even in our time, however, we yet know the great longing and hope of the ever recurrent and still surviving dream, the wishful rebirth fantasy, *Jonah and the Whale—Rebirth Motif*. It's eerie to learn that the fish is the very ancient symbol of the female principle.

In the austere elimination of the accidental for ordered simplification, there is a quality of the abstract and lifeless, but lifeless only contra spurious lifelikeness. Instead of which a purely sculptural attempt by the most simple unambiguous demonstration of tactile relations, the greatest possible preservation of cubic compactness, carved to exclude all chance evasive spatial aspects to approximate the abstract cubical elemental forms and even to preserve the identity of the original rock so that it hardly seems carved, rather to have endured so always—inevitable.

The artistic representation of the organic and living now takes on an abstract lifeless order and becomes, instead of the likeness of what is conditioned, the symbol of what is unconditioned and invariable, as though seeking the timeless, changeless finality of death. Sculpture like this is as inevitable.

All as part of the profound social purpose of art—communication. We communicate something of the record of the human spirit.

JOHN B. FLANNAGAN
June, 1941

8

JOHN B. FLANNAGAN

There is a theory about the origin of art that is exemplified by the oyster that creates the pearl. Art—in this case the pearl—comes about through irritation and pain and suffering. If the theory has any plausibility, it is borne out in the life of John B. Flannagan.

Flannagan had a tragic life. This is not the occasion to analyze his psyche or to enumerate the handicaps and malign forces which frustrated his personal life from childhood on. The story has unfolded to its tragic dénouement, and may some day be told—portrayed in the mood and with the complex overtones of a Dostoyevsky character. He was a distinguished artist and it is as an artist that I shall speak of him. His art was not tragic: it was pure and self-contained, profound yet simple.

He once set forth his credo in a letter*: "My aim is to produce sculpture as direct and swift in feeling as drawing—sculpture with such ease, freedom, and simplicity that it hardly seems carved but rather to have endured so always. This accounts for my preference for field stone: its very rudeness seems to me more in harmony with simple direct statement. There are often necessary compromises, but the shape of the stone does not determine the design; more often the design dictates the choice of the stone. I would like my sculpture to appear as rocks, left quite untouched and natural, and, as you have said, inevitable. Such qualities of humor or the grotesque or whatever may be found therein are for the most part accidental and

subordinate to a conception purely sculptural."

In the above he hints at one of the two leading themes he once elaborated to me as being dominant in his attitude—a passion for anonymity. The work itself, and not the artist, was important; the ultimate end and not the instrument. The work was enduring and timeless, the artist merely human and temporal. Why should there be this modern cult of the so-called creator? Do we know who *created* Egyptian or Assyrian sculpture, who carved the Cathedral of Chartres? "In the Middle Ages the unknown man carved the numberless statues of Romanesque and Gothic cathedrals, and covered chapel and refectory walls with unsigned frescoes. But with the approach to modern times, when the stupid craze for signatures came in, the unknown man ceased his activity and was content to rest. An immense throng of vain fellows, of men who had a name or sought to make a name, began to paint, invent, carve, write. They had less genius than the unknown man and they also had less modesty; they proclaimed to all the winds that they, and none but they, had done these things. They worked not only for their own joy or for others' benefit, but that the world might know that they, and none but they, had done the work." Very few of Flannagan's sculptures are signed, except insofar as they are signed all over. He was medieval in his disinterested and truly mystical passion for humility and anonymity. St. Francis of Assisi was one of his great heroes. He would have felt at home in the Middle Ages, and he might

*A volume of the letters of John B. Flannagan, with an introduction by W. R. Valentiner, is now in preparation.

perhaps have led a happier life in the age of universal faith. He would have liked nothing better than to have had his work merge into the great anonymous plastic tradition of Egypt or medieval Europe, but it seems more than likely that his desire for anonymity will not be granted him.

The other theme he stressed was what he called the philosophy of pity. This philosophy had reverberations in his personal life, but in his art it was related to his sympathy for all living things, particularly the humbler animals (St. Francis again), his *feeling into* whatever subject he approached: "The intense feeling of identification," as he put it, "with which I take up each stone to work upon it." He wrote in his notes: "Embrace all living forms, each for its plastic adjustment to a theme—living for warmth. No narcissistic worship of humanity—contra, the stately dignity of the Mountain Goat, the ironic pensiveness of the apparently thoughtful Monkey, and (in his greater moments) the timeless yet rebellious patience of the Ass." There is an all too human logic in this attitude which he subtly analyzed in *The Image in the Rock* (see page 7).

His work was executed with unbelievable intensity. When the fury of creation descended on him, he worked quite literally night and day without pause. "Creation is revelation," he said. The physical labor of direct carving, intense and exhausting though it be, was merely the stripping away of extraneous material, revealing the image which he had projected in the rock. There was no floundering around in conception or execution. His esthetic intuitions were immediate and absolute, and his hand with practised cunning made them concrete. But there were fallow periods. He who had such spiritual need for certainty fell prey to devastating uncertainty and doubt. He would lose faith in himself, his past work and his future inspiration. Then he would strive to forget, to escape by any means at hand this awful inchoate dread, the dark night of the soul. In this vein he once wrote me: "This past summer has been one of constant strain—a tension that has drawn me as taut as a violin string. Believe me I am trying, but I am not always successful. Always I am seeing with the vividness of a hallucination the wraith-like figure of a child that seems irrevocably lost; and the only way I see to dissipate my own feeling of being equally lost myself, is to give you a show expressing everything I have to say just now. After that I'm safe." "All artists," he said on another occasion, "are close to madness; it is their art that keeps them sane." In another mood, however, he could write serenely: "I feel like a different person. It was a case of going stale before I left, but now I find there is still something eager left in me—so much so, that I don't even feel the need of a drink any more, but feel more intensely just one steady abiding purpose such as it is—to make images out of rock. There is here a certain quiet I have sought for a long time. There is peace in the unhurried and simple existence of life here, so that I, in relishing it, feel out of place in the highly mechanized drift of our time, and have found where I belong."

Paradoxically enough, Flannagan was both apart from and of his time. He stood apart from it in that he was essentially a mystic, one who aligned himself with spirit rather than mechanism. He was modern by reason of his intelligent grasp of the problems of the artist today. What he admired about the Middle Ages was the functional relation, the give and take, between the artist and society, and between art and architecture. Today, he felt, both these relations were to a large extent ignored. He saw the necessity of re-establishing these values. In his application for a Guggenheim Fellowship in 1931 he cited as one of his chief aims a study of the "coordination of sculpture and architecture as expressed notably in 13th century Gothic, the ultimate purpose being the simplification of sculptural design and structure so as to be effective in the severe architectural scheme prevailing now." And in a note recently written: "Just as all really effective art has been an expression of the psyche of its time, so the simplification prevalent in the best contemporary art is quite in step with the severity of our architecture. It would seem also that the very austerity of that architectural style necessarily demands discreet sculptural relief."

Flannagan was always interested in the application of sculpture to building, but he never really had a chance to put his ideas into practice. The nearest he came to it was perhaps the *Design for a Skyscraper Court*, the *Mother and Child*, now in the Fogg Museum (see page 27). He made the design for Rockefeller Center, but it never came officially before the authorities. Nevertheless, he decided to execute it on a large scale. He made an illuminating analysis of the problems involved in a monumental sculpture to be placed in a court surrounded by high buildings. A statue in the round, he reasoned, must be designed to compose well from every angle, in this case not only when seen from the ground but also from above, from the many windows of the surrounding skyscrapers. This complicated set of conditions he solved triumphantly in what is, in my

opinion, one of the most important works of modern sculpture in America.

He was modern, too, in his consistent preoccupation with abstraction. It was always fundamental in his design, but he fused and modified it with other factors. "Pure abstraction is dead," he said. "Make it come alive by the use of living form. Warm the cold geometry of abstraction with a naturalism in which the superficial and accidental have been eliminated by their union with pure form. A withdrawing from the too close view of things in order to see them in their atmospheric content. Use abstraction to achieve a finality, but, in humanizing it with immediacy, retain it always in a state of becoming, rather than being. A thing should never be finished—should rather always be in a state of *becoming* (no end: an evasion or overcoming of time), completed each according to his own psyche by whoever has eyes to see. Use the apparently accidental to avoid formal hardness, and the spontaneous to avoid emotional hardness. A fine composition has the calm ordered elation of a mathematical solution, instead of mock-heroics or maudlin-nostalgic-associational emotionalism." It is obvious that with such a conception of the basis of art, consistently avoiding any formula or superficial mannerism, Flannagan could only be a lone creator and never the founder of a school. Yet, as has happened with John Marin, imitators have managed to discover a bag of surface tricks without ever penetrating to the animating spirit within. Thus Flannagan has not been without influence as a master of direct carving in America today.

He was no escapist. Long ago he spoke of "disciplining myself to think and see and feel so naturally as to escape the precious or the

11

esoteric. My aim is the achievement of a sculpture that should fulfill a definite function in the social consciousness of many instead of a limited few." He accepted the realities of today. Escapism he associated with the romantic attitude and he abhorred it. "Science honest—romance evasion and dishonest. Honesty liberates—cutting away romance and sentiment—deals with hard realities instead of dead moralities and high sentimental purities." In a letter to Curt Valentin enclosing the manuscript of *The Image in the Rock* he wrote: "Here is my credo —some week-end reading—I hope it reads well—it has clarity for those who make the effort toward intelligence. For the others, the Escapists, have their comic strip and Walt Disney. This statement has nothing of that flight from reality, the romantic, and neither have I."

His work was always keyed to the sculptural needs of today: monumental statues when he had the opportunity (the *Design for a Skyscraper Court* and the *Gold Miner* in Fairmount Park, Philadelphia, demonstrate with what success he solved the problems of plastic monumentality); sculpture for gardens, and small pieces designed for the home. His work has a direct human appeal without ever departing from the plastic conventions. Sculpture is an austere art, one that requires mature planning and sustained effort in its execution. Therefore he chose themes of a universal or symbolic nature—woman, man, child, animal. The design, the sculptural form, was, as we have seen, the keystone of his conception, but he vitalized it with living subject matter. Over and above the tactile organization of his lines, planes, and masses there seems to brood the mystery and glamor of a living thing. Thus he created character

and psychological values as well as esthetic forms.

Flannagan had an unusually developed plastic sense, a perception of three-dimensional form. Possibly only a sculptor can appreciate the daring and rightness of his simplification of planes, the solidity of his masses, and the inner logic of his forms. He was a great technician. His knowledge of the idiosyncracies of wood and stone and metal and the mechanics of the sculptor's craft was unsurpassed. But he had gone far beyond mere technique, which he called "hardness— the display of obvious skill and an overdone imitation of the surface aspects of reality." He believed in understatement, disdaining ostentatious facility. He once wrote: "It takes an artist to be a really good craftsman; all that these shop-trained guys know are things one *can't do*; but we artists say *can do* with imagination." "Thinking with his hands," as he used to call it, he could be more receptive to psychological overtones, promptings of the unconscious, suggestions of age-old dreams and fantasies. He has described one such fantasy as the *Dragon Motif* in *The Image in the Rock*. In the following note he alludes to the *Design for a Skyscraper Court*: "As a boy I very rarely saw my mother, and I think that the whole psychological story of what that means to a child is implied in this piece, which is a consistent architectonic statement as well."

He was a searching observer of nature. Endowed with a tenacious visual memory, he would require but a glance or two at an object to add its structure to his wide knowledge of human and animal forms. He never worked directly from a model. If he ever made use of one, it was for purposes of study. On such occasions he would pose the

12

model for a minute or two, walking around and observing intently, and then say, that is enough. He grasped, intuitively perhaps, and managed to suggest in his work the essential nature, the significant gesture of an animal, the cattiness of a cat, the dogginess of a dog, the womanliness of a woman. His drawings have this same rightness and precision of simplification. But, apropos of drawing, he once wrote: "Preparatory drawing seems much like doing one's thinking on paper and then carving the conclusion. I prefer to think the thing out first and last in stone or the medium for which it was intended."

Flannagan had an innate feeling for style. It was apparent in his talk and in his writing, which often had an epigrammatic quality. But it was most evident in his art. He sensed the scope and limitations of his medium and worked within them, using a different approach when carving wood or stone, or modeling clay, or working metal. The great bulk of his work was direct stone carving, but he worked in wood at the beginning and in metal toward the end of his career. His approach to metal working was consistent with his feeling for other materials. "I have used a smooth finish [in the *Rag Doll*] in order to emphasize the form, and because it is truer to the character of the metal. Bronzes lately seem a little inclined to a tricky clay texture. An obvious contradiction. . . ." He was also interested in combining metal and stone.

There was no dross of imitation or second-hand feeling in Flannagan's work. He often spoke of "a realism of feeling rather than a painting or carving of realism." In this sense his sculpture was pure and unalloyed. He was one of the most original of modern sculptors, revealing little outside influence. Each one of his pieces was conceived from within, and grew into an organic and self-contained whole. He never worked with an eye to fashion or the main chance. For every ten artists who function only because conditions are favorable, there is one who cannot help being an artist under any conditions, no matter in what age or country he was born. Flannagan was one of those rare artists.

CARL ZIGROSSER

13

CHRONOLOGY

1895 Born at Fargo, North Dakota, April 7.

1914–17 Studied painting with Robert Koehler at the Minneapolis Institute of Arts.

1917–22 Shipped as an able-bodied seaman with the Merchant Marine, making several trips to Europe and South America.

1922–23 Worked as a farm hand for Arthur B. Davies at Congers, N. Y. Painted at night, using wax technique Davies taught him. With Davies' encouragement, started to carve in wood.

1923 Exhibited for first time, Montross Gallery, New York, Jan. 23–Feb. 10; 5 "wooden pictures" and 2 wax paintings in 7-man exhibition with Davies, Glackens, Kuhn, the Prendergasts, Sheeler.

1924–29 Lived in New York, Rockland County and Woodstock, N. Y., developing sculpture as his ultimate medium. About 1926, began to work in stone as well as wood; after 1928, gave up wood. In extreme poverty, unable to buy stone, began to use field stone (various glacial boulders). Destroyed paintings and devoted himself to sculpture.

1925 Exhibited, Whitney Studio Club, New York, Dec. 8–24; 21 sculptures in 4-man exhibition with Leon Hartl, Charles Howard, Dorothea Schwarcz.

1927 One-man exhibition, Weyhe Gallery, New York, Jan. 5–20; 26 sculptures.

1928 One-man exhibition, Weyhe Gallery, Jan. 23–Feb. 4.

1929 One-man exhibition, Whitney Studio Galleries, New York, Jan. 22–Feb. 9; 15 sculptures. Contract with Weyhe Gallery guaranteeing weekly stipend in return for sculpture. This arrangement lasted intermittently until 1937.

1930 One-man exhibition, Weyhe Gallery, Apr. 7–26. In May, to Ireland where he lived for a year. Brief visit to Paris.

1931 Returned from Ireland in June. One-man exhibition, Weyhe Gallery, Nov. 9–28; 17 sculptures.

1932–33 Granted Guggenheim Fellowship and returned to Ireland. Lived there from March 1932 to March 1933.

1934 One-man exhibition, Weyhe Gallery. One-man exhibition, Arts Club of Chicago, Mar. 16–30; 26 sculptures. Breakdown, followed by 7 months in New York Hospital at White Plains. There, experimented with metal casting and produced *Toward the Sun* (no. 23) and the *Rag Doll*.

1934–35 First monumental sculpture, *Design for a Skyscraper Court* (see page 27).

1936 One-man exhibition, Weyhe Gallery, Feb. 24–Mar. 14; 24 sculptures. One-man exhibition, Vassar College Art Gallery, Poughkeepsie, N. Y., April; 9 sculptures. Exhibited, Brooklyn Museum, New York, Oct.–Nov.; 10 sculptures in 6-man exhibition with Brook, DuBois, Kroll, Sheeler, Sloan. Commission from Fairmount Park Art Association for monument, the *Gold Miner*, as part of Ellen Phillips Samuel Memorial, Philadelphia. This sculpture, in limestone, 6 feet high, was completed in 1938.

1937 One-man exhibition, Bard College, Annandale-on-Hudson, N. Y., Oct. 27–Nov. 10; 10 sculptures.

1938 One-man exhibition, Weyhe Gallery, Feb. 9–Mar. 5; 27 sculptures.

1939 Survived 4 brain operations. Warned against the effort of cutting stone, he turned to metal, working directly on unfinished bronze casts.

1940 Awarded Alexander Shilling prize allocating *Figure of Dignity* to the Metropolitan Museum of Art, New York.

1942 Died a suicide, January 6. One-man exhibition, Buchholz Gallery, New York. Mar. 18–Apr. 11. 24 sculptures.

Christ. 1925. Walnut, 34″ high. Lent by Frederick Zimmermann.

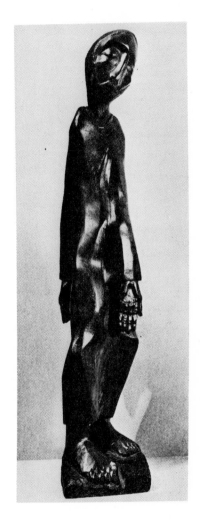

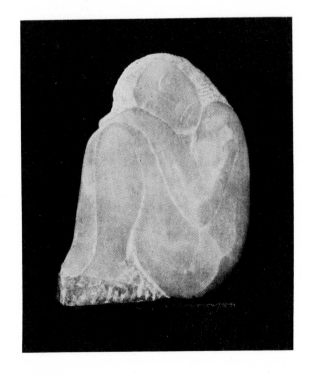

Crouching Woman. 1930. Alabaster, 11 ⅛″ high. Lent by E. Weyhe.

Elephant. 1929–30. Bluestone, 13½″ high. Lent by the Whitney Museum of American Art.

Ram. Ireland, 1931. Granite, 13½″ high. Lent by Edward M. M. Warburg.

Goat. Ireland, 1930–31. Granite, 18½″ long. Lent by the Weyhe Gallery.

Head. Ireland, 1932–33. Granite, 10½″ high. Lent by Mrs. Grace Flannagan.

Sleeping Cat. Ireland, 1932–33. Granite, 21½″ diameter. Lent by Mrs. Malcolm L. McBride.

Dragon Motif. Ireland, 1932–33. Granite, 26″ diameter. Lent by the Weyhe Gallery. (See page 8.)

Note for Dragon Alligator. Brush and ink, 9½ x 8½″. Lent by Curt Valentin.

Evening. Ireland, 1932–33. Black marble, 17″ high. Lent by the Detroit Institute of Arts.

Monkey and Young. Ireland, 1932–33. Granite, 15″ high. Lent by the Addison Gallery of American Art, Phillips Academy.

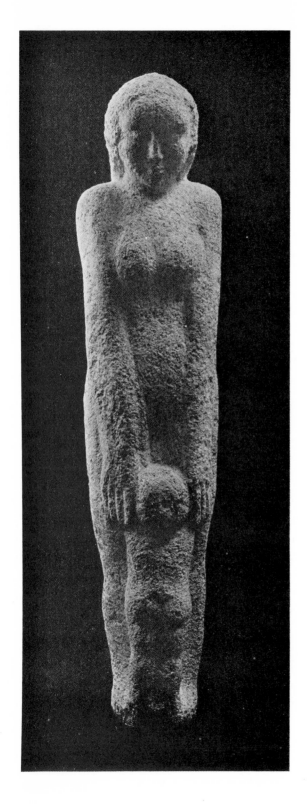

Woman and Child. Ireland, 1932–33. Granite, 41″ high. Lent by the Vassar College Art Gallery.

24

Dragon. Ireland, 1932–33. Granite, 29″ high. Lent by the Weyhe Gallery.

Figure of Dignity. Ireland and
New York, 1932–33. Granite with
cast aluminum horns, 48⅛″ high.
Lent by the Metropolitan Museum
of Art.

Design for a Skyscraper Court: Mother and Child. 1934–35. Red sandstone, 42¾″ high. Lent by the Fogg Museum of Art, Harvard University.

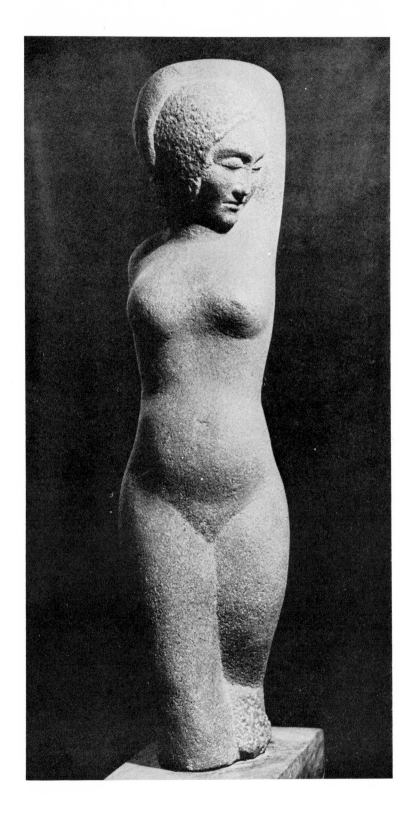

Young Woman (Rondo). 1935. Red sandstone, 36¾" high. Lent by Chauncey Stillman.

Head of a Child. 1935. Quartz, 6½″ high. Lent by the Weyhe Gallery.

Nude. 1941. Brush and ink, 18½″ x 12″. Lent by the Buchholz Gallery.

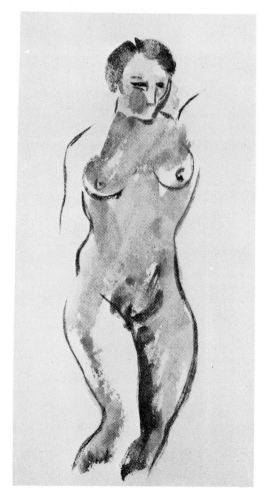

Nude. 1941. Watercolor, 18 x 11 ⅛″. Lent by John Asmussen.

30

New One. 1935. Bluestone, 12⅝″ long. Lent by the Weyhe Gallery.

Restive Acrobat. 1938. Fieldstone, 8″ high. Lent by Mr. and Mrs. Henry Clifford.

Frog. 1938. Sandstone, 7 ⅛″ high. Lent by the Wehye Gallery.

Snake. 1938. Limestone, 25½" high. Lent by R. Sturgis Ingersoll.

Little Creature. 1941. Bluestone, 13″ high. Lent by Edgar J. Kaufmann.

Pelican. 1941. Wrought bronze, 17½" high. Lent by the Buchholz Gallery.

Not Yet. 1940. Wrought bronze, 18" high. Lent by the Buchholz Gallery.

Dragon Motif. 1941. Bluestone, 12½″ long. Lent by the Buchholz Gallery.

New Lizard—Egg. Brush and ink,
9½ x 9″. Lent by Curt Valentin.

36

Triumph of the Egg II. 1941. Bluestone, 9½″ long. Lent by the Buchholz Gallery.

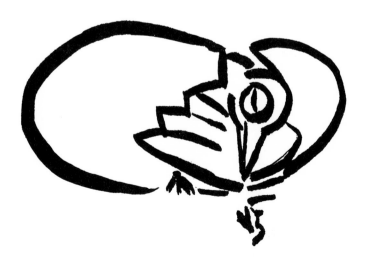

Study for the Triumph of the
Egg. Brush and ink, 9½ x 8½″.
Lent by Curt Valentin.

37

CATALOG OF THE EXHIBITION

An asterisk (*) preceding the number indicates that the work is illustrated.

1. Giraffe. 1924. Walnut, 22¾″ high. Lent by Carl Zigrosser.

*2. Christ. 1925. Walnut, 34″ high. Lent by Frederick Zimmermann.

3. Bust of a Woman. 1926. Rosewood, 14½″ high. Lent by the Weyhe Gallery.

*4. Elephant. 1929–30. Bluestone, 13½″ high. Lent by the Whitney Museum of American Art.

5. Standing Nude. 1929–30. Alabaster, 10⅛″ high. Lent by the Weyhe Gallery.

*6. Crouching Woman. 1930. Alabaster, 11⅛″ high. Lent by E. Weyhe.

7. Ass. Ireland, 1930–31. Granite, 13″ long. Lent by the Weyhe Gallery.

*8. Goat. Ireland, 1930–31. Granite, 18½″ long. Lent by the Weyhe Gallery.

9. Bundle. Ireland, 1930–31. Marble, 16½″ long. Lent by the Weyhe Gallery.

*10. Ram. Ireland, 1931. Granite, 13½″ high. Lent by Edward M. M. Warburg.

*11. Head. Ireland, 1932–33. Granite, 10⅜″ high. Lent by Mrs. Grace Flannagan.

*12. Dragon Motif. Ireland, 1932–33. Granite, 26″ diameter. Lent by the Weyhe Gallery.

13. Dog. Ireland, 1932–33. Granite, 22½″ diameter. Lent by the Weyhe Gallery.

*14. Sleeping Cat. Ireland, 1932–33. Granite, 21½″ diameter. Lent by Mrs. Malcolm L. McBride.

*15. Dragon. Ireland, 1932–33. Granite, 29″ high. Lent by the Weyhe Gallery.

*16. Monkey and Young. Ireland, 1932–33. Granite, 15″ high. Lent by the Addison Gallery of American Art, Phillips Academy.

17. Dark Lady. Ireland, 1932–33; reworked, New York, 1941. Black marble, 18⅜″ high. Lent by Mr. and Mrs. William L. McKim.

*18. Evening. Ireland, 1932–33. Black marble, 17″ high. Lent by the Detroit Institute of Arts.

*19. Woman and Child. Ireland, 1932–33. Granite, 41″ high. Lent by the Vassar College Art Gallery.

*20. Figure of Dignity. Ireland and New York, 1932–33. Granite, cast aluminum horns, 48⅛″ high. Lent by the Metropolitan Museum of Art.

21. Brass Tail Monkey I. 1933. Field stone, bronze tail, 9¼″ high. Lent by the Weyhe Gallery.

22. Crane. 1933. Sandstone, bronze legs, 34″ high. Lent by the Weyhe Gallery.

23. Toward the Sun. 1934. Silver, copper and bronze, 2⅞″ high. Lent by Miss Moira Flannagan.

*24. Design for a Skyscraper Court: Mother and Child. 1934–35. Red sandstone, 42¾″ high. Lent by the Fogg Museum of Art, Harvard University.

*25. Young Woman (Rondo). 1935. Red sandstone, 36¾″ high. Lent by Chauncey Stillman.

*26. Head of a Child. 1935. Quartz, 6½″ high. Lent by the Weyhe Gallery.

*27. New One. 1935. Bluestone, 12⅝″ long. Lent by the Weyhe Gallery.

28. St. Theresa Not Interested. 1936. Bluestone, 20⅞″ high. Lent by the Weyhe Gallery.

*29. Jonah and the Whale: Rebirth Motif. 1937. Bluestone, 30½″ high. Lent by the Weyhe Gallery.

*30. Triumph of the Egg I. 1937. Granite, 12″ high. The Museum of Modern Art, given anonymously. *Frontispiece.*

*31. Restive Acrobat. 1938. Field stone, 8″ high. Lent by Mr. and Mrs. Henry Clifford.

*32. Frog. 1938. Sandstone, 7⅛″ high. Lent by the Weyhe Gallery.

*33. Snake. 1938. Limestone, 25½″ high. Lent by R. Sturgis Ingersoll.

34. Head. 1938. Granite, 8½″ high. Lent by Chaim Gross.

35. Monkey. 1939. Granite, 11½″ high. Lent by Charles A. La Centra.

*36. Not Yet. 1940. Wrought bronze, 18″ high. Lent by the Buchholz Gallery.

37. Bear. 1940. Field stone, 9″ high. Lent by Curt Valentin.

*38. Little Creature. 1941. Bluestone, 13″ high.

Lent by Edgar J. Kaufmann.

*39. Triumph of the Egg II. 1941. Bluestone, 9½″ long. Lent by the Buchholz Gallery.

40. Early Bird. 1941. Bluestone, 17″ high. Lent by the Buchholz Gallery.

*41. Pelican. 1941. Wrought bronze, 17½″ high. Lent by the Buchholz Gallery.

*42. Dragon Motif. 1941. Bluestone, 12½″ long. Lent by the Buchholz Gallery.

43. Beginning. 1941. Bronze, 17¼″ high. Lent by the Buchholz Gallery.

DRAWINGS, WATERCOLORS, PASTELS, PRINTS

44. Nude. Brush and ink, 11¼ x 8″.

45. Nude. Brush and ink, 18⅜ x 9⅛″.

46. Nude. Watercolor, 15½ x 9¾″.

47. Nude. Watercolor, 11¾ x 8¾″.

48. The Arch. Watercolor, 8½ x 12¼″.

49. Nude. Crayon, 11¼ x 16¼″.

50. Nude. Crayon, 15 x 12″.

51. Head of a Girl. Crayon, 10⅛ x 8¼″.

52. Cat. Crayon, 10 x 8″.

*53. Study for Dog. Crayon, 11¾ x 13¾″.

54. Study for Bird. Crayon, 16 x 11½″.

55. Giraffes. Woodcut, 9½ x 6½″.

Nos. 44–55, lent by the Weyhe Gallery.

*56. Study for the Triumph of the Egg II. Brush and ink, 9½ x 8½″.

*57. Note for Dragon Alligator. Brush and ink, 9½ x 8½″.

*58. New Lizard—Egg. Brush and ink, 9½ x 9″.

Nos. 56–58, lent by Curt Valentin.

59. Nude. Watercolor, 18¾ x 12″. Lent by Miss Marjorie Stoker.

*60. Nude. Watercolor, 18 x 11⅛″. Lent by John Asmussen.

61. Design for Pieta. Brush and ink, 8 x 8½″. Lent by Mrs. John B. Flannagan.

62. Landscape with Donkey. Watercolor, 9½ x 12¾″. Lent by Mrs. Grace Flannagan.

63. Landscape. Pastel, 16⅝ x 23″. Lent by Mrs. Grace Flannagan.

64. Landscape. Pastel, 17 x 23″. Lent by Sam Eskin.

65. Nude. 1941. Brush and ink, 18¼ x 12″.

66. Nude. Brush and ink, 18⅝ x 11⅞″.

67. Male Nude. Brush and ink, 12⅛ x 11⅜″.

68. For Triumph of the Egg. Brush and ink, 10⅝ x 12″.

69. Nude. 1941. Brush and ink, 18⅝ x 12⅛″.

*70. Nude. 1941. Brush and ink, 18½ x 12″.

71. Nude. 1941. Brush and ink, 18⅜ x 12″.

72. Nude. 1941. Brush and ink, 18⅜ x 12″.

Nos. 65–72, lent by the Buchholz Gallery.

73. Pelican. 1941. Brush and ink, 11⅝ x 18⅜″. Lent by Miss Betty Chamberlain.

SCULPTURE BY FLANNAGAN IN MUSEUM COLLECTIONS

A number in parentheses indicates that the sculpture is included in this exhibition, and an asterisk (*) that it is illustrated in this book. Several museums own drawings and watercolors, not listed here.

Andover, Massachusetts. Addison Gallery of American Art, Phillips Academy.
    Monkey and Young. 1932–33. Granite, 15″ high (no. *16).
    Kitten Playing with Its Tail. 1933–34. Marble, 9½″ long.

Cambridge, Massachusetts. Fogg Museum of Art, Harvard University.
    Design for a Skyscraper Court: Mother and Child. 1934–35. Red sandstone, 42¾″ high (no. *24).

Cincinnati. Cincinnati Museum.
    Head. 1931. Cast stone version of granite *Head* (no. *11). 10⅜″ high.

Cleveland. Cleveland Museum of Art.
    Buffalo. 1931–32. Granite.

Detroit. Detroit Institute of Arts.
    Evening. 1932–33. Black Marble, 17″ high (no. *18).

Dublin, Ireland. Municipal Gallery of Modern Art.

Mother and Child. First version of *Design for a Skyscraper Court* (no. *24). 1932–33. Caen stone.

Honolulu. Honolulu Academy of Fine Arts.
    Full Hands. 1936. Black granite, about 24″ high.

Lincoln, Nebraska. University of Nebraska.
    Elephant. 1938. Bluestone, 8″ high.

New York. Metropolitan Museum of Art.
    Figure of Dignity. 1932–33. Granite, 48⅛″ high (no. *20).

New York. Museum of Modern Art.
    Triumph of the Egg I. 1937. Granite, 12″ high (no. *30).

New York. Whitney Museum of American Art.
    Chimpanzee. 1928. Black granite, 11″ high.
    Elephant. 1929–30. Bluestone, 13½″ high (no. *4).
    Colt. 1930. Bluestone, 15⅜″ high.

Oberlin, Ohio. Allen Memorial Art Museum, Oberlin College.
    Mother and Child. 1933. Small cast stone version of *Design for a Skyscraper Court* (no. *24), 14½″ high.

Poughkeepsie. Vassar College Art Gallery.
    Woman and Child. 1933–34. Granite, 41″ high (no. *19).

Wichita, Kansas. Wichita Art Museum.
    Head. 1937. Granite, about 10″ high.

FIVE THOUSAND COPIES OF THIS BOOK HAVE BEEN PRINTED IN OCTOBER, 1942 FOR THE TRUSTEES OF THE MUSEUM OF MODERN ART BY THE PLANTIN PRESS, NEW YORK

Photograph by Paul Strand

GASTON LACHAISE

Gaston Lachaise

Retrospective Exhibition

January 30 - March 7, 1935

The Museum of Modern Art, New York

Copyright, January 1935, by the Museum of Modern Art, New York

THE EXHIBITION HAS BEEN SELECTED FROM THE FOLLOWING COLLECTIONS:

Mr. Walter P. Chrysler, Jr., New York

Mrs. W. Murray Crane, New York

Mrs. Edward Cummings, New York

Mr. John A. Dunbar, New York

Mr. Arthur F. Egner, South Orange, New Jersey

Mr. Gustave B. Garfield, New York

Mrs. O'Donnell Iselin, New York

Mr. Gaston Lachaise, New York

Mrs. Gaston Lachaise, New York

Mr. and Mrs. Q. A. Shaw McKean, Boston

Mr. Lyon Mearson, New York

Mr. George L. K. Morris, New York

Mr. Edward Nagle, Charlottesville, Virginia

Mrs. Edward A. Norman, New York

Mrs. Philip Owen, New Haven

Mr. Frank K. M. Rehn, New York

Mrs. John D. Rockefeller, Jr., New York

Mr. Paul Rosenfeld, New York

Mme. Helena Rubinstein, New York

Mr. Gilbert Seldes, New York

Mr. Carl Van Vechten, New York

Mr. Edward M. M. Warburg, New York

Dr. James Sibley Watson, Jr., Rochester

Mr. M. R. Werner, New York

Cleveland Museum of Art, Cleveland

Lyman Allyn Museum, New London

Smith College Museum of Art, Northampton, Massachusetts

Whitney Museum of American Art, New York

Kraushaar Art Galleries, New York

Weyhe Gallery, New York

In addition to those who have lent works of art, the Trustees and the Director wish to thank the following for their help in assembling the exhibition: Mr. Winslow Ames, Director of the Lyman Allyn Museum; Mr. Philip Goodwin; Mr. Lincoln Kirstein; Miss Antoinette Kraushaar of the C. W. Kraushaar Art Galleries; Mr. William M. Milliken, Director of the Cleveland Museum of Art; Mr. Edward M. M. Warburg; Mr. Carl Zigrosser of the Weyhe Gallery; and the artist.

Special thanks are due Mr. Lincoln Kirstein for his contribution to the catalog.

Miss Dorothy Miller and Miss Ernestine Fantl of the Museum Staff have been in charge respectively of assembling the exhibition and supervising the catalog.

Mr. Lachaise has coöperated in selecting the exhibition. Only works approved by him have been included.

ALFRED H. BARR, JR., *Director*

TRUSTEES

A. Conger Goodyear, *President*
Mrs. John D. Rockefeller, Jr., *1st Vice President*
Stephen C. Clark, *2nd Vice President*
Samuel A. Lewisohn, *Secretary and Treasurer*

William T. Aldrich
James W. Barney
Frederic C. Bartlett
Cornelius N. Bliss
Mrs. W. Murray Crane
Frank Crowninshield
The Lord Duveen of Millbank
Philip Goodwin
Mrs. Charles S. Payson
Duncan Phillips
Nelson A. Rockefeller
Paul J. Sachs
Mrs. John S. Sheppard
Edward M. M. Warburg
John Hay Whitney

GASTON LACHAISE

His Life

The sculptor Gaston Lachaise was born in Paris, March 19, 1882. His father, Jean Lachaise, was a cabinet maker who came up from Auvergne to the capital and installed himself in his own workshop. He married Marie Barrée, a Parisian of Alastian descent. Jean Lachaise executed the woodwork for the private apartments of the engineer Eiffel at the very top of the great tower constructed for the Exposition of 1889. As a small boy Lachaise climbed with his father out upon the exterior framework of the tower, conceiving a terror of heights.

At the age of thirteen, encouraged by his father who had an artisan's respect for an artist, Lachaise entered the Ecole Bernard Palissy. Named after the great Renaissance ceramist, this school was one of the most thorough and imaginative training grounds for the artist-craftsman in the whole of Europe. A remarkable standard of practical work in carving stone, wood and ivory, in drawing, painting, anatomy and the history of art was maintained by an excellent academic faculty. Lachaise studied there for three years. He was instructed by the director Aube, a distinguished academician, and particularly by Moncel, the master in sculpture. To complete his course Lachaise should have a stayed a fourth year, but he was eager not to waste his time, as he thought, so he applied for admission to the Académie Nationale des Beaux-Arts, to which he was admitted in 1898 at the age of sixteen.

Moncel had been a pupil of Gabriel Jules Thomas, the most conservative of the classicists and head of one of the three sculpture ateliers at the Beaux-Arts. Lachaise therefore entered the studio of Thomas rather than of either of the two other eminent official sculptors, Falguière or Barrias. At the same time Charles Despiau and Paul Landowski were studying at the Beaux-Arts; of the three hundred odd students of the time only Despiau, Landowski and Lachaise have, in any real sense, become eminent.

Lachaise learned a great deal more at the Ecole Bernard Palissy than at the Beaux-Arts, but his new position as a student of the state gave him for a time a sense of security. He had a small studio on the Avenue du Maine near the Gare Montparnasse. He was a good student but worked without any particular impulse. He was trying, as he was taught, to express "interesting" subjects. His natural dreaminess began to assert itself and he found himself more and more prone to wander in the Louvre and other museums rather than to work. He went to studio parties, to the Bals Musettes, the Concerts Rouges. He read Baudelaire, Rimbaud and Verlaine.

One day he met by chance an American who later became his wife and who was to have a profound influence on his art and life. She was leaving for America and he would have followed at once if he had had the money. To his wife Lachaise has constantly given all credit for a courage and fortitude of which he himself was not capable. She had been the directing emotional and spiritual force in his creative endeavor.

Though he could not leave France Lachaise now abandoned the Beaux-Arts. He had already twice been chosen in the first twenty of three hundred students to compete for the Prix de Rome. This twenty was to be reduced to ten, the ten to the winner. But Lachaise threw over all his chances for such academic ease and went to work for René Lalique, the successful designer and manufacturer of jewelry and objects in glass. The style of the Art Nouveau with its use of motives from nature was rampant. Lachaise went around with a snake in his pocket to study its undulations as ideas for jewelry designs. During these years he exhibited frequently at the Salon des Artistes Français.

He worked with Lalique for a year to save enough money to go to America. He sailed from Liverpool on the S. S. Ivernia. His decision to leave Europe was the turning point of his life. Since then he has never left this continent, and he feels that in spite of his foreign heritage he has become, in his thirty years of creative life here, entirely naturalized.

When he arrived in Boston on January 13, 1906, he could not speak a word of English. He had tried to learn it at night school in Paris but soon gave it up. He had thirty dollars in his pockets and no prospects. But he got a job for a short time with John Evans, a commercial sculptor on Huntington Avenue, who told him to do a Gothic Virgin for a church. Lachaise found himself, after all his study at the Bernard Palissy and at the Beaux-Arts, wholly untrained to turn out this kind of work. He had not learned to construct a figure in any style at a day's notice. In Paris he would have been given the problem of expressing a "subject-composition" and he would have had six months to do a full-length figure.

He found a room on Beacon Hill. Through his landlady who knew the eminent American academic sculptor, Henry Hudson Kitson, he secured his second position. Kitson, who lived at Quincy not far away, was working on an enormous Civil War memorial to the Confederate dead at Vicksburg, a project involving soldiers, horses, men and guns. When Lachaise started to work for Kitson he found again that what he had been taught at the schools was of little practical use to him. But

8

his training with Lalique and his mastery of the jeweler's craft stood him in good stead. He worked on the uniform trimmings, belt buckles, buttons, epaulets, harnesses and saddles. Kitson was a stickler for military accuracy. He well knew the eagle-eyed committees of C. S. A. veterans with whom he had to deal. Kitson was also working on the Fenway memorial to Patrick Andrew Collins and Lachaise did the delicate tracery on the Irish Harp of Tara's Muse. Lee Lawrie, later the sculptor of Bertram Goodhue's Nebraska State Capitol, was at this time Kitson's chief assistant. Lachaise was amazed at the facility with which Lawrie could throw up a figure, wrinkles in the sleeves, creases in the pants, all complete in practically no time. But his Beaux-Arts training always made him look for the anatomical structure, the bone beneath the surface.

Lachaise had been of an indolent, delicate and dreamy disposition. In the spring of 1906 he took a room in Quincy. Every day he swam in Dorchester Bay and at the end of a month he could swim a mile at a stretch. This changed his nature physically and mentally. For the first time he really felt that he was an American, although he had made little progress in American methods of working. He rented a studio on Tremont Street near Park, but continued to earn his living by enlarging buttons, medals and swords for Kitson. As work of his own he modeled a series of masks in honor of the birth of a friend's child. They were faces of such men as Abraham Lincoln and others who he felt would have a benign influence over a new life.

Kitson then came to New York, opening a studio on MacDougal Alley. In the previous two years Lachaise had made himself very useful around the studio, so that he was left, with Mrs. Kitson in charge, to finish enlarging a big equestrian statue, the central figure of the Vicksburg memorial, which in all took four years to complete. Lachaise followed Kitson to New York in 1912. He took a small studio on Fourteenth Street, and first felt the impulse to model the small human figures which were to be the basis of his subsequent sculptural activity.

The severing of his connection with Kitson in one sense relieved Lachaise. He was at least free, but he had absolutely no means by which to live. He took a room in a boarding house on Washington Square South kept by a Miss Case. It was a house in which Edgar Poe might have lived, full of dark corners, strange sounds and smells, and even boasting a mad poet. Lachaise had two first floor windows which looked on the Square, and in this room, by no means a studio, he commenced the life-sized *Standing Woman* (No. 16) which was to take ten years to complete. His wife posed for this figure in its earliest state, but after that he amplified the form from his own imagination. This figure he considers to be the nucleus and spring of his entire development and in some ways his best work. His mother managed to help him with what little money she could spare, but after six months he had to look for another job.

9

At about this time Lachaise went to the studio of Paul Manship, whose assistant, an Italian sculptor Buffano, was leaving to work on the decoration of the San Francisco's World's Fair. Manship did not feel that he needed an assistant, however, and Lachaise continued his search elsewhere. Suddenly the mad poet at Miss Case's decided that he wanted to study sculpture and asked Lachaise if he knew who could teach him. Lachaise had been fascinated by the behavior of this strange man. He took him to Manship's studio. Manship refused to teach the poet, but said that if Lachaise himself would come back the next day there would be work for him.

Manship was doing considerable sculptural detail on private houses for the architect Platt. Lachaise worked on decorative arrangements of leaves, fruit and the like. The training at Lalique's again proved useful. Manship was pleased, and Lachaise worked on the detail of the pedestal of Manship's *Nymph and Centaur*, putting more character into his work than would an ordinary bronze chiseller.

In 1913 Lachaise rented his first really good studio. It was on West Twenty-third Street and had a skylight but no elevator. He could now take the cast of the *Standing Woman*, which was already in plaster, out of storage. On this he now worked a great deal, and also at this time composed the series of statuettes, a few of which, cast in bronze from the wax, are exhibited in the present exhibition (Nos. 1-5). He was starting to express his own personality freely for the first time. Lachaise was now able to marry, as he had long wished to do. Then he became ambitious on his own account; he wanted to have a show himself. When the preparations for the famous Armory Show of 1913 were under way, Gutzon Borglum and Arthur B. Davies had come to Kitson's studio to see if he had anything for the exhibition. Kitson had not, but after they had left, Lachaise, who was in his overalls working around the studio, asked Kitson if he could not show them something of his own. Lachaise overtook them halfway down the alley, led them to his room nearby, and showed them a clay figure of a woman (No. 3). He had no money for bronze or plaster, but it was exhibited in the Armory Show under glass.

Lachaise had planned a show for 1916 at the Bourgeois Galleries. Toward this he worked intensively, sending plasters to the foundry, the casting to be paid for when the bronzes should be sold. The World War and unsettled conditions forced the postponement of his exhibition until 1918, and debts started to mount up grimly.

Lachaise's life has never been easy, but strangely enough, it has always been on the verge of ease without his ever achieving, even for a month at a time, anything like economic security. Yet Lachaise however much he has been misunderstood has always impressed academic sculptors and critics by his innate crafts-

10

manship and ability; and his decorative work, always somewhat of a compromise for him, has usually won immediate and wide-spread popularity. An American academician once approached him, telling him that it would be easy for him to join the National Academy, thus gaining prestige and the probability of subsequent commissions. At the same time he was informed that if he chose to compete as an American for the Prix de Rome it would be possible to suspend the rules disqualifying a married man. But Lachaise had no desire for three years' study in Rome. His one idea was to establish himself independently as a sculptor in his adopted country. He felt that any academic approbation or affiliation was a step in the very direction he had abandoned when he left France. Lachaise has persistently refused any alliance with official groups. In 1930 he was asked to join the Art Commission of the City of New York, but he declined to serve because he felt that he could not be sympathetic with the policies of such a body.

His first one-man show at the Bourgeois Galleries was comparatively well received. Two pieces were sold. Henry McBride praised the work, but the *Standing Woman*, now complete in plaster but not to be cast in bronze for another ten years, was ridiculed as fat, heavy, grotesque.

Manship moved from his old studio at Twenty-third Street and Lexington Avenue to the large studio in Washington Mews which Lachaise himself now occupies. He was at work upon the memorial to J. P. Morgan, commissioned by the Trustees of the Metropolitan Museum of Art. This large marble plaque was, of course, designed by Manship, but Lachaise worked on both the clay and the plaster and did all the stone cutting. Some four years were expended on its execution.

During this period Lachaise had a difficult time making both ends meet. He was working toward his second show. There was hardly enough time in the twenty-four hours of a day to fulfill his obligations to Manship, and do his own work. In his own studio on Fourteenth Street he was modelling a large work, an heroic nude group of a man with a woman in his arms. This he later destroyed in the plaster for he felt that it was unrealized. He wishes to return to the idea, but as yet has not.

In 1920 his second one-man show was held at the Bourgeois Galleries. Albert Gleizes, the French painter, was a friend of Lachaise and much interested in his sculpture. They exchanged examples of their work. In spite of Lachaise's considerable fame in America, the small figure which he gave Gleizes is his only work owned in Europe. The French, so eager as a nation to claim their artists, have never had a chance to see Lachaise's work. Nothing was sold from the second show. There was little result from it except more debts. But a little later Lachaise began to sell a few works directly to collectors, and Kraushaar, the Fifth Avenue dealer, for some time bought nearly everything Lachaise would bring him.

11

Soon after this time Lachaise decided to sever his connection with Paul Manship.

In 1919 *The Dial* was taken over by Dr. James Sibley Watson and Scofield Thayer. They made it a magazine distinguished by contributions from the important creative artists and writers of America and Europe. The frontispiece of the first issue was a drawing by Lachaise. Later several photographs of his sculpture and drawings were used for its monthly posters and his work was frequently reproduced in its pages. Lachaise did portraits of Watson and Thayer, and other contributors to *The Dial* also sat to him, notably Marianne Moore, E. E. Cummings, Gilbert Seldes, Edward Nagle, Edgar Varese, and Henry McBride. Thayer bought *La Montagne* cut in a bluish stone, which was reproduced along with a crayon drawing in the *Dial* portfolio "Living Art," published in 1923. In 1924 A. E. Gallatin published a book of plates of the work of Lachaise, with an appreciative essay and a check list of works so far achieved. In 1927 Alfred Stieglitz gave Lachaise a one-man show at his Intimate Gallery, and did a great deal to help the sculptor's position and to justify him before the New York world of art. Stieglitz' propaganda for Lachaise came at an excellent time, for Lachaise was being bitterly attacked for his innovations in form. Lachaise did portraits of Stieglitz and of John Marin in bronze and of Georgia O'Keeffe in alabaster.

Some years before, Lachaise had done some architectural decoration. A large house in Miami built in 1920 by the Chicago millionaire, James Deering, had a small allowance for decorative sculpture. The architect Paul Chalfin offered Manship the job, but he declined. Lachaise accepted. He designed two handsome peacocks which were admirably suitable for garden sculpture. Unfortunately they were badly executed in stone in Florida. Welles Bosworth, architect of the New York Telephone and Telegraph Building at Broadway and Fulton Street, had Manship design a frieze around half of its great hall. In 1921, when Manship was in Europe, Bosworth asked Lachaise to superintend a duplication of the frieze for the other half of the hall. Lachaise refused, but it was happily suggested that he might design something of his own, which he did. In 1922 he executed cement panels of the four seasons for Bosworth's house at Locust Valley, Long Island. He considers these panels his finest architectural sculpture previous to the completion of the reliefs for the International Building in Rockefeller Center.

In 1928 Joseph Brummer gave his handsome galleries for a retrospective one-man show. The *Standing Woman* was finally shown in bronze, as well as the plaster of the large *Floating Woman* (No. 31).

Meigs of the Philadelphia firm of architects Mellor, Meigs and Howe became interested in Lachaise through seeing a photograph of one of his works reproduced in a magazine, and asked him to do a sea gull for his apartment. George Howe of the same firm had received the commission to design a federal memorial to the men of the United States Coast Guard for the National Cemetery at Arlington. He realized that the work of an unofficial sculptor would be accepted with difficulty by the Government Art Commission, but he fought successfully for Lachaise's design, which is of a comparatively tranquil nature.

In 1931 plans for Rockefeller Center were in the air. The late Raymond Hood, one of the architects, was also planning the Chicago Century of Progress Exposition and commissioned Lachaise to do a portal for the Electricity Building. Lachaise now asked him for a job on the Rockefeller Center project. All sculptural commissions were in the hands of Harvey Wiley Corbett. Finally Lachaise was given a commission. But instead of being allowed to do the large bronze over-door of the Maison Française on Fifth Avenue and Forty-ninth Street, he was relegated to a relatively obscure position on the Sixth Avenue side of the R. C. A. Building. The Art Commission unanimously approved his designs, but they were so placed that they can be properly seen only when the elevated railway is removed, if ever.

Lachaise's portal for the Electricity Building at the Chicago World Fair was twenty feet high, fifteen wide. It was executed in polychromed plaster, at first black and gold, then changed to white in the second year of the Fair. This panel was an interesting experiment in the use of the human male figure against a pattern of telegraphic wires and insulators. It was destroyed at the close of the Fair.

Lachaise has just finished two large reliefs for the International Building in Rockefeller Center, now in process of construction. These panels show figures of typical working men, in one panel blasting for the foundation of a building, in the other balancing in the air on a steel beam. These panels, also, are to be placed in a rather awkward and unflattering position, but they are nevertheless his preeminent achievement in this branch of his medium.

His Work

It is probable that Lachaise is one of the most important sculptors alive today, but the magnitude of his achievement is not readily grasped, and this for no merely superficial reason. In his work there is a concentrated dynamism which is so intense that it repels while it attracts. His subject matter is not ultimately men and women, nor even Man and Woman. His subject matter is the glorification, revivification and amplification of the human body; its articulate structure clothed in flesh. He is an idol maker. He risks the dangers, derisions and rewards of a man, not creating a religion, but at least supplying the documents corroborating a religion. Just as his figures frequently transcend the factually physical, so does their physicality transcend the immediately sexual; but since much of his work has sexual implications, there have been numerous inevitable confusions in his reception as an innovator.

Lachaise, above all other sculptors since the Renaissance, is the interpreter of

13

maturity. He is concerned with forms which have completed their growth, which have achieved their prime; forms, as he would say, in the glory of their fulfillment. Amplitude and abundance are not in themselves concepts unpleasing to most people, so long as the expression of them in sculpture is not far removed from a young Greek girl banked with a flowering cornucopia representing Plenty. Acceptance of the idea of maturity today would imply a change in popular psychology. It is no wonder that to a nation predominantly adolescent Lachaise's insistence upon the mature is frightening.

Considered a violent offender against rules of good taste in sculpture, Lachaise can nevertheless rely on many witnesses from the past in art to justify him, should he need them. Michelangelo, Titian, Dürer, Rubens, Rembrandt, Courbet come easily to mind. He feels that he is a link in the tradition of the handling of developed forms, but far more as a re-creation than as a reminiscence of previous epochs. His preferences in the art of the past illuminate his present activity. The past he loves best is remotest, the very earliest dawn of European culture when men inscribed tusked mammoths and bison on the walls of their stone caverns, beasts with shaggy mountainous bodies delicately balanced on small, careful hoofs. Or small paleolithic objects carved from ivory or stone, female bodies of refined grossness, with huge mounded breasts capable of suckling whole tribes; earth-goddesses which were in ten thousand years to be corrupted into the softer, many-breasted Diana of the Ephesians. Next, he admires the clarity, precision and anonymity of the Egyptian stone carvers, craftsmen who were capable of taking human models, priest or king, and elevating them into godhead, the cut stone becoming not only a portrait but an expressed fragment of divine vitality, an idol worthy of worship. Lastly he feels himself close to the Hindu sculptors of India and the Malay archipelagos, who allowed themselves great freedom with the human body, adopting hieratic rearrangement and refinement to produce interlocking friezes of terrible dances and scenes of loving and destructive gods. He feels that the cavemen had already all the reverence, simplicity and fervor of subsequent "great" periods, that their painting too had a majesty never revived in later inventions. He admires the force of barbarians and feels there is not nearly enough of their directed impulse in art today. He feels that his own work has a barbarian impulse which, taking nature as its base, makes nature idol-like or god-like. For the well-achieved work of other more civilized periods he has the good craftsman's respect for good craftsmanship. But that is about all. He thinks, for example, that negro sculpture, considering its conditioning in fear, magic and ceremonial aims, is far more relevant to Africa and to ourselves than is Greek sculpture of the middle or late periods and the decadence of classic traditionalism in the West. A simple, unbiased vision has been difficult for the paler European. He believes that Renaissance imitation of Greek ideals and its various mutations

14

down to our own time are without much inherent energy and in the last analysis only well-executed imitations of a reality far more moving in the flesh. The cavemen knew as much about the relationship of animals to natural forces as contemporary artists despite their advantage of the whole realm of scientific research and developed cosmologies. Not that Lachaise would stop at the mammoth. Only, he would share the grandeur and inevitability of the earlier impulsive awe, unfettered by secondary considerations of decoration or surface refinement or a preconceived idea of what is fitting or beautiful.

Lachaise keenly feels himself to be of his own time. He is constantly motivated by a tense desire to express his reactions, to clarify impressions received immediately around him in his daily existence. When he left the declining French heritage of the nineteenth century at the age of twenty, he foresook all that the European continent had to offer him. He came to an America which was and is, for him, explicit in its many vivid, brutal, fragmentary energies and techniques. He has loved and studied the ample crassness of strip-tease burlesque shows, the miraculous human equilibrium of circus tightrope walkers and six-day bicycle racers, the transitory revelations of women's fashions, the irresistible controlled force of hydraulic presses and steam drills, the lift and pull of derricks, and the suspension of riveted steel beams. His files are full of pictures torn from newspapers, wind blowing a woman's skirt, workmen balanced on the final height of a building's skeleton, airplanes, automobiles, and wild animals. Of the sculptors of his own time he respects Lehmbruck, Epstein and Brancusi.

Many of his American contemporaries have sat to him for their portraits. Sometimes the likeness has been achieved in a few sittings. But in other cases it has been far longer. On one head he worked for fifty-eight separate sittings, on another small full-length portrait, longer. Often a portrait has been done in the initial clay, later cast in bronze from plaster, and subsequently even carved in marble. The portraits are a great deal more than likenesses. Like Roman and Egyptian portrait heads they preserve at the same time not only the man but his epoch. Lachaise's portraits, like the rest of his work, are essential rather than factual. Except for Epstein, there is no one in our own time who so comprehensively presents a whole personality in a portrait head.

The whole personality can of course be inferred from a head. But often over the past few years Lachaise has preferred to portray the entire nude figure whenever the model can be persuaded. There are numerous barriers against such portraiture today, primarily in the minds of his subjects. But the Romans and the Egyptians were not dismayed by this frankness, and gradually we are becoming less so.

Lachaise has in his life done a great deal of work which, though he is by no means ashamed of it, he considers to be of a secondary nature. This includes

15

numerous decorative treatments of birds, fish and animals, all studied carefully for the fullest expression of their character but with full understanding of the slightness of the subject matter. It is not difficult to understand why these amiable objects have been widely popularized and even imitated. His architectural work of the past he also considers of a subordinate character. He always hopes for the day when he will be offered the chance to produce a work of sculpture in relation to architecture which is neither an apology for a blank wall or an incidental detail in the design. It is not too unlikely to expect that such a time will come. However, most architects are jealous of any competition with their own rigid elevations. They placate the sculptor by placing his work where it amounts to little more than an irritated surface. They do not sufficiently understand that sculpture in high relief or even free-standing can definitely enhance the monumental volumes of modern building.

However, Lachaise has not allowed himself to be discouraged from attempting heroic sculpture merely because of lack of large commissions. Aside from the first *Standing Woman* he has completed four large figures, each suitable for an architectural setting. The so-called *Floating Woman* was completed in plaster in 1927. At this time Lachaise had been much impressed by contemporary theories of space and time. He had been considering the almost unimaginable curve of the earth's ocean horizon line, straight to the physical eye, but progressing into an infinite curve; over and above this, even more incredible, the convolutions of the earth's curves enclosed in other more enormous orbits, of which our whole universe is possibly but a fragment. He has always felt the most sentient, universal subject of sculptural expression to be the human figure, and in his *Floating Woman* he attempted an embodiment of cosmic concepts.

The heroic nude *Woman* (No. 39), is a culmination in this direction, the maturity of his maturity. Her strong legs seem almost forced deep in the ground, yet her large haunches exert little pressure. She exists in air as much as on the earth. She is a calmly savage figure, an idea of the feminine that has a serenity more dominating than tender. This figure is an uncompromising statement, not easy to regard with complacency.

The *Man* (No. 41), considerably refined and altered since it was first shown at the Museum of Modern Art in 1930, is this *Woman's* peer. The pride of this figure is staggering. Its benediction is an ultimate gesture of triumphant, active, sympathetic control. No model was used. The anatomy of the torso reveals the sublimated, crystallized design and firm amplification which Lachaise's profound knowledge of the architecture of the human body has brought him.

Lachaise's physical types have about them an ambiguous quality. The faces of his women often partake of masculine strength and the female figures have a male musculature. His men's heads are sometimes almost androgynous, and mysteri-

16

ously may be implicated with their opposites. This is not decadence but a clear understanding of the mutual nature of the two sexes which arose from the same source.

La Montagne (No. 60), has achieved finality in an heroic mould, after several intermediary developments in bronze and stone. The sculpture is cast in cement, a material which Lachaise feels is appropriate for out-of-doors. *La Montagne* will be placed on a rise of ground in a tall pine wood, raised in all its buoyant weight on six high pillars. This sculpture is a clear phrasing of Lachaise's conception of weight, the balance of breathing sumptuousness, a mountain raised into air, earth sharing the shape of clouds, not swollen or inflated but placid with a concentrated luxurious fullness.

In his own studio at present there are a number of pieces in plaster and bronze which have not been included in this retrospective exhibition. Lachaise feels these works to be of paramount importance to himself and to the world's knowledge of him as an artist. If they were to be shown today, however, they might give offence and precipitate scandal obscuring the importance of the rest of his creation. He is proud of these works and he is not afraid of scandal, and he believes that the original elements in these sculptures will have a healthful effect when they are courageously displayed in a favorable setting. The elements characterizing these works are not new to him. But in them his previous tendencies have been pushed so far as to constitute almost a new revelation. He has fixed in these works heroic incarnations of flesh so violent, so disturbing, that for some time to come they can only provoke wonder.

The organs and spasms of birth are universal symbols for the source and continuation of human life. Lachaise has not been timid in using these symbols. Here again he has personified and canonized sexuality. But his sexuality has not the qualities of superficial, titillating attractiveness, which easily becomes obscene or absurd when rendered in stone or bronze. The lust he shows is heavy, cleansing, weighted with implications of earth and the sprung seed.

No discussion of Lachaise's work, however brief, would be complete without a word about his drawings. Though entirely in outline and very much the work of a sculptor as opposed to that of a painter, the drawings are in no way studies for sculpture. They are independent expressions in their own medium; swift, exuberant, economical and bold. They show his gifts of imaginative metamorphosis, his profound understanding of the articulation, motive processes and capacities of the human body.

His Position

Lachaise is now recognized, even by the daily press, as one of America's outstanding artists. The show at the Museum of Modern Art is a sign of his importance. Nevertheless, it is illuminating to consider him, an acknowledged artist of superior talent, in relation to one factor that qualifies this kind of recognition—economic security.

Lachaise is not represented in the Metropolitan Museum of Art nor in many other American museums. Until this year and the commission for the Fairmount Park Memorial in Philadelphia, Lachaise has had to wait for a public monument worthy of his talent, although they are continually handed out to acceptable academicians even in these lean times. It is true that he is well represented in many private collections. For his patrons a considerable amount of work of secondary character has been accomplished; a smaller amount of primary importance. His life has been filled with difficulties about money, debts and ensuing misunderstandings involving the exhaustion or estrangement of successive patrons, as has so often been the case with artists. A reputation for being difficult, particularly in combination with his naturally reticent character, has not enhanced his standing with possible selection committees. He is not a humorous nor a particularly engaging man. Neither is he resentful. But his intense earnestness has become a way of life, apparent in his manner and his speech. By nature soft and agreeable, he has often forced himself to be harsh and arbitrary almost to save his soul by his own brutality. He has a very just notion of his position in the present and the future. His work, achieved and to be achieved, is of course far more important than the attitude of his patrons about the way he accomplishes this work. If he had followed their solicitous prudent counsel he might have been out of debt, but much of his work would not have existed in the bronze, or at all. Too often patrons have been confused as to the motives of their patronage. Genuinely attracted by something in an artist's work, they will often wish to possess it. Gradually they become involved in the artist's personal life. Patronage imperceptibly shifts to charity, charity to indignation and exasperation. It remains to be seen if patronage by the state has any advantage over the accidental interest of private individuals.

As for Lachaise's future, there is the commission for the monument in Fairmount Park, Philadelphia. There will be portrait heads to do, and the possibility of casting in bronze some of the large figures already in plaster. What else? That is in the hands of the architects of whatever building still goes on. Most of it is controlled by government commissions, and their diffident attitude toward such a sculptor as Lachaise is only too well known. Lachaise has constantly refused to teach. He believes that anyone with a character so well defined as his own could only hand down mannerisms to sensitive pupils. He feels that, as in his own case, the best teachers are well instructed pedagogues. His influence, as such, upon American sculpture has been negligible.

One may hope that some really unselfish interests concerned with the fine arts

18

will give Lachaise a commission for an even more important civic or public work. Many possibilities suggest themselves. For example, there is no worthy memorial to Thomas Jefferson at the University of Virginia, a project which interests Lachaise intensely. There is no fitting monument to Herman Melville, or to Winslow Homer or Thomas Eakins. John Reed is unhonored by Harvard College. There is no stone to the memory of Hart Crane, whom Lachaise knew and admired. Lachaise has twenty years or more of work ahead which should be the crowning period of his life. Not to make the fullest use of such a talent would be heartless waste.

LINCOLN KIRSTEIN

CHRONOLOGY

1882	Born in Paris, March 19
1895	Entered the Ecole Bernard Palissy
1898	Entered the Atelier Gabriel Jules Thomas at the Académie Nationale des Beaux-Arts
1899-1903	Exhibited at Salon des Artistes Français
c.1905	Left the Beaux-Arts. Met Isabel Nagle, his future wife. Went to work for René Lalique
1906	Landed in Boston, Massachusetts, January 13.
1906-1912	Worked for Henry Hudson Kitson
1912	Moved to New York City. Began the *Standing Woman*
1913	Small clay figure exhibited in the Armory Show. Met Paul Manship and became his assistant. Married
1916	First show planned and postponed
1918	First one-man show at the Bourgeois Galleries
1920	Second one-man show at the Bourgeois Galleries
1919-1925	*The Dial* period. Portraits
1921	Frieze for Telephone Building, New York. Work at the Kraushaar Galleries
1922	Cement plaques for Welles Bosworth's house, Long Island
1923	*The Dial's* portfolio, "Living Art," published
1924	Monograph by A. E. Gallatin published. Cleveland Museum purchase of marble head
1927	One-man show at Stieglitz' Intimate Gallery
1928	One-man show at the Brummer Gallery. *Floating Woman* shown. National Coast Guard Memorial, Washington
1930	Heroic *Man* (first state) exhibited at Museum of Modern Art
1931	Reliefs for R. C. A. Building, Rockefeller Center
1932	Portal for Chicago Century of Progress Exposition
1933	Heroic *Standing Woman* in bronze placed in New London. Nude portraits
1934	Reliefs for International Building, Rockefeller Center. *La Montagne* in cement
1935	Commission for Memorial to the Peoples of America, for Fairmount Park, Philadelphia

BIBLIOGRAPHY

Cummings, E. E.   Gaston Lachaise. *Creative Art*, Vol. III, Aug. 1928, pp. xxvii-xxviii

——————————   Gaston Lachaise. *The Dial*, Vol. LXVIII, Feb. 1920, pp. 194-204

Fierens, Paul.   Sculpteurs d'Aujourd'hui. Paris, Editions des Chroniques du Jour, and New York, E. Weyhe, 1933; pl. 18-19, page opp. pl. 15

Gallatin, A. E.   Gaston Lachaise; sixteen reproductions in collotype of the sculptor's work, edited with an introduction by A. E. Gallatin. New York, E. P. Dutton & Co., 1924

——————————   Gaston Lachaise. *The Arts*, Vol. III, June 1923, pp. 397-402

——————————   Letter from U. S. A. *Formes*, No. VI (English edition), June 1930, pp. 22-23

Lachaise, Gaston.   A Comment on My Sculpture. *Creative Art*, Vol. III, Aug. 1928, pp. xxiii-xxvi

Living Art; a portfolio. New York, The Dial Publishing Co., 1923; pl. 4, 9-10

McBride, Henry.   Here's to Lachaise; introduction to catalog of Lachaise exhibition. New York, The Brummer Gallery, 1928

——————————   Modern Art. *The Dial*, Vol. LXXXII, June 1927, pp. 530-32; Vol. LXXXIV, Mar. 1928, pp. 262-64; Vol. LXXXVI, May 1928, pp. 442-44

Mayor, A. Hyatt.   Gaston Lachaise. *Hound & Horn*, Vol. V, July-Sept. 1932, pp. 563-80

Seldes, Gilbert.   Lachaise: Sculptor of Repose. *The New Republic*, Vol. LIV, Apr. 4, 1928, pp. 219-20

——————————   Profiles: Hewer of Stone. *The New Yorker*, April. 4. 1931, pp. 28-31

The work of Lachaise has also been reproduced in many periodicals, such as *The American Magazine of Art, Architectural Forum, Arts and Decoration, The Art Digest, The Art News, The Dial, Fine Arts*, and *Parnassus*, and in the catalogs of the Museum of Modern Art, *Painting and Sculpture by Living Americans, American Painting and Sculpture*, and *Modern Works of Art*.

CATALOG

An asterisk before a catalog number indicates that the item is illustrated by a plate which bears the same number. Dates have been supplied by the artist.

*1. Woman (1910)
Bronze, 12 inches high
Collection Edward M. M. Warburg, New York

2. Woman Walking (c. 1911)
Bronze, 11¼ inches high
Collection Kraushaar Art Galleries, New York

*3. Woman (1912)
Plaster, 10½ inches high
Exhibited: Armory Show, New York, 1913
Collection Mrs. Gaston Lachaise

4. Woman (c. 1912)
Bronze, 7¼ inches high
Collection Weyhe Gallery, New York

5. Statuette (c. 1912)
Bronze, 7¾ inches high
Collection Mrs. Gaston Lachaise, New York

*6. La Montagne (c. 1913)
Bronze (1930), 6⅞ inches high
Collection Weyhe Gallery, New York

*7. Woman (1913-1918)
Bronze, 12½ inches high
Collection Smith College Museum of Art, Northampton, Massachusetts

*8. Woman (c. 1918)
Bronze, 11⅞ inches high
Collection Gustave B. Garfield, New York

*9. Woman's Head (1918)
Marble, 10½ inches high
Collection Mrs. Q. A. Shaw McKean, Boston

10. Woman's Head (1918)
Stone, 14½ inches high
Collection Dr. James Sibley Watson, Jr., Rochester, New York

11. **Relief—Woman (1918)**
Marble, 28½ x 19¾ inches
Collection Mrs. Gaston Lachaise, New York

12. **Seated Woman (c. 1918-1925)**
Bronze, 11¼ inches high
Collection Mme. Helena Rubinstein, New York

*13. **Woman on Sofa (1918-1923)**
Bronze (1928), 9¼ inches high
Collection Weyhe Gallery, New York

14. **Woman's Head (1919)**
Stone, 14¾ inches high
Collection Mrs. W. Murray Crane, New York

*15. **Woman's Head (1920)**
Marble, 20¼ inches high
Collection Cleveland Museum of Art, Cleveland, Ohio

*16. **Standing Woman (1912-1927)**
Bronze, 68 inches high
Collection John A. Dunbar, New York

17. **Torso (Fragment of No. 16)**
Plaster (1934), 47 inches high
Collection the Artist

18. **Woman's Head (1922)**
Alabaster, 13½ inches high
Collection Arthur F. Egner, South Orange, New Jersey

*19. **Woman Walking (1922)**
Bronze, 19 inches high
Private Collection, New York

20. **Mask (1922)**
Alabaster, 7 inches high
Collection Mrs. Gaston Lachaise, New York

21. **Mask (1922-1925)**
Bronze nickel-plated, 15½ inches high
Collection Arthur F. Egner, South Orange, New Jersey

22. **Portrait of E. E. Cummings (1924)**
Bronze, 15 inches high
Collection Mrs. Edward Cummings, New York

23. **Portrait of Edward Nagle (1924)**
    Bronze, 14 inches high
    Collection Edward Nagle, Charlottesville, Virginia

*24. **Portrait Head (1924)**
    Plaster, 13½ inches high
    Collection the Artist

*25. **Standing Woman (1924)**
    Bronze, 15¼ inches high
    Collection Mrs. O'Donnell Iselin, New York

*26. **Woman in Chair (c. 1924)**
    Bronze, 12⅞ inches high
    Collection Weyhe Gallery, New York

27. **Floating Figure (c. 1924)**
    Bronze, 13¼ inches high
    Collection the Artist

*28. **Standing Woman (1926)**
    Bronze, 15¾ inches high
    Collection Frank K. M. Rehn, New York

29. **Woman (1926)**
    Bronze, 11⅝ inches high
    Collection Paul Rosenfeld, New York

30. **Relief—Woman (1927)**
    Alabaster, 13⅝ x 7⅜ inches
    Collection Mrs. Gaston Lachaise, New York

*31. **Floating Woman (1927)**
    Bronze (1935), 53 inches high
    Collection the Artist

*32. **Portrait of John Marin (1927)**
    Bronze, 11 inches high
    Collection The Museum of Modern Art, New York
    Anonymous Gift

*33. **Head (1928)**
    Bronze nickel-plated, 13¼ inches high
    Collection Whitney Museum of American Art, New York

34. **Woman (1928)**
Bronze, 17 inches high
Collection Mrs. Edward A. Norman, New York

*35. **Woman (1928-1931)**
Plaster, 17¾ inches high
Collection the Artist

*36. **Reclining Woman (1928-1931)**
Plaster, 13½ inches high
Collection the Artist

*37. **Torso (1928)**
Bronze, 8¾ inches high
Collection Walter P. Chrysler, Jr., New York

37A. **Hand of a Pianist (1928)**
Plaster, 21 inches high
Collection the Artist

*38. **Woman (Acrobat) (1929)**
Bronze, 20 inches high
Illustrated with No. 57
Collection M. R. Werner, New York

*39. **Standing Woman (1930-1933)**
Bronze, 8 feet high
Lent through Lyman Allyn Museum, New London, Connecticut

*40. **Torso (Fragment of No. 39)**
Plaster (1934), 45 inches high
Collection The Museum of Modern Art, New York
Gift of Edward M. M. Warburg

*41. **Man (1930-1935)**
Plaster, 8½ feet high
Collection the Artist

42. **Torso (1930)**
Bronze (1935), 9 inches high
Collection the Artist

*43. **Torso (1930)**
Bronze, 12 inches high
Collection the Artist

*44. Portrait of Timothy Seldes (1931)
Alabaster, 10 inches high
Collection Gilbert Seldes, New York

*45. Portrait of Carl Van Vechten (1931)
Bronze, 16 inches high
Collection Carl Van Vechten, New York

46. Statuette (1932)
Bronze, 6¼ inches high
Collection Mrs. Philip Owen, New Haven, Connecticut

*47. Portrait Head (1932)
Bronze, 15½ inches high
Private Collection, New York

48. Portrait of Evelyn Gerstein (1932-1935)
Bronze, 15½ inches high
Collection Gustave B. Garfield, New York

*49. Portrait Bust (1933)
Marble, 32 inches high
Collection George L. K. Morris, New York

*50. Boy with a Tennis Racket (1933)
Bronze, 23 inches high
Collection George L. K. Morris, New York

*51. Portrait Figure (1933)
Bronze, 20¾ inches high
Private Collection

*52. Portrait of Edward M. M. Warburg (1933)
Alabaster, 14½ inches high
Collection Edward M. M. Warburg, New York

53. Breasts (1933)
Marble, 7¾ inches high
Collection Edward M. M. Warburg, New York

*54. Knees (1933)
Marble, 19 inches high
Collection Edward M. M. Warburg, New York

27

55. **Torso** (1933)
Marble, 14 inches high
Collection Edward M. M. Warburg, New York

56. **Woman** (1933)
Bronze, 13¼ inches high
Collection Lyon Mearson, New York

*57. **Woman** (1934)
Bronze, 19¾ inches high
Collection the Artist

*58. **Relief—Woman** (1934)
Plaster, 87 x 50 inches
Collection the Artist

*59. **Portrait Figure** (1934-1935)
Bronze, 45 inches high
Private Collection, New York

*60. **La Montagne** (1934-1935)
Cement, 4 feet high, 9 feet long
Collection George L. K. Morris, New York

DRAWINGS

Crayon Drawings

*61. Collection the Artist
62. Collection Mrs. Gaston Lachaise, New York
63. Private Collection, New York

Ink Drawing

64. Collection Mrs. Gaston Lachaise, New York

Pencil Drawings

*65-*74. Collection Edward M. M. Warburg, New York
75. Collection Lyon Mearson, New York
76-77. Private Collection, New York
*78-84. Collection the Artist
85-86. Collection Mrs. Gaston Lachaise, New York
87. Private Collection, New York

PLATES

The plates bear the same numbers as the items of the catalog. Not all the items are illustrated.

3. Woman (1912)

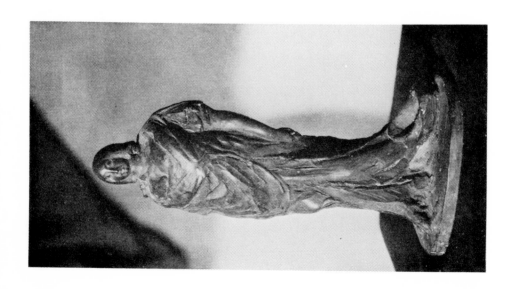

1. Woman (1910)

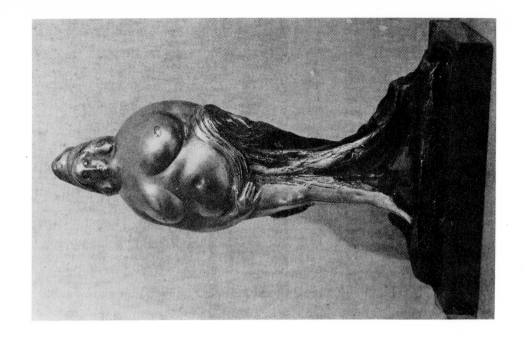

8. Woman (c. 1918)

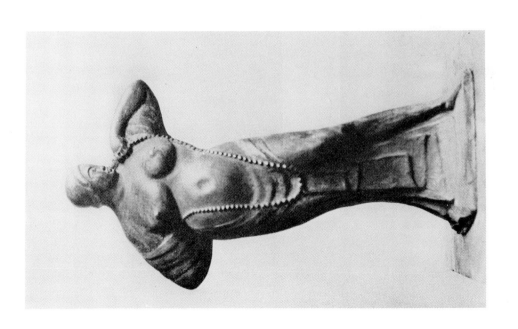

7. Woman (1913-1918)

15. Woman's Head (1920)

9. Woman's Head (1918)

6. La Montagne (c. 1913)

13. Woman on Sofa (1918-1923)

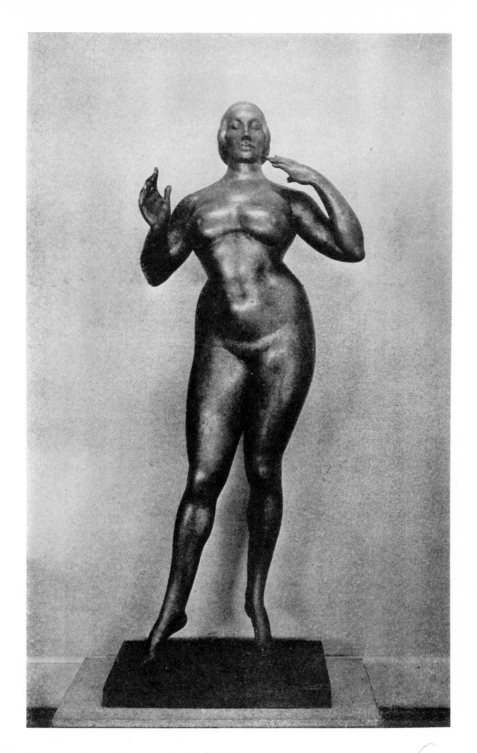

16. Standing Woman (1912-1927)

19. Woman Walking (1922)

28. Standing Woman (1926)

25. Standing Woman (1924)

26. Woman in Chair (c. 1924)

31. Floating Woman (1927)

24. Portrait Head (1924)

32. Portrait of John Marin (1927)

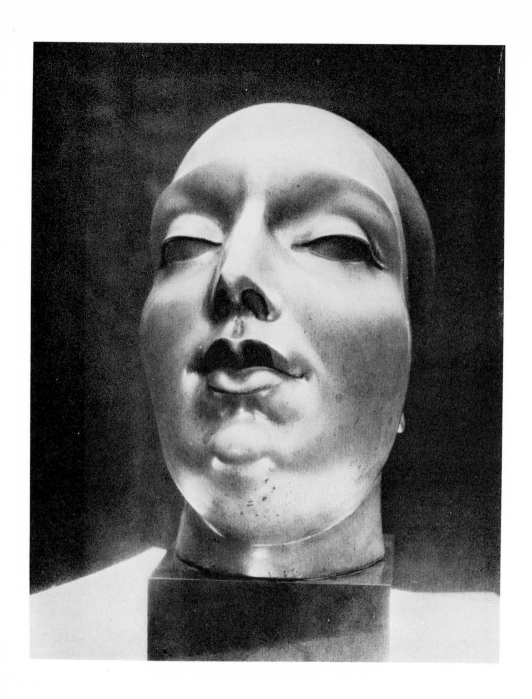

33. Head (1928)

35. Woman (1928-1931)

36. Reclining Woman (1928-1931)

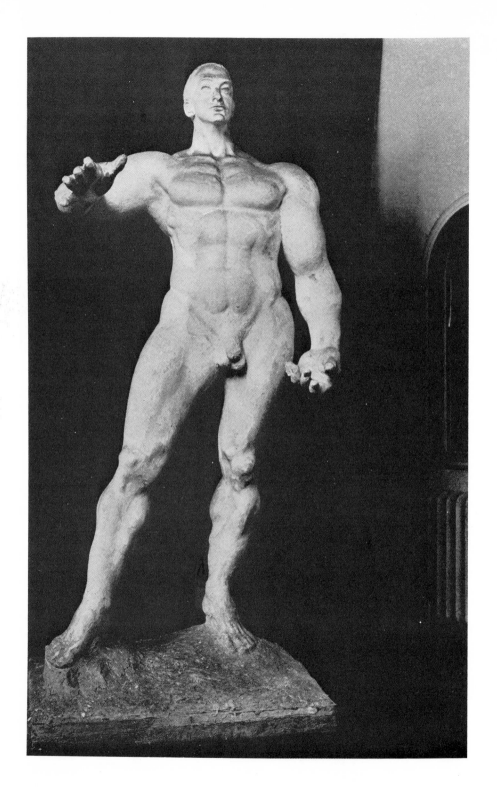

41. Man (1930-1935)

39. Standing Woman (1930-1933)

40. Torso (1934)

43. Torso (1930)

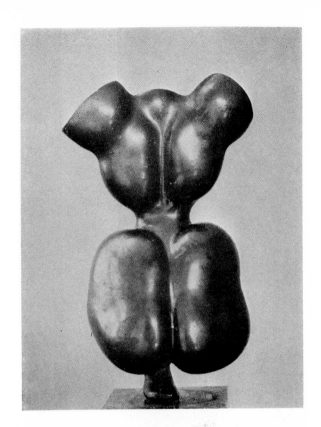

37. Torso (1928)

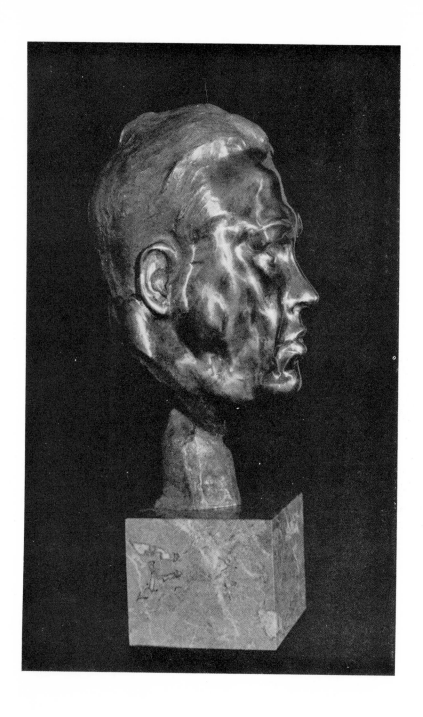

45. Portrait of Carl Van Vechten (1931)

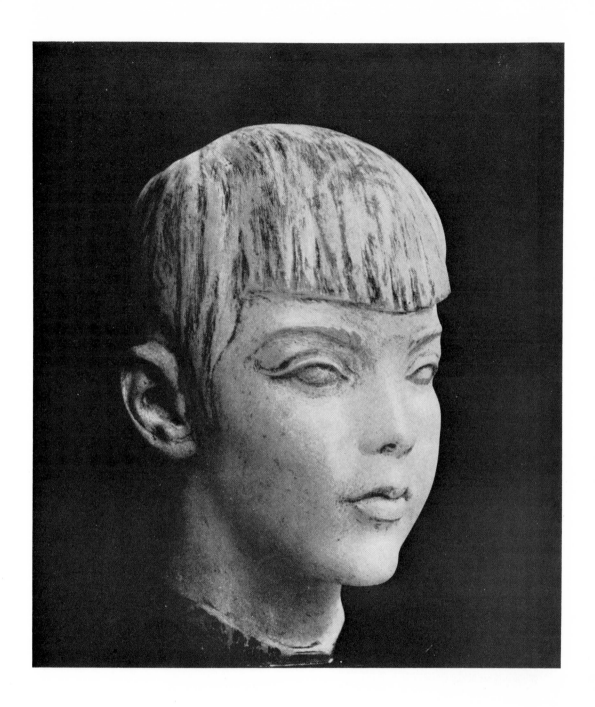

44. Portrait of Timothy Seldes (1931)

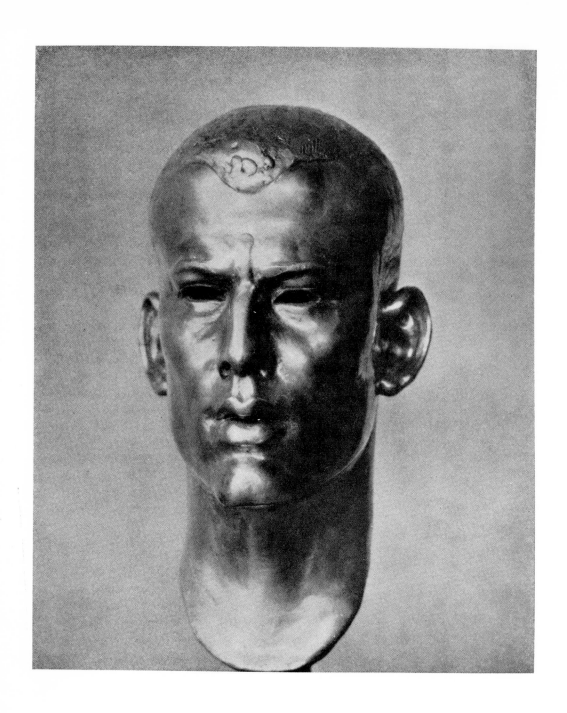

47. Portrait Head (1932)

52. Portrait of Edward M. M. Warburg (1933)

50. Boy with a Tennis Racket (1933)

51. Portrait Figure (1933)

49. Portrait Bust (1933)

54. Knees (1933)

59. Portrait Figure (1934-1935)

58. Relief—Woman (1934)

57. Woman (1934)

38. Woman (Acrobat) (1929)

60. La Montagne (1934-1935)

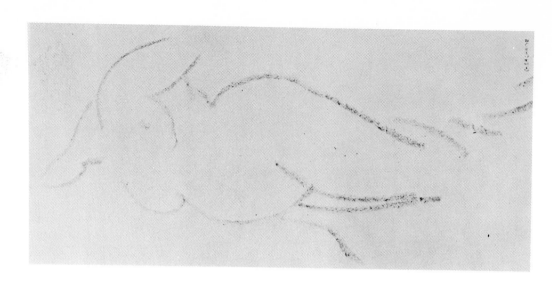

61. Crayon Drawing

74. Pencil Drawing

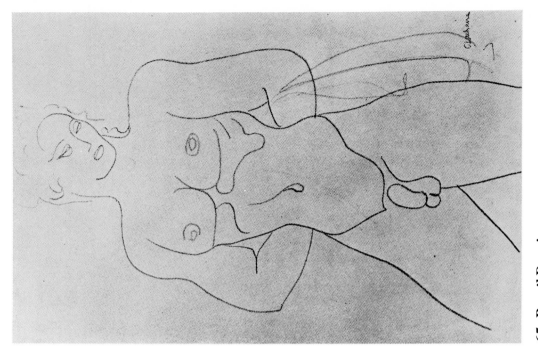

65. Pencil Drawing

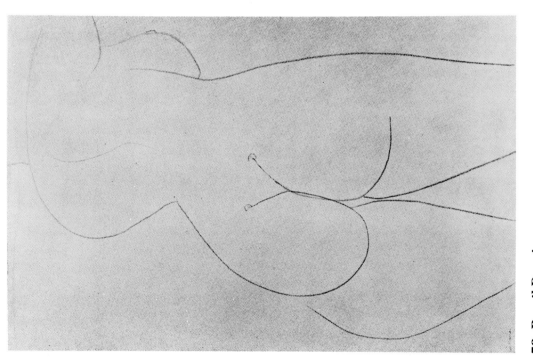

78. Pencil Drawing

PUBLICATIONS OF THE MUSEUM OF MODERN ART

Painting and Sculpture

Cézanne, Gauguin, Seurat, van Gogh. Critical and biographical studies by Alfred H. Barr, Jr. 152 pages; 97 plates. Paper bound—$2.00; bound in boards—$3.50.

Painting in Paris. Foreword and critical notes by Alfred H. Barr, Jr. 88 pages; 50 plates. Paper bound—$2.00; bound in boards—$3.50.

Paintings by 19 Living Americans. This and the following catalog are anthologies of work by the best known contemporary American artists. Biographical notes by Alfred H. Barr, Jr. 88 pages; 38 plates. Paper bound—$2.00.

Painting and Sculpture by Living Americans. 67 pages; 34 plates. Paper bound—$1.50.

Homer, Ryder, Eakins. Essays by Bryson Burroughs, Frank Jewett Mather and Lloyd Goodrich. 68 pages; 34 plates. Paper Bound—$2.00.

Corot and Daumier. Introduction by Alfred H. Barr, Jr. 128 pages; 108 plates. Paper bound—$2.00.

Toulouse-Lautrec and Odilon Redon. Introduction by Jere Abbott. Notes on Lautrec's circle by Daniel Catton Rich. 72 pages; 39 plates. Paper bound—$2.00.
German Painting and Sculpture. Work of the leading German artists, with foreword and extensive notes by Alfred H. Barr, Jr. 91 pages; 49 plates. Paper bound—$2.00.

Murals by American Painters and Photographers. Essays by Lincoln Kirstein and Julien Levy. 62 pages; 61 plates. Paper bound—$.50.

American Painting and Sculpture, 1862-1932. Introduction by Holger Cahill. 128 pages; 79 plates. Paper bound—$1.50; bound in boards—out of print.

American Folk Art. Most comprehensive survey of this subject so far published. Introduction by Holger Cahill. Bibliography. 131 pages; 80 plates. Paper bound—$1.50; bound in boards—$3.50.

American Sources of Modern Art. Introduction on the art of ancient America and its relationship to the art of today by Holger Cahill. Bibliography of over 100 titles. 104 pages; 56 plates. Paper bound—$1.50; bound in boards—$3.50.

Painting and Sculpture from Sixteen American Cities. Contemporary work by 119 artists, with biographies. Edited by Alfred H. Barr, Jr. 61 pages; 116 illustrations. Paper bound—$1.00; bound in boards—$2.50.

A Brief Survey of Modern Painting. Revised edition. A simple introduction to modern painting with notes on each artist by Alfred H. Barr, Jr. Paper bound—$.25.

The Lillie P. Bliss Collection. 1934. Catalogue raisonnée of the collection bequeathed to the Museum. Forewords by A. Conger Goodyear and Alfred H. Barr, Jr. Essay on Cézanne by Jerome Klein. 164 pages; 93 plates. Paper bound—$1.50; bound in boards—out of print.

Modern Works of Art. Introduction by Alfred H. Barr, Jr. Biographies of 111 artists. 152 pages; 147 plates. Paper bound—$1.75; bound in boards—$3.50.

Monographs on Individual Artists

Henri-Matisse. "Notes of a Painter" by Henri-Matisse; only publication in English. Essay by Alfred H. Barr, Jr. 128 pages; 82 plates. Paper bound—$2.00; bound in boards—$3.00.

Charles Burchfield, Early Watercolors. Foreword by Alfred H. Barr, Jr., and notes by the artist. 24 pages; 10 plates. Paper bound—$1.00.

Max Weber, Retrospective Exhibition. Foreword by Alfred H. Barr, Jr., and notes by the artist. 40 pages; 16 plates. Paper bound—$1.00.

Maurice Sterne. Introduction by Horace Kallen and notes by the artist. Biography by Holger Cahill. 52 pages; 23 plates. Bound in boards—$2.50.

Edward Hopper. Notes by the artist. Essays by Charles Burchfield and Alfred H. Barr, Jr. 81 pages; 48 plates. Paper bound—$1.00; bound in boards—$2.50.

George Caleb Bingham, "The Missouri Artist." Essays by Meyric R. Rogers, James B. Musick and Arthur Pope. 32 pages; 14 plates. Paper bound—$.50.

Architecture and Industrial Art

Modern Architecture. By Henry-Russell Hitchcock, Jr., and Philip Johnson. Essay on housing by Lewis Mumford. Introduction by Alfred H. Barr, Jr. Complete bibliographies. 200 pages; 65 plates. Paper bound—$1.50; bound in boards—out of print.

Machine Art. Introduction by Alfred H. Barr, Jr. Brief history of industrial art by Philip Johnson. Catalog of 1,000 industrial objects. 116 pages; 121 plates. Paper bound—$1.50; bound in boards—$3.50.

America Can't Have Housing. Edited by Dr. Carol Aronovici. Articles by 16 American and European housing experts. 64 pages. Paper bound—$.50.

Theatre

Theatre Art. Four centuries of Theatre Art in fourteen countries. Edited and with introduction by Lee Simonson. Articles by John Anderson, John Mason Brown, Paul Alfred Merbach, Allardyce Nicoll, Oliver M. Sayler. 146 pages; 76 plates. Paper bound—$1.50; bound in boards—$3.50.

Riviera Portfolio

Diego Rivera—A Portfolio of Color Reproductions of Mexican Frescoes. Notes by Jere Abbott. The first color reproductions published of the famous frescoes in Chapingo, Cuernavaca and Mexico City. 19 full-color plates and 15 monotones. Autographed by Diego Rivera—$30.00.

Out of Print

Lehmbruck and Maillol; The Bliss Collection, Memorial Exhibition, 1931; Paul Klee; Diego Rivera.

Fifteen hundred copies of this catalog were printed for the Trustees of the Museum of Modern Art by William E. Rudge's Sons, New York, January, 1935.

Frontispiece: two circus women, c.1930. Papier-mâché, 61¼″ high

The Sculpture of Elie Nadelman

BY LINCOLN KIRSTEIN

THE MUSEUM OF MODERN ART · NEW YORK
IN COLLABORATION WITH: THE INSTITUTE OF CONTEMPORARY ART, BOSTON;
THE BALTIMORE MUSEUM OF ART.

Trustees of The Museum of Modern Art

John Hay Whitney, *Chairman of the Board;* Henry Allen Moe, *1st Vice-Chairman;* William A. M. Burden, *2nd Vice-Chairman;* Sam A. Lewisohn, *3rd Vice-Chairman;* Nelson A. Rockefeller, *President;* Philip L. Goodwin, *1st Vice-President;* Mrs. David M. Levy, *2nd Vice-President;* Ranald H. Macdonald, *Treasurer;* John E. Abbott, Alfred H. Barr, Jr., Mrs. Robert Woods Bliss, Stephen C. Clark, Rene d'Harnoncourt, Walt Disney, A. Conger Goodyear, Mrs. Simon Guggenheim, Wallace K. Harrison, James W. Husted, Henry R. Luce, William S. Paley, Mrs. E. B. Parkinson, Mrs. Charles S. Payson, David Rockefeller, Beardsley Ruml, James Thrall Soby, Edward M. M. Warburg, Monroe Wheeler.

HONORARY TRUSTEES

Frederic Clay Bartlett, Mrs. W. Murray Crane, Duncan Phillips, Paul J. Sachs, Mrs. John S. Sheppard.

Copyright, 1948, The Museum of Modern Art. Printed in the U.S.A.

Acknowledgments

Many people have been helpful in gathering information for this book. Without them, especially those in Paris, little would have been precise about Nadelman's early career. In particular, I wish to express appreciation for the unstinted labor of Mlle Liliane Yacoël who saw people who knew the sculptor in his Parisian period. Her detailed reports have been of the first importance, not only for this brief survey, but towards an eventual biography. Mrs. A. Stewart Walker, one of the sculptor's oldest American friends, was continually helpful with information and advice.

Special thanks are due to Mrs. Elie Nadelman for invaluable advice and assistance.

In addition, the author and The Museum of Modern Art wish to thank: Alexander Archipenko, Alfred H. Barr, Jr., George Baillie, Adolphe Basler, Clive Bell, Bernhard Berenson, Edward L. Bernays, Martin Birnbaum, Ernest Brummer, Mrs. Joseph Brummer, Dr. Ruth Cohn, Mrs. Henry T. Curtiss, Prof. Szczesny Detloff, Mrs. Muriel Draper, Donald C. Gallup (and the Collection of American Literature, Yale University), Philip L. Goodwin, Princess Gourielli-Tchkonia, The Misses Gutheridge, Philip C. Johnson, Miss Constance Lloyd, Henry McBride, Thadée Natanson, David Rosen, Meyer Schapiro, Mrs. Marie Sterner, Marek Swarcz, Virgil Thomson, Edward Titus, Roy Titus, Miss Alice B. Toklas, Carl Van Vechten, Glenway Wescott, Dr. Edgar Wind and Count Auguste Zamoyski.   LINCOLN KIRSTEIN

Photograph Credits

Henri Cartier-Bresson courtesy of Harper's Bazaar, p. 9
Druet, pp. 8, 10, 17
Robert Ganley, frontispiece, pp. 11, 25, 40, 44, 45, 46, 47, 48, 49, 50, 51, 52, 53
Mattie Edwards Hewitt, pp. 60 below, 61 above and right
Peter A. Juley, pp. 16, 19, 20, 21
R. V. Smutný, pp. 15 above, 24, 28, 29, 30, 31, 32, 35, 36, 37, 38, 39
Soichi Sunami, pp. 12, 13, 22, 23, 33, 41, 42, 43, 54, 55, 57, 59
Yale University Library, Collection American Literature, pp. 6, 60

Note

All sculptures and drawings unless otherwise indicated are in the collection of Mrs. Elie Nadelman, Riverdale, New York.

Elie Nadelman. Paris, c.1909

Elie Nadelman was born February 20, 1882 in Warsaw, Russian-Poland, at Marszalkowski 143, a house destroyed in the Second World War. He was the seventh child of Hannah Arnstan and Philip Nadelman. His father was a jeweler of liberal opinions and extensive philosophical background. His mother's family numbered among them artists, writers and musicians. He was schooled at the Warsaw *Gymnasium* and High School of Liberal Arts. He spoke and wrote French, German, later English, besides his native Polish and Russian. His childhood seems to have been happy; although he left Poland at nineteen, never to return, he was devoted to his parents until their deaths. His nature was cheerful, energetic and extroverted; he had no conflict in his wish to be an artist. He was briefly sent to the Art Academy maintained in Warsaw. In 1900 he volunteered for the Imperial Russian Army, Poland then being a province of the Tzar. An enlisted man, he received preference owing to his volunteer status. He served a year; but most of the time was spent in teaching drawing to officers' children and decorating barracks with paintings which were almost his last.

After 1901 he studied again at the Warsaw Academy, and a year later went to Kracow to investigate the artistic atmosphere, in hopes it would be less provincial and academic than the capital. There, Konstantin Laszczka (b. 1865) taught a dilute Impressionism derived from Rodin. Nadelman found little to learn, and indeed discovered he was more advanced than either local masters or students; he returned to Warsaw. At this time, as had been the case for a century, Paris was the focus for all progressive Polish thought and art. To be a Polish patriot presupposed Parisian exile. A large and influential colony of Poles led a rich cultural

Rodin

6

life in France. Count Anton Potocki, with the art critic Adolphe Basler, founded a luxurious art journal *Sztuka*. Published in Polish, at once nationalist and international, with lavish illustrations, it held annual competitions. The prize in 1902 went to young Nadelman for his project of a memorial to Frédéric Chopin. The drawing was recognized at once as the work of a sculptor.

Nadelman next reached Munich where he remained six months. Here the dominant artistic influences were the school of anecdotal Romanticism as practiced by Arnold Böcklin and Franz von Stuck. Nadelman was also affected by the piquant modernity of Aubrey Beardsley, whose drawings were very popular in Germany. Some of the characterization in Nadelman's early bronze heads, memories of Herod and Herodias from the illustrations to Oscar Wilde's *Salome*, echoed the perverse, ambiguous amplitude of Beardsley's snaky curls (page 17). Nadelman disliked the artistic climate of Munich, except for its music, theatre, circus and such popular satirical magazines as *Simplicissimus* and *Jugend*. But Munich also contained the Glyptothek with its unrivalled collection of fifth-century pediment figures from the temple of Aegina. This was Nadelman's first contact with the antique. All through his long, variable artistic development there would be continual anchorage to the mature Hellenic ideal, which he later studied more closely in the Louvre.

Lasting memories Nadelman owed Munich were of the wood, plastic and china-headed dolls of the eighteenth and early nineteenth centuries. A great collection of these, with their accessories, furniture and animals, was housed at that time in the Bayerisches Nationalmuseum. These small serious images, made by grownups for children in Bavaria and Thuringia, remained equally in his mind, alongside the heroic simplicity of the archaic gods and warriors. For all his life, the antiquities of the Aegean, and the folk arts of Western Europe were the opposing poles of Nadelman's imagination, revolving around a central focus of the observation of the human body. But Munich was only a step on his path to Paris.

Here Nadelman found by himself, through study of models and museums, the basis for his education as thinker and artist. His father, the jeweler, had given him a sense of craft, together with a passion for luxurious material and rich surface. From the start, Nadelman felt at home manipulating metal, stone and wood — painted, stained or polished. Little is evident from 1903 to 1946 of improvisation or a tentative approach. Even his drawings or small plaster figures were seldom sketchy. Nadelman never worked at the Beaux Arts or with a master. Briefly around 1904, he drew from short poses at the Atelier Colarossi; there was no critique, attendance was merely an inexpensive method of sharing a living model. Here he perfected his ability to catch the salient characteristics of the body, although after 1913, except for portraits, he used no model.

The most famous living artist was then Auguste Rodin, installed, at the end of a life still full of battles, in the state's Dépôt des Marbres on the rue de l'Université. Nadelman admired Rodin as the greatest modeler in bronze since the Renaissance. The bearded, benevolent satyr seemed,

7

as Guillaume Apollinaire wrote, a veritable God-the-Father-Eternal of world art. Rodin's influence on Nadelman is apparent in reproductions of two early plaster groups, now lost, which appeared in *Sztuka* for 1904, as well as in the fine portrait sketch of Thadée Natanson of 1909 (page 60). Later, Rodin's denial of the integrity of stone as a material, the textural softness of his marble cut by his *praticiens* and *metteurs au point* (roughers-out) oppressed Nadelman, who never failed in his admiration for *The Age of Bronze* or *Balzac*. Later, something of Rodin's looming suggestive vagueness may be found in Nadelman's heads in galvano plastique (plaster coated with copper) c. 1924 (page 37).

At the start Nadelman was poor, although aided by his parents, and then by the brothers Natanson (also Poles), founders of *La Revue Blanche* to which so many writers and artists contributed, from Octave Mirbeau and the young Gide, to Bonnard and Vuillard. Nadelman early exhibited a solitary temperament; he immured himself with his companion model, and up to the time of his first show was rarely seen in cafés. He was a creature of personal grace, physical magnetism and an amazingly facile talent. Success could have come easily: Apollinaire speaks of him as working *couronné de roses.*

Some time in 1905, after two months of introspection, he made his decision to devote himself entirely to the root problems of sculpture, which had not been faced seriously for years. He wished to find out, since no one could tell him, of what plastic form was composed: how volume could be described, filled and balanced. This devotion was not towards self-expression, but to researches comparable to an investigation of the nature of physical matter. By analytical drawings of the human nude and head, (page 14) and sculpture projected from these analyses, he sought the construction underlying form and volume. This was an intellectual

Exhibition of Nadelman's work, Galerie Druet, Paris, April 1909

Sculpture in the artist's home, 1947.

rather than an emotional problem undertaken as a moral as much as a manual discipline. Hence he retired from café and salon; later retirement became an increasing compulsion. In his last twenty years it grew complete. Yet, three times within a decade he enjoyed international success. Now, for six years (1903-09) he lived frugally. Gertrude Stein, who met him around 1908, said he rarely quit his studio by daylight; she knew he meditated for hours on the Seine bank. André Gide called his studio a *tanière,* an animal's lair, when Alexandre Natanson took him there in the summer of the same year. At night, Nadelman went on lonely walks about the city of Verlaine, Rimbaud and Baudelaire, whose verses became his bible, and whose spirit could be fully illustrated by his sculpture and drawings.

His early analytical experiments are the key to Nadelman's entire *oeuvre,* which seems planned from the start as an organic unit, having less development or progression than sequential exhaustion of a number of ways of seeing, of stylistic expression, all of which were apparent in essence at his beginning. Commencing by the demarcation of big forms in the nude, he outlined them arbitrarily, or "abstractly" although his contours were always based on concrete observation. The outlines were suites of curves expressing a general direction of gesture of the limbs. After the gross shapes were blocked out, he made further decomposition towards analysis; descriptive arcs were bisected and trisected, reciprocals encompassed the interior masses; finally there was an enveloping unification. The only titles Nadelman gave his figures from 1905 through 1915 were *Research in Volume* or *Accord of Forms.*

Praying figure, c.1904. Plaster, 56″ high

The American collector and critic, Leo Stein, Gertrude's brother, took his friend Picasso to Nadelman's studio in late summer of 1908, the critical year of the analytical movement that Apollinaire (with the phrase of Matisse) was to popularize as Cubism, and which is responsible, historically speaking, for one of the most influential esthetic tendencies of our century. Stein bought a number of Nadelman's early drawings, as well as a small plaster comment on the *Venus of Knidos*. They were placed with the early Picassos in their apartment on the rue de Fleurus, (page 60)

Standing female nude, c.1907. Bronze, 30″ high

where they remained until the Steins split their ménage, Leo moving
to Florence. Gertrude kept the plaster for twenty years, when it was
cast in bronze (above). Most of the drawings were returned by Stein
to Nadelman for reproduction in his portfolio *Vers l'unité plastique*, which
was announced for 1913, but which did not appear until 1914.

Picasso saw in Nadelman's studio the head of a man in plaster (page 15),
which he did not fully understand, but from which, as so often happened
in his voracious career, he appropriated stylistic mannerisms. Nadelman's

11

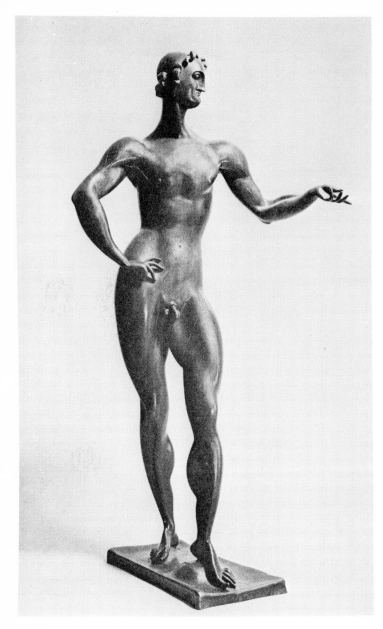

Standing male nude, c.1909. Bronze, 25¾″ high

head was a fragmentation of curves with their logical echoes; he was not decomposing form as much as he was drily describing its anatomy. The head by Picasso (page 15), dated 1909, in the collection of the Museum of Modern Art, is close to Nadelman's, now lost, which in plaster was exposed at the Galerie Druet in April 1909. Comparison of the two illuminates the capital differences between Nadelman's personal research and Analytical Cubism of 1909. Nadelman's head, based on knowledge from his mirror, is a bold demonstration of emphatic planes and curved-edged

Standing female nude, c.1909. Bronze, 22″ high

forms. The volumes repeat the normal anatomy of the skull; the distortion is neither accidental nor Expressionist, but accentuates the underlying geometry.

In 1921, Nadelman published through E. Weyhe of New York, at his own expense, the drawings issued in Paris in 1914, but with the title changed to *Vers la beauté plastique*. They bore the following inscription, reduced by Nadelman to a brief paragraph from several original and extant manuscript pages:

Two drawings, c.1906. Pen and ink

These drawings, made sixteen years ago (1905), have completely revolu-
tionized the art of our time. They introduced into painting and sculpture
abstract form, until then wholly lacking. Cubism was only an imitation of the
abstract form of these drawings and did not attain their plastic significance.
Their influence will continue to be felt more profoundly in the art of the future.

When the American art historian, collector and painter Walter Pach
together with Arthur B. Davies was collecting examples of advance-guard
painting and sculpture for the Armory Show of 1913, they selected a dozen
Nadelman drawings, plus the *Head of a Man* cited above as affecting
Picasso. Oddly enough, the drawings had already been in the United
States. Alfred Stieglitz had imported them, through Basler, in the summer
of 1910, after the interest aroused by the Druet show of the year before.
Stieglitz however never exhibited them, for Nadelman needed them for
his London show of 1911. But Stieglitz printed Nadelman's statement
intended as a preface, in *Camera Work* (No. 32; October 1910). In it,
there is the first enunciation of "significant form," later to become one of
the rally-cries of "modern art," through the evangelism of the English
critic, Clive Bell. Nadelman wrote:

. . . But what is this true form of art? It is significant and abstract: i.e. composed of geometrical elements.

Here is how I realize it. I employ no other line than the curve, which pos-
sesses freshness and force. I compose these curves so as to bring them in accord

14

Head of a man, c.1907. Plaster. Destroyed

Picasso: Head, 1909. Bronze, 16¼″
high. The Museum of Modern Art

Head of a woman, c.1909. Marble, 12⅞" high. Collection
Princess Helena Gourielli-Tchkonia

or opposition to one another. In that way I obtain the life of form, i.e. harmony.
In that way I intend the life of the work should come from within itself. The
subject of any work of art is for me nothing but a pretext for creating significant
form, relations of forms which create a new life that has nothing to do with life
in nature, a life from which art is born, and from which spring style and unity.

In later years, Nadelman always spoke of his responsibility for the in
semination of Cubism. He is unmentioned in official histories. The few
remarks in seldom read works of Leo and Gertrude Stein are unnoticed,
Gide's *Journal*, with the two apposite entries (December 24, 1908: April
25, 1909), was only recently translated. At the start, Nadelman fought
for his historic rights. Among his papers are many drafts of a letter written to Henry Goddard Leach, editor of *The Forum*, a magazine dedicated
to controversy, for a symposium on "Is Cubism Pure Art?" in which
Nadelman's letter was printed (July, 1925). Here Nadelman offered to
debate with anyone, anywhere, any time, on his priority over Picasso.
The challenge was ignored. His final word was scribbled on a scrap, a
few years before his death: "Cubism . . . towards external (*rather than
interior*) form . . . feverish changes while unsatisfied."

16

Head of a boy, c.1906. Bronze, 16¾″ high

It was already well known by 1909 that Nadelman was an important talent. Alexander Archipenko, who came to Paris a little later, relates that Nadelman was then the chief exponent of extreme Modernism. The brothers Natanson, arbiters of literary and artistic taste, owned examples of his work, and prevailed upon their associates, Octave Mirbeau, the playwright Romain Coolus, André Gide, and Frank Haviland to buy pieces. Joseph Brummer, later a great dealer, then a student of Rodin, told Philip Goodwin, architect of the Museum of Modern Art, that Matisse,

17

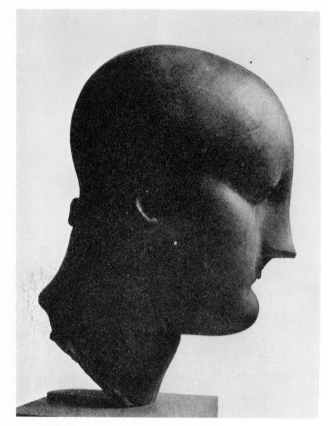

Head of a man, c.1909. Bronze. Whereabouts unknown

briefly maintaining an atelier on the Boulevard d'Orléans where he taught, posted a sign on the wall: *Défense de parler de Nadelman ici.*

André Gide, having been escorted by Alexandre Natanson to Nadelman's studio the winter before, feeling he had underestimated him since he had been so amused by Natanson's patronizing attitude, took care to describe the *vernissage* of Nadelman's one-man show at the Galerie Druet, April 25, 1909:

Nadelman draws with a compass and sculpts by assembling rhomboids. He has discovered that every curve of the human body is accompanied by a reciprocal curve, which opposes it and corresponds to it. The harmony which results from these balancings smacks of the theorem. The most astonishing thing, however, is that he works from the living model.

The Druet show was the marvel of the studios and bistros of Montparnasse. It created the greatest interest of a sculpture show since Rodin's retrospective at the International Exhibition of 1900. Gide wrote that Leo Stein bought two-thirds of the drawings; Brummer later obtained many from Stein, and Nadelman had them back from Brummer for their American publication in 1921. Bernhard Berenson, rediscoverer of Italian painting, wrote Stein from Settignano, April 1909:

18

I found Nadelman's work interesting and have sent influential people to see it. Of course it is hard to say what will become of a person who begins with such a pronounced and echoing manner.

Echoes of this manner, of this new method of analytical construction, of rendering plastically through abstract line and volume were later felt in such a diversity of talents as Brancusi (*La Tête de Madame Pogany*), Arthur B. Davies (the early Detroit murals), Joseph Bernard (*La Porteuse d'Eau*), Modigliani, Eugen Zak, Paul Thévenaz, Marie Laurencin, and many others. In 1928, twenty years after the Druet show, Basler wrote in *La Sculpture Moderne en France*:

The initial figures of the Pole, Nadelman, astonished the élite of Parisian art

Horse, c.1914. Plaster, 36¼″ high. Collection Princess Helena Gourielli-Tchkonia. A smaller bronze version is owned by the polo champion, Winston Guest, and other versions by the Worcester Museum and Mr. J. B. Neumann.

19

Standing woman (Spring), c.1912. Terra cotta, 30¾" high.
Collection Princess Helena Gourielli-Tchkonia

amateurs fifteen years ago. His researches had even the power of disturbing
Picasso, that eternally nervous creature, who is rendered ill by any novelty.
The principle of spherical decomposition in the drawings and sculptures of
Nadelman preceded in effect, the inventions of the Cubists. But Nadelman not
only pretended to have discovered the mechanics of Greek sculpture, but also
to establish laws of plastic construction. An artist as able as he was intelligent,
he had assimilated the Hellenistic formulae of the second century. In his

Standing woman (Winter), c.1912. Terra cotta, 31″ high. Collection Princess Helena Gourielli-Tchkonia

bronzes, chiseled with the virtuosity of the Renaissance Florentines, and in his marbles polished as in antiquity, he united a rational science of proportion with a refined elegance of form.

Facing the range of Nadelman's forty years of productivity, we are moved both by its unity within diversity, and its superficial lack of connection between each style, material or period. This must have been even more true at the Druet show which contained only six years of work.

21

Wounded bull, 1915. Bronze, 11½″ long. The Museum of Modern Art, New York

Here was concentrated labor which would have been remarkable for an entire workshop; from the hand of a single young man it was astonishing.

There was a series of standing nudes, deliberate comment on the antique with slight generalization (page 10); beside them, in almost the same pose, as if to prove a formal thesis, another series reducing the body to chartlike abstraction. Another series of small bronzes, had a swaggering finesse recalling, without direct reminiscence, the court ornaments of Giovanni da Bologna. There was a whole other family of tubular nudes expressing a suave continuum of flowing limbs, and a group of plaques (page 60), projections in low relief from pen-and-ink drawings, so closely derived it is impossible to tell which was first, the drawing or the relief.

Finally, there was a series of marble heads, recalling the antique, which was also his completest exposition of analysis (page 16). These white heads distress people today, since they are smooth, symmetrical, harmonious and complete. To eyes nourished on the accidental distortion and battered surface of Expressionism, they are cloying. But they differ from the antique in the massiveness of their grand rondure and heavy bosses;

22

Standing bull, 1915. Bronze, 11¼″ long. The Museum of Modern Art, New York

they can best be understood in relation to drawings which support them. With their porcelain surfaces polished high to reject any speck of dust, they are living illustrations of Baudelaire's great sonnet:

> . . . *J'unis un coeur de neige à la blancheur des cygnes;*
> *Je hais le mouvement qui déplace les lignes;*
> *Et jamais je ne pleure et jamais je ne ris . . .*

Their sentiment, of an immobile spirit that detests dislocation of linear boundaries (either from softness or imprecision), of lips that neither laugh nor weep; their bland, impersonal, seraphic smile of ambiguous consciousness is shared by all art with an esoteric base, whether Vedic, neo-Platonic or Christian. Its foundation in Nadelman was a religious belief in the principles of antiquity which produced works of unrepeated beauty, plus his confidence in a concrete canon of plane and solid Euclidean geometry.

The Druet show was an active lecture on the essence of sculpture whose nature had been taken for granted, or unquestioned since Rodin's first appearance. Nadelman served as a Socratic instructor: Do you want to see how this is done, of what mass is composed, how style is added to form

23

Man with a hat, c.1914. Plaster. Destroyed

or manner to volume? And he exposed all his means, but the smooth surfaces combining decomposition and construction were less experimental
sketches than beautiful lessons.

After the close of the Druet show, Nadelman intended to join Leo Stein,
who had sent him photographs of the Giottos in the Arena Chapel and
at Assisi. Instead, he took a short vacation near Dieppe. On the way back,
he sent Gertrude Stein a post card from Rouen of the church of Saint
Maclou:

Here is a veritable museum of cathedrals; I have never seen such marvels.
God must pardon me, but their great beauty astonishes me far more than the
sea [which he had never seen before] . . .

The most vivid portrait of Nadelman at this time is in the unpublished
notebooks, full of direct psychological analyses of friends, which Gertrude
Stein kept as the groundwork for her "Making of Americans," now in the
Yale University Library:

Man in the Open Air, c.1915. Bronze, 53¾″ high

Nadelman, like Pablo [Picasso] and Matisse have a maleness that belongs to genius . . . Nadelman attacks [as opposed to a list of people who resisted] . . . is very like Paderewski; he has that same kind of sensibility . . . Nadelman exalted . . . the light would be glad to bathe itself in his statues . . . a complete (rather than a split) thing. An artist, an exalted sensitive scientist like Goethe . . . really passionate, insight and realization of women, men and beauty . . . Pure passion concentrated to the point of vision . . . Nadelman, like Leonardo, when he is a scientist is not an artist . . . gives real sense of beauty directly, not derived (as in the case of X.) who has . . . emotion for beauty rather than direct realization of it . . . The magnetic pole, that queer paleness they all have, only Nadelman has the steady brilliant inside flame that gives his outer thing alive and moving . . . °

He returned to Paris to a larger studio in the impasse off the rue Campagne Première, and immured himself again in preparation for proposed shows in Berlin, Barcelona and London. However, over the next three years he was seen somewhat more often at those cafés, then tiny, now legendary — the Dome, Rotonde, and the bar of the Gare Montparnasse — with Picasso, Brancusi, later Modigliani (whom he met through his Polish dealer Zborowski), Zak, Kisling, Marcoussis, Halicka, Marie Laurencin, Hermine David, Pascin and Derain. Ernest Brummer, brother of Joseph, whom the Douanier Rousseau portrayed, recalls the young sculptor in his turtle-neck sweater, hair *blond-cendré,* so handsome he was known as Nadelman *Le Beau,* and because of his attachment to the Greeks, Praxitilman or Phidiasohn. *"Il faisait partie du décor de cette époque-là."* An incisive, didactic talker, he carried himself erect with an elegance apparent under his work-clothes. Fierce to the point of arrogance when esthetics were involved, he was anti-Fauve and anti-Cubist. He was respected but not known intimately by other artists, who were rarely asked to his studio. Aside from Natanson, Gertrude and Leo Stein, and two or three women who posed for him, he had no close friends.

In 1911 Nadelman went to London for a comprehensive exhibition at Paterson's Gallery, Bond Street. Besides earlier pieces, there were shown fifteen highly polished white marble heads, less generalized than before, the amplitude more developed, the roundness more personal. There was also a charming horse in plaster, a handsome reclining polished bronze nude set on elaborate drapery and the quizzical head of Mercury, which might also have been a contemporary boy in a bowler hat.

Into Paterson's Gallery walked a compatriot of Nadelman's, Madame Helena Rubinstein, later Princess Gourielli-Tchkonia, a sympathetic collector. She did not acquire merely one or two heads; she purchased the entire exhibition outright. Her patronage of Nadelman, coming when it did, was the most influential of his career. Madame Rubinstein mounted his pieces in her handsome establishments in London, Paris, Boston, New York and Buenos Aires; they became her trademark-symbol for the scientific beautification of modern woman. Later, Nadelman executed in terra cotta large high-relief plaques for the billiard room of her house in Putney Park Lane. Through these decorations and *Four Seasons* (pages 20 and

---

° Quoted by permission of Carl Van Vechten, literary executor for Gertrude Stein.

26

21), in the same spirit, Nadelman affected a whole school of commercial art, almost to the same degree as the engraved models of Piranesi which served as guides for Directoire and Empire interior design. Nadelman was responsible for a style of rendering *l'art décoratif moderne*, taken over by fashion artists for Paul Poiret, and popularized in Madame Rubinstein's advertising, which became the next step in decorative art after *L'Art nouveau* of 1900, and which was powerful in world taste through the Paris Exposition of 1925.

In 1912, the Italian journalist Marinetti gave a lecture on his Futurist doctrine in the Galerie Bernheim-Jeune. There was excitement on the floor when Nadelman asserted "M. Marinetti declares he will demolish all the arts of the past. He shows he does not in the least comprehend the nature of the art of the past." Marinetti jumped from the podium, slapped Nadelman, and precipitated a free-for-all. Lights were switched off, and discussion adjourned to nearby cafés. Nadelman, who seemed at the Druet show a revolutionary now presented himself to the students of Montparnasse almost as a reactionary; they held his work *trop mou*, too soft; even worse, he spoke well of Rodin. The poet André Salmon, writing in 1914 of the superb *Balzac*, then refused by its sponsors, said "The *Balzac* is not a work; it is a demonstration. It is a plastic lecture, similar to those given by Elie Nadelman."

In 1911 Nadelman held a show in Barcelona together with the sculptor Manolo, another progressive artist of the period, later collected by John Quinn, but now almost forgotten. Nadelman was well received; he made drawings from bull fights, recalling the cave paintings of Les Eyzies in the Dordogne, which resulted in the fine pair of bronze bulls (1915) presented by his widow in 1947 to the Museum of Modern Art (pages 22 and 23). He also showed at a Non-jury Salon in Berlin in 1913, and was purchased by German collectors.

In June 1913, Nadelman held his second Paris exhibition at the Galerie Druet; it was smaller than that of 1909, and could not have been expected to repeat the same sensation. The supplement of the *Gazette des Beaux-Arts* observed:

M. Elie Nadelman is clever in noting the essential in physiognomy, in endowing the female face with sweetness, and in combining his taste for the archaic with the trembling nervousness of nature. He stylizes his attitudes in order to express their roundness, dominated by his willful fantasy, in all human gesture . . .

The first full-length article devoted to Nadelman appeared in the semi-official *L'Art décoratif*, March 1914; it was by André Salmon, to whom Apollinaire had dedicated his charming *Marriage Ode*. The titles attached to the many reproductions of sculpture or drawings were always "Research in Form and Volume: Identification of Forms." The article was soberly sympathetic, a guarded introduction:

A great number of his admirers take him for a precious young master — almost Byzantine, although all of his work tends towards a unity, a great plastic whole. Neither, although it is often said of him, is he a sterile imitator of the Greeks. Nadelman is above all a theorist, a theorist in spite of himself . . . Let us not

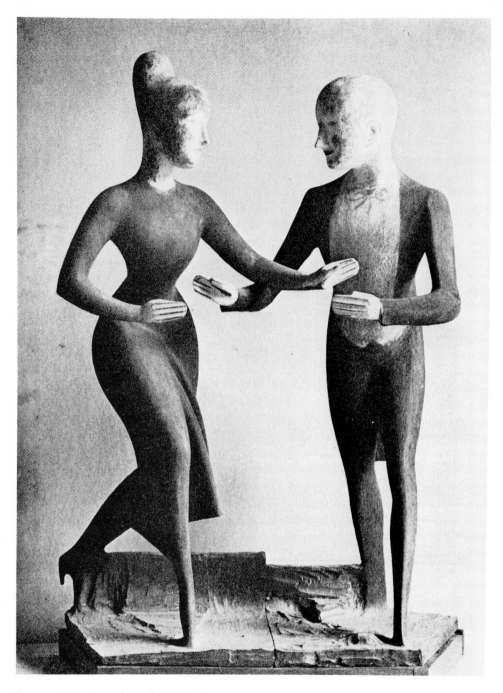

Tango, c.1918. Painted wood, 33¾″ high

forget that Nadelman sacrificed everything to the relations of volumes a long
time before the Cubists . . .

The illustrations included the witty study of a horse, which with others
related to it, forms the basis of the spirited thoroughbred with tiny, pranc-

ing hooves (page 19). Nadelman admired the horses of Eugène **Lami** and Constantin **Guys**; one could have said of him as Baudelaire of **Guys**: "He not only understood the generalized horse, but also applied himself to the personal beauty of horses."

Nadelman owned Champfleury's *Histoire de la Caricature*. From 1914 on, he was preoccupied with the passing scene of fashion and high society. His drawings and free-standing figures in bronze and wood, clothed in simplifications of modern dress, would emerge as serious jokes, loving if ironic definitions of the mundane mask. They have important connections

Host, c.1917. Painted wood, 28½″ high

Caricatures.
generalizations

Woman at the Piano, c.1917. Painted wood, 36″ high. Collection Philip L. Goodwin

with the vital, expressive profiles of Seurat; in the same number of *L'Art décoratif* which contained Salmon's article, Nadelman read Lucie Cousturier's appreciation of the charcoal sketches of Georges Seurat, all but unknown at this time. Nadelman tore out a reproduction of a woman in silhouette; it was among his cherished scraps found after his death.

Nadelman spent the summer of 1914 near Ostend. He made sketches of his concierge, her daughter and their poodle for future use. The declaration of war caught him unaware. He went at once to Brussels and offered himself as reservist in the Russian army, but the consul told him it was useless to try to cross Europe. The Germans were already advancing on

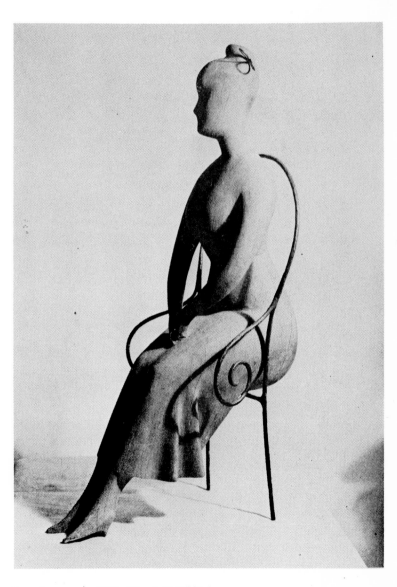

Seated woman, c.1917. Wood, 31½" high

The Orchestra Conductor, c.1919. Painted wood, 37¼″ high

Dancer, c.1918. Wood, 28¼″ high. Dr. and Mrs. David M. Levy.

Liége. He reached England; through the generosity of Madame Rubinstein, he managed to obtain passage to New York, with most of the contents of his Paris studio. He sailed on the *Lusitania,* arriving October 31, 1914.

Madame Rubinstein put at his disposal her garage in Rye, New York, to prepare his first New York show. Nadelman had already been in contact with Americans — Stieglitz, Davies, Pach, the painter Ann Goldthwaite and others. However, his first active aid in the United States was Martin Birnbaum, connoisseur and critic, who helped form the great collection of paintings, drawings and Chinese sculpture left by Grenville Winthrop to Harvard University.

Joining the firm of Scott & Fowles, art dealers, as junior partner, Birnbaum had heard of Nadelman in Paris from the Natanson brothers; and Adolphe Basler, who was then in New York, insisted he visit the walk-up studio on West 14th Street. To Birnbaum, the sculpture seemed a revelation. He made immediate arrangement for an important show, and prepared an article appearing in *The International Studio* for December 1915. He brought to the studio Mrs. Radeke of Providence, who presented a marble head to the Rhode Island School of Design, the first American museum to own a Nadelman, although in the next years he was to be included in the permanent collections of Brooklyn, Detroit, Cleveland, Worcester, the Corcoran and the Carnegie. Birnbaum introduced him to the influential Canadian collector, Sir William van Horne. In the meantime Nadelman had made arrangements for a small exhibition at Alfred Stieglitz' Photo-Secession Gallery, "291," for December 1915.

Here, Nadelman showed his *Man in the Open Air* (page 25), recently completed in plaster, a figure in a bowler hat, supported by a tree-trunk whose slim branch quite simply grew up through his left arm. The single adornment of its elegant attenuation was a small bow-tie in free relief, casting echoing shadows on its broad shirt-front. At once comic, supple and worldly, this was a culmination of a new development, a turn towards his full comment, as personal and precise as Guys, on *la vie moderne*. And yet the pose and its relationship to the supporting tree stump were a kind of whispered echo of the *Apollo Sauroktonos*, the *Boy with the Lizard*, of classical antiquity. In France, Nadelman had made numerous drawings and plaques of match-limbed creatures, recalling both cave drawings and dolls. There had already been two heads of Mercury, in bronze and marble, on which, with a single line, or roll of form capping the skulls, he had indicated a cloche or derby hat.

He now worked feverishly preparing his real American debut which was tastefully arranged in February 1917 at the handsome Fifth Avenue galleries of Scott & Fowles. Martin Birnbaum was a master of publicity; not only had he sold a number of important pieces before the opening; he printed an elaborate catalog, and his rooms were carefully lit in their succession of bronze and marbles with some in wood, besides plaques and drawings. The exhibition, one of the first so carefully installed in New York, was a vast success, and all but sold out; Nadelman was swamped with commissions for figures and portraits. He could have made a fortune a year on portraits alone, if he had cared to accept them. Using a formula of stylish verisimilitude in the line of Laurana and Houdon, cutting wood and marble with his perfect fluency, he created some fifty busts of men, women and children. Perhaps the most memorable of these are of Mrs.

Acrobat, c.1916. Bronze, 14⅞″ high

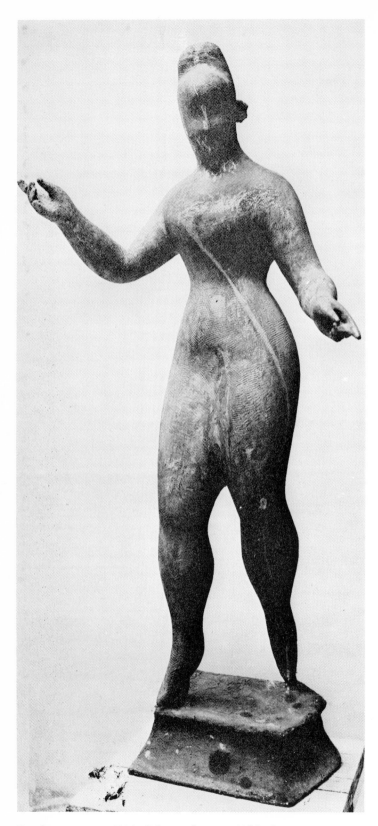

Standing woman, c.1924. Galvano plastique, 61″ high

Standing woman, c.1924. Galvano plastique, 58¾″ high

Circus woman, c.1924. Galvano plastique, 49¼″ high

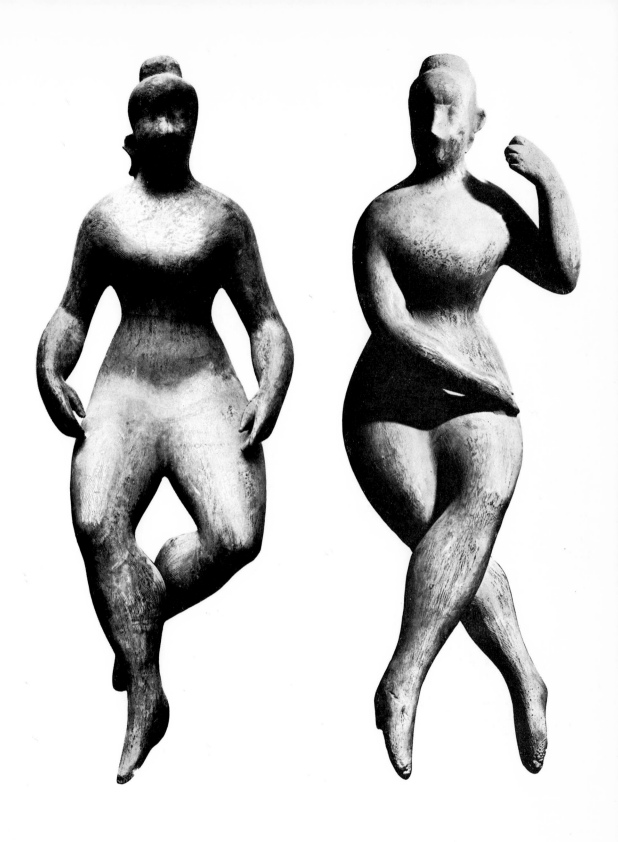

Two circus women, c.1924. Galvano plastique, left: 46½″ high; right: 44¾″ high

Head of a woman, c.1922. Polished marble, 18¼" high

Templeton Crocker (now Mrs. Paul Fagan of San Mateo) (page 61), Mrs. Clarence Hay, Senator Carter Glass, the small son of the architect A. Stewart Walker, and the Garvan children.

Nadelman loved the great moral tapestries of Henry James; his library is full of first editions, which he bought from time to time. The people he portrayed with candid elegance, beyond cynicism, would not have been unfamiliar to characters in "The Wings of the Dove" or "The Ambassadors." Gide described him ten years before as a figure out of Balzac, the provincial who by his wits laid siege to the city. Now he seemed the epitome of the dandy, but essentially, Nadelman was a type of spiritual stoic less like George Brummel than Charles Baudelaire:

40

Head of a woman, c.1942. Rose marble, 15¼" high

Dandyism is not even, as many unthinking people believe, an immoderate taste for the toilette or material elegance. These things are merely, for the perfect dandy, a symbol of the aristocratic superiority of the soul . . . Dandyism is, before anything else, the passionate need to create out of oneself an originality, contained in the external limits of convention . . . The nature of the beauty in the dandy consists above all in the cold manner which comes from the unshakeable resolution not to be moved; one might say of a latent fire which makes one guess its presence; which could, but which does not choose to, burn . . .

Nadelman now installed himself in a functioning studio-shop, in the line of a Rodin. He sent for Albert Boni, his faithful *praticien*, from Paris. At one time he employed three assistants; besides Boni, there were the Italians Ferdinand Terenzoni and Julius Gargani. Several replicas were

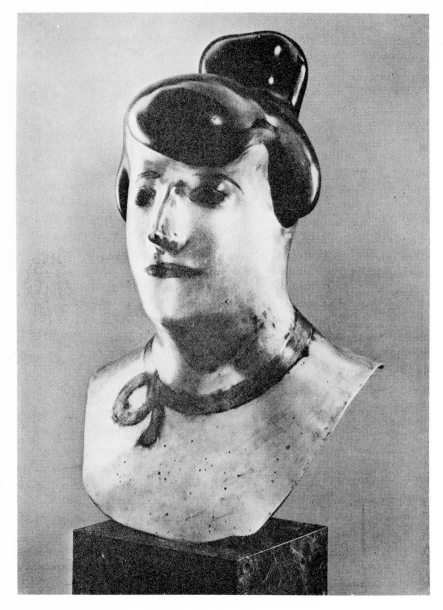

Bust of a woman, c.1927. Painted bronze, 23⅝″ high

made of many figures, even in wood and stone. In his Riverdale studio, after his death, there were found dozens of roughed-out, unfinished blocks, versions of other works completely achieved in a different material. Nadelman chose blocks of perfectly clear stone; if on cutting he found a flaw or vein, he abandoned the block.

The press for the Scott & Fowles show established his local position as a leading figure. Henry McBride of *The New York Sun*, Nadelman's earliest and ever most loyal supporter among critics, had greatly praised the earlier Stieglitz show and now defined a general impression.

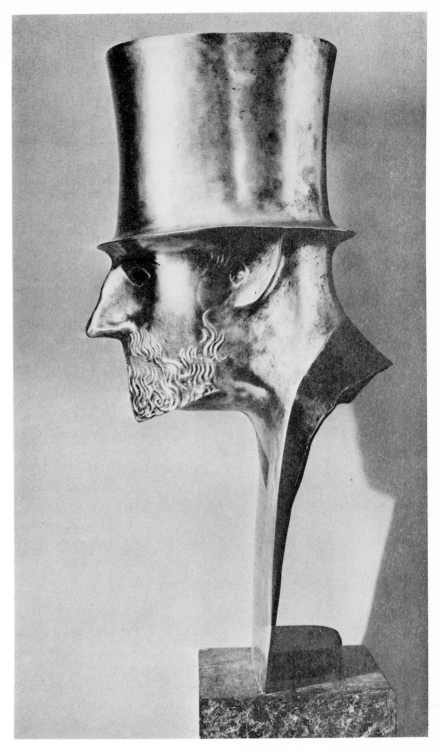

Man in Top Hat, c.1927. Painted bronze, 25¾″ high

Two female nudes, c.1931. Papier-mâché, 59″ high

Two women, c.1934. Terra cotta

It is, in a word, refined. It is in the highest degree a before-the-war art. It is culture to the breaking point . . . It seems to breathe out all the rare essences that were brought by the wise men from all the corners of the earth to be fused by the Parisians . . . into the residuum called 'modern civilization,' which now, so many millions are dying for . . . In this sculpture, the past and present are blended almost cruelly.

By 1918 Nadelman was a force in the artistic life of New York, a prominent member of that "High Bohemia" so admirably depicted in the early novels of Carl Van Vechten. He was a member of the Penguin Club, whose annual banquet menus were etched by Jules Pascin; a friend of

45

Woman, c.1934. Terra cotta, 16¼" high

George Bellows and Eugene Speicher (his sponsor when he became an American citizen), of Alfred Frueh, the cartoonist, of Gari Melchers, the painter. He had particular respect for sculptors whom he considered good craftsmen; so much the professional himself, he seldom questioned the quality of talent if skill were present. Particularly, he knew George Grey Barnard, with whom he shared a passion for the Gothic, Edward Mac-

Standing woman, c.1934. Painted papier-mâché, 11¾″ high

Cartan, Edmund Quinn, MacMonnies (who often asked his advice), Manship, Mahonri Young and Gertrude Whitney. He was active in artistic organizations and taught for a time at the Beaux Arts Institute of Design. He designed floats for the annual Beaux Arts Ball and participated in improvising an example of "indigenous sculpture" for an exhibition at Mrs. Whitney's Studio Club.

Kenneth Hayes Miller, respected master of many American painters, once said to him at the opening of an exhibition: "You know, Nadelman, we all go by what you do." There is not room here for a complete record of the immense influence Nadelman's fresh way of seeing had on our painters and sculptors. From 1915 on, he provided precedents for George Bellows, Guy Pêne du Bois, Rockwell Kent, Hunt Diederich, Gaston Lachaise, to the caricaturists John Held, Jr. and Fish of *Vanity Fair*, just as he himself had been affected by Daumier, Gavarni and Constantin Guys. He provided a vision of New York society, not as an echo of a richer, more interesting Europe, but as a place which, almost for the first time, was feeling its own promise. There was an awakening in contemporary patronage, not from alien prestige but as American possibility. Muriel Draper was decorating the fabulous Villa Viscaya for Henry Deering in Palm Beach. Robert Chanler was painting his huge decorative screens of porcupines and giraffes. Christian Brinton was publicizing Léon Bakst, Russian folk art and Ignacio Zuloaga. Diaghilev's Ballet Russe was spending the war in America, backed by Otto Kahn.

In December 1917 a group of society women and conservative sculptresses arranged as a war charity an exhibition called "Allies of Sculpture," which was held on the Ritz-Carlton Roof. Nadelman showed his *Femme Assise*, in plaster, the small figure of a hostess or *saloneuse*, her hair indicated by pale Prussian blue. Magically witty, designed with a mature

Group of plaster figures, c.1944

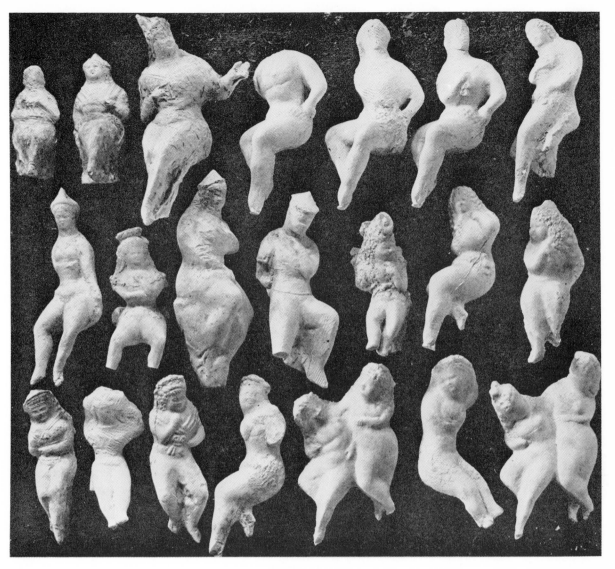

Group of plaster figures, c.1944

enchantment, delicately balanced in her wrought-iron skeleton of a chair on her tiny sharp shoes, it is hard to see today why she caused a scandal. Perhaps because the organizing committee felt she was a proto-Hokinson caricature of their busy sponsoring, she was removed amid a welter of publicity. Gertrude Whitney spoke in her defense; Muriel Draper and Christian Brinton were photographed defending her right to be seen. Nadelman wrote to the *New York World*, December 19, 1917:

At the "Allies of Sculpture," where, as in all exhibitions of sculpture, the subject matter of almost all works represents nude men, nude women, and nude men having the bodies of nude women, I have exhibited some works whose subjects are dressed women as one sees them in everyday life.

Figure, c.1944. Plaster, 9″ high

Well, the majority of the visitors on seeing the dressed women found them indecent and were so shocked that they removed them from their original place to a remote corner where they could not be seen. This fact is significant.

It proves the tenacity of habits and especially of bad habits. It proves that habit and not logic makes people accept or reject things; when the public does not find nude women in sculpture, they wonder whether the works are artistic or not . . .

For the next two years, Nadelman would be primarily devoted to creat-

Figure, c.1944. Plaster

Societal
comment

ing a world derived from type figures of the society he daily observed.
First he made drawings, of many sorts of people, from direct observation
and from photographs in magazines and newspapers; only a few he felt
suitable for projection into plaster. There was a further selection for those
finally achieved in red-cherry, a grainless wood, grateful to carve, which
the Biedermeier craftsmen particularly esteemed. This wood took gesso
well; Nadelman made indications of features, dresses, boiled (and stuffed)
shirts, hair and gloves. The feet were attached to the base with the

51

slightest support possible, to heighten the sense of the preposterously fashionable. His poses derived from two theatres, either the circus, vaudeville or concert hall, or the arena of the drawing room, whose ring-masters were *Host* (page 29) and *Hostess*. Nadelman had a genius for gesture, for approximating all the authority, expectancy, queenliness and self-satisfaction, not alone in posture but in the very forms of dress — alert, arrested or stolid — which clad their personal stance in the costume of 1918. He had always loved the circus as the apogee of the performing arts. In America, he found our vaudeville at its sunset glory, just before Hollywood killed it. It was the age of Vernon and Irene Castle, of Florence Walton and Maurice. Nadelman's *Tango* (page 28) shows an understanding of theatrical dancing such as no one had had since Seurat and Lautrec; like them, he knew how to extract from the rich gross ore of the music halls the pure ritual entrance and electrifying display. The *Host* (which might have been a portrait of Adolphe Basler), was enthroned in his armchair as a prince of permanent smugness. His *Hostess* had the hauteur of Goya's Duquesa de Alba with her two arms held at high tremble, as eager to insert darts as to extend her fingers. *Woman at the Piano* (page 30) by the very arch of her back and poised hand attracts the attention of an entire world to her single struck note. *The Orchestra Conductor* (page 32), a monolith of suave domination gloved in swallow-tails is the solemn doll which accompanies his orchestra like a virtuoso.

Late in 1919, Nadelman married Mrs. Joseph A. Flannery, a widow of considerable means. He was himself well off now, at the height of an expanding prestige. Since his wife was at this time unwell, they purchased Alderbrook, the old Percy Pyne estate at Riverdale-on-Hudson. Many assumed Nadelman had married rich and stopped working, or else it was rumored he had no further interest in sculpture since he was forming a huge collection of folk art. This collection, the finest assembled in America, was primarily started by Nadelman as an interest for his wife, who, before they met owned an important group of laces and embroideries. Nadelman was interested in our popular handicrafts as soon as he came here. There was then so little interest in local carving or Pennsylvania Dutch ceramics and calligraphy, that when he spoke of folk art it was assumed he meant Navajo weaving or pottery. He planned to demonstrate the entire gamut of popular crafts in the United States, together with prime examples of their European sources. Within a few years, the Nadelmans spent a fortune on their collection, later housed in a stone building on their property.*

It has been suggested Nadelman's sorties into society and the energy spent in collecting impeded the development of his own gift. On the contrary, his art was nourished by both. He was so familiar from association with his subjects, that his cherry-wood figures are not symbols for stock characters, they are portraits of epitomes. The style he gave them

---

* When the Nadelmans lost their money, the contents of the museum was distributed among the New York Historical Society (which shortly dispersed part of the collection), Colonial Williamsburg, the Museum of Modern Art (both through Mrs. John D. Rockefeller, Jr.), the Brummer Galleries, Henry F. DuPont, and the Metropolitan Museum of Art.

Figure, c.1944. Plaster, 9⅜″ high

is no pastiche of naïve expression, but a personal vision, so imbued with the entire fabric of popular art that they seem but the latest addition to a long traditional line.

In 1929, with the Stock Market Crash, their fortune, largely over-extended in real estate was all but wiped out. The town house was first rented, then lost through arrears. They retired to Alderbrook in Riverdale, which was also subsequently lost. However, before his death Nadelman managed to regain its title. The period of his final seclusion commenced.

Nadelman's last period is a complex problem, psychologically as well

final period

53

Family, c.1914. Pen and ink wash, 10 x 7⅜"

as esthetically. There is no easy explanation for his absolute refusal to exhibit or sell in the face of his enormous productivity, or to discuss his work with colleagues when he was making so many experiments, or for his refusal to seek commissions when he needed them. Living in Riverdale, less than an hour from 57th Street, he was nevertheless removed from the heart of the world of art. When people came to call, as they often did, from friendship as well as curiosity, and asked Nadelman what he was doing, he would show them nothing but his fine white raspberries.

54

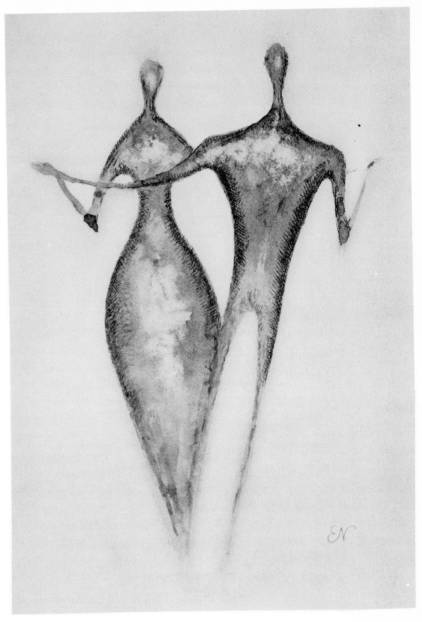

Tango, c.1917. Pen and ink wash, 12¼ x 8¼"

His neighbors in Riverdale hardly knew he had been an artist. His single relaxation was playing bridge at the Cavendish Whist Club, a few times a week for low stakes.

In 1935, after the loss of his large studio which had been made over from an old coach house, workmen, sent to remodel, destroyed many plaster figures, as well as some of his wooden carvings; a great deal of his work was irreparably hurt or lost. This was a grievous blow, one from which he never fully recovered, although he seldom referred to any period of his past during his obscurity. Nadelman stuffed everything he could salvage of his work prior to 1935, just as it was, damaged or tarnished, in the attic or cellar of the Riverdale house where it remained disintegrating until its complete restoration in the year and a half following his death. No one visiting him in the last decade would have seen a single example of his work. Removed physically and mentally from participation in the currents of local artistic activity, it is slight wonder he began to be forgotten. In 1938, refusing the request of a loan to a group show, he wrote Alfred H. Barr, Jr., then Director of the Museum of Modern Art, indicating he was not yet ready for a retrospective exhibition, but when he should be, would like to have it held there. He was granted no work under P.W.A. or W.P.A., although for two years twenty W.P.A. workers were in the Riverdale house, rendering objects from his collection of folk art for the Index of American Design. No example of his own work was ever purchased by a New York City museum.

Through the firm of Walker and Gillette he obtained two large architectural jobs, the Fuller Building on East 57th Street, and the Bank of the Manhattan Company in Wall Street. Nadelman made use of everything that came his way. Society portraits were at the root of his sardonic, luxurious late heads in painted brass, with Prussian-blue coiffure, his final devastating mummification of his world of fashion (pages 42 and 43). From the clay model (entirely altered when transformed into stone) for the overdoor of the Fuller Building (page 61), we have in embryo the last fifteen years of Nadelman's achievement, at once the most fascinating and baffling of his life.

Nadelman was amused to work on a large scale, and performed with dispatch and facile thoroughness. He made a pair of elaborate stags for the gates of the Myron Taylor estate in two days; his huge reclining *Aquarius* for the Bank of Manhattan took less than three weeks. The figures of construction workers for the Fuller Building were the direct source of two huge groups in papier-mâché, impregnated with plaster, which inaugurate, like a Wagnerian fanfare, his final contribution.

These vast Amazonian pairs (frontispiece and page 44), impassive, benevolent as the huge Percheron mares they might have mounted, throned like circus queens, are as big in size as they are in scale, the physical and spiritual mothers of innumerable smaller figures he was to multiply until the end. Their size is certainly impressive, and never more so than when discovered, shrouded under quilts in the high attic of his all but deserted house, on a cold winter afternoon following his death. But Nadelman realized their dimensions would impede their chances of finding many permanent homes and the nature of their material would be considered not serious enough for museums. He was too enthusiastic about the possession of art by all the people to care any longer for important isolated purchases of his large sculptures. He had built his own kiln for experimental pottery, glazed and unglazed, and he worked towards producing inexpensive sculpture on a small scale in papier-mâché, terra cotta, plaster with an electrically deposited layer of bronze, etc. But he

Hen, c.1919. Pen and ink wash, 6½ x 5″

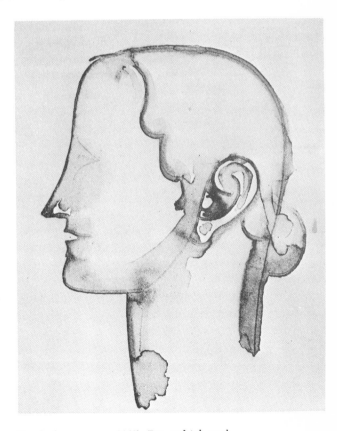

Head of a woman, c.1915. Pen and ink wash

lost the kiln together with his studio, and henceforward worked only in plaster, although he cut a few exquisite small nudes in lovely marble, in the same spirit as the figurines. His last work diminished in size when he moved into a small studio almost secretly attached to his home.

On his work bench lay a collection of actual Tanagrine fragments; his large art library contained the best books on classical terra cottas in famous collections of Europe and America. He knew Greek sculpture as a conductor knows the symphonic repertory; and he was as familiar with the by-paths, the so-called minor arts, as with famous monuments. Nadelman's late figurines (pages 48 to 53), inspired by Hellenistic fired-earth objects are in the scale of chamber works. They are not easy to assimilate; they are a recapitulation of all he had learned, discovered and liked about fashion and form, texture and volume, gesture and ornament. Their miniature splendor seems at first hardly more than playful comment on the *Ares Ludovisi*, the *Diadoumenos, Demosthenes* adjusting his cape, the *Spinario* and *Idolino*, or on innumerable Myrinan or Tarentine statuettes. They contain a humane spirit echoed from antiquity, of a civilization past its primal innocence, but the forms are by no means identical with any earlier work. At once dolls, babies, men and women; goddesses, queens, burlesque dancers, they seem intended as ritual objects for some cult whose nature is as yet unknown. Entering his old studio, where the dozens of small bodies are laid out by families for reference and comparison, is like stumbling suddenly upon some important archeological discovery. It is a collective rather than an idiosyncratic art.

All his knowledge of anatomy, his sense of style and scale, instead of being shrunk by the confines of the small plasters, actually expanded, was glorified, became mature and final. A few days before his death he told his wife that he felt he had achieved the purpose to which he had devoted his life, a rediscovery of the principle of absolute formal harmony in sculpture.

Nadelman's last years were both tragic and heroic. He felt the war keenly; his son was fighting across France and Germany, and Nadelman followed him with the only series of letters he wrote. In February 1942, he enrolled in the local Air Warden Service and, in spite of a bad heart condition which he never mentioned, always took the late night or early morning watches. He volunteered for work in occupational therapy at the Bronx Veterans' Hospital, where he provided all the materials, supplying and working the kiln as well. He was devoted to his work with men suffering from shock which affected their hands, and he helped in some notable cures. After his death, December 28, 1946, the manager of the Veterans' Administration wrote his widow:

In bringing his highly developed skill in sculpture and ceramics to the disabled boys, twice weekly for two years, he brought much beauty and inspiration to their lives. His bright enthusiastic personality did much to combat their suffering and fatigue.

French poodle, c.1914. Watercolor, 7⅞ x 10⅜"

Cow, c.1912. Pen and ink

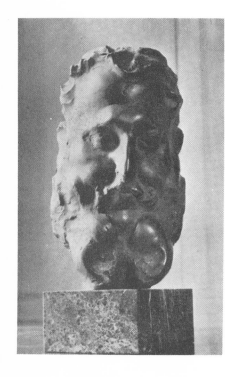

Above: Corner in the apartment of Leo and Gertrude Stein. rue de Fleurus, c. 1909. The plaster statuette is from the first Druet show. On the walls are paintings by Picasso and Matisse.

Left: Thadée Natanson, 1909. Bronze. Collection Thadée Natanson, Paris. Before the first Druet show, Natanson feared that the exhibits were "too exclusively abstract, . . . too uniformly theoretic"; he describes in *Peints à leur tour* (Paris, 1948) how Nadelman in two sittings modeled this realistic head, as a contrast to the other figures.

Below: Autumn, c. 1912. Bronze, 9 x 18″. Collection Princess Helena Gourielli-Tchkonia. This style, evolved by drawing in the round with thin rolls of clay, was widely imitated for twenty years in decorative, commercial and fashion art, its source in Nadelman forgotten or ignored.

Above: Head of a boy, c. 1922. Polished marble, 14½″ high. Nadelman's single ideal male head in stone; drawings explain it as an imaginative self portrait. A bronze variant exists.

Right: Mrs. Templeton Crocker, c. 1922. Marble. Perhaps the finest of Nadelman's stone salon heads which he executed between 1916 and 1925. His last important portrait was of Senator Carter Glass of Virginia (1933), now in Washington, D. C.

Below: Clay model for the overdoor of the Fuller Building in New York City, 1931. Through A. Stewart Walker of Walker and Gillette, Nadelman obtained two large architectural commissions. This composition for the corner of 57th Street and Madison Avenue was altered in execution. But the figures shown here are the first statement of his final period, corresponding to early papier-mâché figures and small late plasters.

Exhibitions of Elie Nadelman

1905–08 *Salon des Indépendants; Salon d'Automne*
Sculptures, shop of Mme Weill, rue Victor
Massé, Paris
1909 Galerie Druet, Paris. First one-man show
1911 Barcelona (with Manolo)
Paterson's Gallery, London. One-man show
1913 January: Non-jury Salon, Berlin
February: The Armory Show, New York. Drawings and plaster head
June: Galerie Druet, Paris. One-man show
1915 December: Photo-Secession Gallery ("291"),
New York
1917 February: Scott & Fowles Gallery, New York
December: "Allies of Sculpture" Exhibition,
Ritz-Carlton Roof, New York
1919 October: M. Knoedler & Co., New York
1920 September: Galerie Bernheim-Jeune, Paris
1925 March: Scott & Fowles Gallery, New York
May: The Arts Club of Chicago (at the Art Institute of Chicago)
1927 January: M. Knoedler & Co., New York
May: Galerie Bernheim-Jeune, Paris
1932 April: early purchases of Mme Helena Rubinstein, Mrs. Marie Sterner, New York
1938 May: Exhibition of American sculpture, Carnegie Institute, Pittsburgh (two marbles)
May: Three Centuries of American Art, Jeu de
Paume, Paris (horse)
1948 October: Memorial Exhibition, The Museum of
Modern Art, New York

Catalog of the Exhibition

LENDERS

Philip L. Goodwin, New York; Princess Helena Gourielli-
Tchkonia, New York; Dr. and Mrs. David M. Levy, New
York; Mrs. Elie Nadelman, Riverdale, N. Y.; William S.
Paley, New York; Mrs. John D. Rockefeller, 3rd, New
York.

*A star preceding the catalog number indicates that the
work is illustrated. All works unless otherwise noted are
in the collection of Mrs. Elie Nadelman.*

* 1 Praying figure, c.1904. Bronze, 56" high. *Plaster
version Ill. p. 10*
* 2 Head of a boy, c.1906. Painted bronze, 16¾" high.
Ill. p. 17
* 3 Head of a woman, c.1909. Marble, 12⅞" high.
Princess Helena Gourielli-Tchkonia, N. Y. *Ill. p. 16*
* 4 Standing female nude, c.1907. Bronze, 30" high. *Ill.
p. 11*
 5 Standing female nude, c.1908. Wood, 15" high
 6 Seated female nude, c.1908. Bronze, 16" high
* 7 Standing male nude, c.1909. Bronze, 25¾" high.
Ill. p. 12

* 8 Standing female nude, c.1909. Bronze, 22" high.
Ill. p. 13
 9 Standing woman, c.1912. Terra cotta, 30" high. Collection Princess Helena Gourielli-Tchkonia, New York
*10 Horse, c.1914. Plaster, 36¼" high. Collection Prin-
cess Helena Gourielli-Tchkonia, New York. *Ill. p. 19*
*11 Man in the Open Air, c.1915. Bronze, 53¾" high.
Ill. p. 25
*12 Standing bull, 1915. Bronze, 11¼" long. The Mu-
seum of Modern Art, New York. *Ill. p. 23*
*13 Wounded bull, 1915. Bronze, 11½" long. The Mu-
seum of Modern Art, New York. *Ill. p. 22*
*14 Acrobat, c.1916. Bronze, 14⅞" high. *Ill. p. 35*
*15 Tango, c.1918. Painted wood, 33¾" high. *Ill. p. 28*
*16 Woman at the Piano, c.1917. Painted wood, 36"
high. Collection Philip L. Goodwin, N. Y. *Ill. p. 30*
*17 Seated woman, c.1917. Wood, 31½" high. *Ill. p. 31*
*18 Host, c.1917. Painted wood, 28½" high. *Ill. p. 29*
*19 Dancer, c.1918. Wood, 28¼" high. Collection Dr.
and Mrs. David M. Levy, New York. *Ill. p. 33*
*20 The Orchestra Conductor, c.1919. Painted wood,
37¼" high. *Ill. p. 32*
 21 Circus woman, c.1919. Painted wood, 31¾" high
 22 Female torso, c.1922. Marble. Collection William
S. Paley, New York
*23 Head of a woman, c.1922. Polished marble, 18¼"
high. *Ill. p. 40.*
*24 Head of a boy, c.1922. Marble, 14½" high. *Ill. p. 61*
*25 Standing woman, c.1924. Galvano plastique, 58¾"
high. *Ill. p. 37*
*26 Standing woman, c.1924. Galvano plastique, 61"
high. *Ill. p. 36*
*27 Circus woman, c.1924. Galvano plastique, 46½"
high. *Ill. p. 39*
*28 Circus woman, c.1924. Galvano plastique, 44¾"
high. *Ill. p. 39*
*29 Circus woman, c.1924. Galvano plastique, 49¼"
high. *Ill. p. 38*
 30 Bust of a girl, c.1925. Galvano plastique, 25¼"
*31 Man in Top Hat, c.1927. Painted bronze, 25¾" high.
Ill. p. 43
*32 Bust of a woman, c.1927. Painted bronze, 23⅝"
high. *Ill. p. 42*
*33 Two female nudes, c.1931. Papier-mâché, 59" high.
Ill. p. 44
*34 Two circus women, c.1930. Papier-mâché, 61¼"
high. *Frontispiece*
 35 Two women c.1933. Terra cotta, 16" high
 36 Two women, c.1934. Painted papier-mâché, 14¼"
*37 Standing woman, c.1934. Painted papier-mâché,
11¾" high. *Ill. p. 47*
 38 Woman with a poodle, c.1934. Terra cotta, 11½"
 39 Seated woman, c.1934. Terra cotta, 14¾" high
*40 Head of a woman, c.1942. Rose marble, 15¼" high.
Ill. p. 41
 41 Standing female nude, c.1942. Marble, 11½" high
 42 Standing female nude, c.1942. Marble, 11¾" high
 43 Seated female nude, c.1943. Orange marble, 14½"
high. Collection Mrs. John D. Rockefeller, 3rd
*44 A group of small plaster figures, c.1944. *Ill. pp. 48-53*
*45 A group of drawings.

Bibliography

The following material, with few exceptions, is in the Museum Library either in original or photostat. In addition, the reader is referred to Elie Nadelman's *Publicity Scrapbook*, also in the Library, which contains, besides much ephemera, the exhibition catalogs of the *Arts Club* Chicago (1925), *Bernheim-Jeune* Paris (1920 and 1927), *Druet* Paris (1913), *International Gallery* New York (1932), *Knoedler* New York (1919 and 1927), *Photo-Secession Gallery* New York (1915-16), and *Scott & Fowles* New York (1917). An extensive bibliography is noted in *The Index of Twentieth Century Artists* for March 1936.   BERNARD KARPEL

THE WORK OF NADELMAN

1 [Statement on his drawings] Camera Work no. 32, p. 41 Oct 1910. *In "Photo-Secession notes" prepared for the catalog of the Little Gallery of the Photo-Secession. The drawings had to be returned before the exhibition.*
2 Quarante dessins de Elie Nadelman. Paris, La Belle Edition, 1913. *Announced for publication but never issued except as a de luxe prospectus with 3 reproductions. See bibliography item 3, 8.*
3 Vers l'unité plastique. 51 drawings in folio Paris, 1914. *Originally announced as "Quarante dessins" (bibl. 2) but published without the promised gloss under this title. The edition of 1921 (bibl. 8) omittted 19 drawings from this edition, but used the original Paris zinc cuts.*
4 [Statement for exhibition at the Photo-Secession] Camera Work no. 48, p. 10 Oct 1916. *"The text of the leaflet which accompanied the Nadelman exhibition."*
5 [Statement in Current Opinion. Mar. 1917] *See bibliography item 17.*
6 [Statement at the Allies of sculpture exhibit] New York World Dec 19 1917. *Commentary on Ritz-Carlton show.*
7 [Interview. Nov. 1919] *Commentary reported by Henry Tyrrell in the World Magazine Nov. 30, 1919. See bibliography item 52.*
8 Vers la beauté plastique, thirty-two reproductions of drawings. 2p. plus 32 plates New York, E. Weyhe, 1921. *Introductory note by Elie Nadelman says "175 sets of these reproductions of the drawings were printed at Paris in 1912. The blocks have been destroyed." Reprinted in small halftone format in Younger Artists Series.*
9 Elie Nadelman, edited by William Murrell, with 6 reproductions in color and 40 in black and white. 50 leaves. Woodstock, N. Y., W. M. Fisher, 1923. (Younger artists series, nr. 6). *This consists almost entirely of plates, with no editorial contribution. Material listed as drawings no. 30-46 is a miniature reprint, including introduction, of "Vers la beauté plastique."*
10 [Letter to the editor on "Is cubism pure art?"] The Forum v.74 no.1, p.148 July 1925.

ARTICLES ON NADELMAN

11 America & Alfred Stieglitz, a collective portrait, ed. by Waldo Frank [and others] 2 illus. p. 110, 314 Garden City, N. Y., Doubleday, Doran, 1934.
12 APOLLINAIRE, GUILLAUME. Anecdotiques. p.10 Paris, Librairie Stock, 1926.
13 BASLER, ADOLPHE. Eli Nadelman. 5 illus. Sztuka p.72-4 Mar-Apr (?) 1912. *Two early sculptures reproduced in Sztuka no. 8-9 1904.*
14 BASLER, ADOLPHE. La sculpture moderne en France. 1 illus. p.36,48 Paris, Crès, 1928 (Peintres et sculpteurs).
15 BEAUNOM, ANDRÉ. Ein Hellenist: Elie Nadelman. 6 illus. Das Zelt v. 1 nr.3, p.94-5, 97, Mar 1924.
16 BIRNBAUM, MARTIN. Eli Nadelman. 4 illus. International Studio v. 57 no. 226, p.LIII-LV Dec 1915. *Subsequently published, with modifications in text and illustration, in the Scott & Fowles exhibition catalog, New York 1917; in his book of essays "Introductions" p.59-68, New York, F.F.Sherman, 1919; and in The Menorah Journal v. 11, p.484-8 Oct 1925.*
17 Breaking loose from the Rodin spell. 3 illus. Current Opinion v. 52no.3, p.206-8 Mar 1917. *Includes statements by Nadelman, Birnbaum, McBride and Forbes Watson.*
18 BROOKGREEN GARDENS. Brookgreen gardens sculpture, by Beatrice Gilman Proske. 1 illus. p. xxxvi-vii, 302-4, 410 Brookgreen, S.C., Printed by order of the trustees, 1943. *Bibliography.*
19 BÜLOW, DR. J.v. Paris auf der juryfreien Kunstschau in Berlin. Kunstchronik v. 24nr. 18, p.250-1 Jan 31 1913.
20 [BURROUGHS, CLYDE H.] The sculpture of Elie Nadelman. 3 illus., Bulletin of the Detroit Institute of Art v. 1no.5, p.73-4 Feb 1920.
21 DAVIS, VIRGINIA H. Heads by Elie Nadelman. 5 illus. International Studio v.80, p.482-3 Mar 1925. *In the Helena Rubinstein collection.*
22 Eli Nadelman. Tygodnik Polski (The Polish Weekly, N. Y.). v.4 no.50, p.15 Dec 29 1946.
23 Eli Nadelman, in a modernist mood. 4 illus. Vanity Fair v.10, p.64 May 1918.
24 Eli Nadelman, of Paris. Camera Work no.48, p.10, 42-5 Oct 1916. *On the exhibit held Dec 8 1915 - Jan 19 1916. Reprints text by Nadelman which was not included in illustrated leaflet issued for the "291" show. Press notices by Caffin, McBride, Watson and Carey are printed on p.42-5.*
25 Eli Nadelman – sculptor. The Index of Twentieth Century Artists, v. 3 no.6, p.259-61 Mar 1936. *Bibliography, list of exhibitions and reproductions.*
26 EVANS, JEAN. Sculptor passes but his marble lives on. 2 illus. New York Star (Magazine Section) v.1 no.33, p.4-5 July 31 1948.
27 [FLINT, RALPH] Nadelman exhibits in triple capacity. The Art News v. 23 no.23, p.1-2 Mar 14 1925. *Review of Scott and Fowles exhibit.*
28 FORNARO, CARLO DE. Elie Nadelman, vers la beauté plastique. Social (Havana) p.37, 64-5 July 1929. *Revised text published in The Tatler p. 52 Dec 1929.*

29 GIDE, ANDRÉ. The journals of André Gide. v.1, p.234-7 New York, A. A. Knopf, 1947.

30 HUYGHE, RENÉ. ed. Histoire de l'art contemporain: la peinture. p.143-6 Paris, Félix Alcan, 1935. *Originally published in L'Amour de l'Art v.14 no.6 June 1933.*

31 KIESLER, FREDERICK. Contemporary art applied to the store and its display. 3 illus. p.28,32-3 New York, Brentano's, 1930.

32 [KING, FREDERICK A.] A "hellenist" sculptor driven here by the war. 3 illus. The Literary Digest v.54 no.9, p.550-1 Mar 3 1917.

33 KIRSTEIN, LINCOLN. Elie Nadelman, 1882-1946. 9 illus. Harper's Bazaar v.82 no.2840, p.132-5, 186 Aug 1948.

34 [LYNES, RUSSELL] After hours [by Mr. Harper] 4 illus. Harper's Magazine v.196, p.381-4 Apr 1948.

35 McBRIDE, HENRY. Elie Nadelman. 2 illus. Creative Art v.10 no.5, p.393-4 May 1932. *Published on the occasion of the Marie Sterner exhibition, but originally written for the New York Sun, Feb 5 1927, as a review of the Knoedler show. Other McBride reviews were published in Fine Arts Journal v.35, p.227-8 Mar 1917; The Dial v. 78 no.6, p.528-9 June 1925; The Dial v. 82 no.4, p.353-4 Apr. 1927.*

36 McBRIDE, HENRY. Neglected sculpture, the odd story of a brilliant artist who escaped critical attention. New York Sun p.23 Feb 28 1947.

37 MONTJOIE! (Paris) no.4, p.4; no.9-10, p.7; no.11-12, p.1,11 1913. *Only illustrations cited in this periodical.*

38 Nadelman. *In* National Cyclopedia of American Biography current volume E, p.282 New York, James T. White, 1938.

39 NATANSON, THADÉE. Elie Nadelman. *In his* Peints à leur tour. 1 illus. p.239-43 Paris, Albin Michel, 1948. *Cultural life in Paris in the epoch of Nadelman, circa 1910.*

40 A new sculptor: two examples of the work of Elie Nadelman. 2 illus. Black & White Apr 1 1911(?) *Review of forthcoming exhibition at Paterson's gallery, London.*

41 NIRDLINGER, VIRGINIA. Eli Nadelman, International Gallery. Parnassus v.4 no.4, p.13 Apr 1932. *Review of "the best of the season's sculpture exhibitions."*

42 PARKES, KINETON. After futurism comes "significant form"; a Polish sculptor, Elie Nadelman, introduces the newest phase in sculptured art. 3 illus. The Sphere v.107, p.18 Oct 2 1926.

43 PARKES, KINETON. Sculpture of today. v.2, p.237-9, 242 New York, Scribner's [1921] (Universal art series).

44 READ, HELEN APPLETON. Eli Nadelman, 2 illus. The Arts v.7, pp.228-9 Apr 1925. *Review of Scott and Fowles exhibit.*

45 Rediscovered genius. 6 illus. Life v.24 no.21, p.119-20,122 May 24 1948.

46 "Reverie," by Elie Nadelman. 2 illus. Bulletin of the Detroit Museum of Art v.12 no.8, p.54,56-7 May 1918.

47 SALMON, ANDRÉ. Elie Nadelman. 9 illus. L'Art Décoratif v.31 no.201, p.107-14 Mar 1914. *Later published as "Humanisme," p.77-82 in his "La jeune sculpture française" Paris, Société des Trente, 1919.*

48 SALMON, ANDRÉ. La sculpture vivante, III. 3 illus. L'Art Vivant v.2 no.31, p.259-60 Apr 1 1926.

49 Sculpture of mystery by Elie Nadelman. Vanity Fair v.9, p.58 Sept 1917.

50 STEIN, ERNA. Nadelman. *In* Thieme-Becker. Allgemeines Lexikon der bildenden Künstler. v.5, p.323 Leipzig, E. A. Seeman, 1931.

51 STEIN, GERTRUDE. Nadelman. *In her* Portraits and prayers. p.51-3 New York, Random house, 1934. *Essay dated 1911, originally published in Larus v.1 no.4, p.19-20 July 1927.*

52 TYRRELL, HENRY. At a musical tea with Nadelman. 6 illus. The World Magazine Nov 30 1919. *Interview.*

53 WATSON, FORBES. A museum of the folk arts. American Magazine of Art v.28 no.5, p.312 May 1935. *For additional material on the Nadelman collection see Art News v.36 no.19, p.17 Feb 5 1938; International studio v.91 no.379 p.50-1 Dec 1928, v.92 no.388, p.51-3 Sept 1929; House & Garden v.56 no.2, p.84-5, 122 Aug 1929.*

54 WEICHSEL, JOHN. Eli Nadelman's sculpture. 10 illus. East and West v.1 no.5, p.144-8 Aug 1915. *First American notice on Nadelman.*

55 WRIGHT, WILLARD HUNTINGTON. The aesthetic struggle in America. The Forum v.55 no.2, p.214-17 Feb 1916. *On Nadelman at the "291" gallery.*

Eight thousand copies of this book have been printed in September 1948 for the Trustees of The Museum of Modern Art by the John B. Watkins Company, New York.

Frontispiece: *Sacrifice II*. 1948-52. Bronze, 49¼″ high.
Whitney Museum of American Art, New York

HENRY R. HOPE **The Sculpture of Jacques Lipchitz**

The Museum of Modern Art NEW YORK

IN COLLABORATION WITH

THE WALKER ART CENTER, MINNEAPOLIS; THE CLEVELAND MUSEUM OF ART

TRUSTEES OF THE MUSEUM OF MODERN ART

JOHN HAY WHITNEY, CHAIRMAN OF THE BOARD; HENRY ALLEN MOE, 1ST VICE-CHAIRMAN; PHILIP L. GOODWIN, 2ND VICE-CHAIRMAN; WILLIAM A. M. BURDEN, PRESIDENT; MRS. DAVID M. LEVY, 1ST VICE-PRESIDENT; ALFRED H. BARR, JR., MRS. ROBERT WOODS BLISS, STEPHEN C. CLARK, MRS. W. MURRAY CRANE*, RENE D'HARNONCOURT, MRS. EDSEL B. FORD, A. CONGER GOODYEAR, MRS. SIMON GUGGENHEIM*, WALLACE K. HARRISON, JAMES W. HUSTED*, MRS. ALBERT D. LASKER, MRS. HENRY R. LUCE, RANALD H. MACDONALD, MRS. SAMUEL A. MARX, MRS. G. MACCULLOCH MILLER, WILLIAM S. PALEY, MRS. BLISS PARKINSON, MRS. CHARLES S. PAYSON, DUNCAN PHILLIPS*, ANDREW CARNDUFF RITCHIE, DAVID ROCKEFELLER, MRS. JOHN D. ROCKEFELLER, 3RD, NELSON A. ROCKEFELLER, BEARDSLEY RUML, PAUL J. SACHS*, JOHN L. SENIOR, JR., JAMES THRALL SOBY, EDWARD M. M. WARBURG, MONROE WHEELER

*HONORARY TRUSTEE FOR LIFE

TRUSTEES OF THE CLEVELAND MUSEUM OF ART

HAROLD T. CLARK, PRESIDENT; LEONARD C. HANNA, JR., VICE-PRESIDENT; EDWARD B. GREENE, VICE-PRESIDENT; LEWIS B. WILLIAMS, VICE-PRESIDENT; RALPH M. COE, MRS. ALBERT S. INGALLS. SEVERANCE A. MILLIKIN, LAURENCE H. NORTON, MRS. R. HENRY NORWEB, RALPH S. SCHMITT, G. GARRETSON WADE

BOARD OF DIRECTORS OF THE WALKER ART CENTER

EDGAR V. NASH, PRESIDENT; ELEANOR HARRIS, VICE-PRESIDENT; H. H. ARNASON, SECRETARY-TREASURER AND MUSEUM DIRECTOR; THEODORE W. BENNETT, E. HJALMAR BJORNSON, WINSTON A. CLOSE, D. W. JUDKINS, LOUISE W. MCCANNEL, ELEANOR MOEN, FRED V. NASH, J. E. RATNER, JUSTIN V. SMITH, MALCOLM M. WILLEY, LOUIS N. ZELLE, PRESIDENT, CENTER ARTS COUNCIL; EX OFFICIO: HON. ERIC G. HOYER, GEORGE M. JENSON, ARCHIE D. WALKER

Contents

Acknowledgments

On behalf of the Trustees of The Museum of Modern Art and the Cleveland Museum of Art, and the Board of Directors of The Walker Art Center, Minneapolis, I wish to thank the collectors, museums, the artist and his dealer, Curt Valentin, whose generosity in lending has made the exhibition possible.

Above all, our gratitude goes to Henry R. Hope, Head of the Department of Art of Indiana University who has served as director of the exhibition and prepared this monograph on the artist. The selection of works for exhibition was made jointly by Mr. Hope and the staff of the Department of Painting and Sculpture of The Museum of Modern Art, with the close collaboration of the sculptor.

We are also particularly indebted to Philip L. Goodwin, the Hanna Fund, Bernard J. Reis, John L. Senior, Jr., H. Harvard Arnason and William M. Milliken for their generous assistance and cooperation.

ANDREW CARNDUFF RITCHIE
Director, Department of Painting and Sculpture

DEPARTMENT OF PAINTING AND SCULPTURE
Andrew Carnduff Ritchie, *Director*
Margaret Miller, *Associate Curator*   Alice Bacon, *Research Assistant*
Ellen Mary Jones, *Research Assistant*   Alicia Legg, *Secretary*

The Sculpture of Jacques Lipchitz

1 Introduction

Jacques Lipchitz is one of the great sculptors of our time. For over forty years, he has been an important figure in modern art. Long recognized as a master in the School of Paris, he was forced in 1941 to take refuge in the United States, and since that time has chosen to remain here.

This exhibition provides his fellow citizens with a unique opportunity to see his sculpture and judge its quality. It is a rich accumulation, for in his long career he has been very productive. Always a pathfinder, seeking to "liberate sculpture from its traditional imprisonment,"[1] he has continued to grow, to find new images that express his ideas.

It is a long line of growth with many variations, going all the way from the abstract to the naturalistic, yet there is an unbroken continuity: "In my work there have never been abrupt changes. Each new sculpture grew out of those which preceded it."

In technique Lipchitz is a modeller. Almost every sculpture he ever made was first conceived in clay. Direct carving, because of its slowness, never appealed to him. His stone sculptures were cut after clay models; he deemed it sufficient to finish the surface once the groundwork had been "pointed" by a stone cutter. It is the same when he makes a plaster model: the cast may be filed, sawed, or remodelled, but the essential realization of the form is in the clay that preceded the plaster.

Consequently, very many of his sculptures are in bronze, and Lipchitz has become a master craftsman in exploiting the potentialities of cast metal. When he works his clay, he seems to visualize the effect it will have in bronze, as a composer hears the sounds of his orchestration. The bold pattern of bosses and recessions and the endless rhythm of broken surfaces he sees as metallic reflections, adding sparkle and variety to his composition. At the foundry he is a major-domo, supervising every operation, often at great length — it took him three weeks to repair the arm of a wax mold that had melted during a heat wave. He hammers, files and polishes the bronze with great care, and then applies

Sketch for *Mother and Child*. 1931. Terra cotta, c.5″ high. Owned by the artist

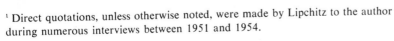

[1] Direct quotations, unless otherwise noted, were made by Lipchitz to the author during numerous interviews between 1951 and 1954.

the patina like a painter, selecting tints — from bright gold to deep reddish browns — as they seem to fit the mood and scale of the piece at hand.

Perhaps his sculpture is more effectively described in terms of poetry than in the vague language of current art criticism. In a broad sense, Lipchitz is a poet employing images no less for symbolic and associational values than for the beauty of their forms, and expressing in his later work some of the great themes common to both literary and artistic tradition. His sculpture reaches its deepest significance in its capacity to move us with reference to the life of the spirit, beyond the ephemeral glitter of pure form. His major monuments, like the *Song of the Vowels* or *Prometheus Strangling the Vulture* are epic, the sculptural expression of sweeping metaphors — of man confronted by the world, by his fellow man, by himself. In work of a more intimate character Lipchitz is often lyrical, especially in his later "transparents" such as *Chimène, Blossoming,* or *The Bride,* where feeling is raised to the pitch of ecstasy. Occasionally he approaches the tragic, as in the Hebraic themes of the *Prayer* and the *Sacrifice,* but with Lipchitz the tragedy is never allowed to unfold. Its ulterior presence is a challenge which strengthens his faith in the indomitable spirit of man. Throughout his work one finds the recurrent themes of life, energy, love, virility. Every sculpture he ever made, he claims, was conceived in a spirit of optimism — which he has summed up in the inscription to accompany his forthcoming statue of the Virgin Mary for a Catholic church in France; "Jacques Lipchitz, juif, fidèle à la foi de ses ancêtres, a fait cette vierge pour la bonne entente des hommes sur la terre afin que l'esprit règne."[2]

For all his poetry, Lipchitz is first a modern sculptor; his art is entirely free of the literary and neo-classic clichés which have stultified academic sculpture for the past hundred years. Like other artists of our time, he has found it necessary to forge a new language capable of giving shape to the images in his mind. In the mysterious dualism of art, his forms and images react upon each other to create sculpture. Often his style is of such force and originality that it is not readily grasped at first glance — nevertheless, he is right in claiming that it is in the great stream of European sculpture from Michaelangelo and Bernini to Rodin. More than any contemporary sculptor, he shares — perhaps inherits — their legacy.

Lipchitz was not always a sculptor of epic and lyric themes. In his beginnings he had little interest in subject matter. The language of pure form was his passion, and in this he achieved his first success with the

[2] "Jacques Lipchitz, Jew, faithful to the religion of his ancestors, has made this Virgin to foster understanding between men on earth that the life of the spirit may prevail."

distinguished sculpture of his cubist period. A glance at some of the titles, *Standing Figure, Seated Harlequin with Guitar, Bather,* indicates the passivity of his subject matter. New rhythms and combinations of forms were his main preoccupation, as they were for most young artists of the pre-World War I generation. These ideas were a part of the milieu which Jacques Lipchitz entered when he first came to Paris — and we shall see how rapidly he absorbed them.

2 Early Work, 1911-1914

When Jacques Lipchitz became an art student he was almost wholly in-experienced, but thanks to his intelligence and talent, and to his com-plete devotion to work, his progress was very rapid.

The *Head of Mlle S.,* one of several portraits made during the winter of 1911-1912, is a good example of his early sculpture. Early work, even by a genius, is apt to be uncertain, and this is no exception. It gives us a glimpse of his talent and promise; at the same time one need not over-look the thinness of modelling and rather vague treatment of planes. Nevertheless this head passed the jury of the conservative Société Nationale, and was admired there by Rodin — a good beginning.

His early figure style can be seen in *Woman and Gazelles* (p.22), a competent if somewhat contrived composition, begun as a single gazelle to which the nude, and later the second animal, were added.

Months before exhibiting this group at the Salon d'Automne of 1913, Lipchitz had begun to veer away from the precepts of the Académie Julian and undertake a series of experiments. It is generally assumed that his first radical work was stimulated by the revolutionary trends in current sculpture, especially those of Archipenko and Boccioni. While not unaware of them, nor of cubist painting, which his friend Diego Rivera kept praising ("Voilà de la sculpture!" he told Lipchitz, pointing out Picasso's painted bronze *Absinthe Glass),* Lipchitz was too deeply involved with his own sculptural problems to pay much at-tention. The nature of these problems can be seen in *The Meeting* (p.23), *Woman with Serpent* (p.25), and *Acrobat on Horseback* (p. 24). In *The Meeting* he was trying to compose a better integrated group than his *Woman and Gazelles,* while *Woman with Serpent* is a study in the opposition of verticals and diagonals. At the same time it is an effort — eminently successful — to make the sculpture seem to turn, to impel the spectator to walk around it, to be aware of its existence in space. Seen in retrospect, this bronze contains many predictions of his later work.

The *Acrobat on Horseback* is a study in geometric curves. Although the emphasis upon angularity and flattened planes seems to be — and

Head of Mlle S. 1911. Bronze, 19¾" high. Owned by the artist

9

indeed is — in the spirit of the time, Lipchitz tells us that "my ideal was then Villard de Honnecourt, for I had just discovered that in his geometricized human figures, drawn in the thirteenth century, he had done exactly what I was trying to do in the twentieth."

A profound change in his outlook on art occurred in Mallorca where he spent the summer of 1914. Away from the rapid tempo of life in Paris, he had time to reflect. The southern sun and spectacular natural surroundings gave him a revelation, a sculptor's vision of nature: huge, sharply-defined mountains of stone rising out of a transparent blue sea. He dreamed of a geometry of shapes, as yet undefined, which one day would materialize in his clay and actually did begin to appear some eight or nine months later — after a proper period of gestation.

In the meantime, moving to Madrid after the outbreak of war, he modelled the *Sailor with Guitar* (p.26) from drawings done in Mallorca. Here he introduced for the first time the abrupt angular planes of cubist painting, modelling them sharply and in clear relationship of parts to whole.

The Prado Gallery played an important part in the education of the artist, for hitherto, engrossed in the art of sculpture, he had admired painting rather distantly. Seeing and re-seeing the masterpieces of Tintoretto, Bosch, El Greco and Goya, he says, made him understand, "all of a sudden, how to enter into the life of the painting, to breathe it." Yet Lipchitz was ill at ease in Madrid, where he was forced to depend upon the generosity of his friends, and before the end of the year he made plans to return to Paris. The memory of Spain went with him, and it has always remained very vivid, perhaps because this Spanish journey marks a turning point, the end of his formative years and the beginning of his career as a sculptor who would make his own revolutions.

3 Cubist Period, 1915-1919

In the grim atmosphere of war-time Paris, Lipchitz went to work with a devotion and frugality that is reflected in the austerity of the new style. It was at this time that the Mallorcan vision began to materialize. The first new sculpture was a thin statuette in clay, a human figure with all details eliminated, organic shapes transformed to geometric, and volume reduced to a thin shaft (p.27). Soon this abstract image appeared in wood — flat boards, cut out and fitted together like prefabricated toys. Entitled *Dancer* or *Figure* (p.28), these wooden demountables were almost non-representational and were among the forerunners of constructivism.

Then his vision enriched these thin forms, by transferring them to stone, where they at once acquired weight, solidity and a clean, geometric rhythm. He preferred to hire a stone cutter for all but the finishing touches, but with his meager resources this was difficult. In 1916 a contract with Léonce Rosenberg, providing extra payment for labor and material, gave him what he needed. Thus liberated, he created a series of tall, thin shafts of great beauty. One of these, the *Man with a Guitar* (p.30), made a sensation when first exhibited because of the hole cut through the center.

Promising though it seems, this non-representational direction was foreign to his nature, and he soon turned away from it. He continued to work in bold cubic forms, but in place of architectonic shafts he now introduced articulated sequences of the seated or standing figure, and for representation of details he invented a kind of geometric shorthand. The importance of this change can be seen when we look at the *Man with Mandolin* (p.33), for it stares back at us like a Cyclops from its astonishing single eye.

In the sculpture which followed, Lipchitz began to show his grasp of the cubists' analysis and penetration of form. His figures were represented as if seen from many angles and perspectives, often with a richly broken up surface of deep and shallow facets, as in the *Bather III* (pp. 31-2). Yet the subordination of parts to whole, and the over-all effect of agitated movement, conflicting with the sheer, static mass of stone gives these sculptures a quality that is unique in cubist art.

At this time his friendship with Juan Gris had brought Lipchitz into the inner circle of cubism. Like Gris, and some of the poets, he delved into occult science, looking — in vain — for a deeper meaning in cubism. He also read in metaphysics and philosophy and had many talks with Gris, whose searching intellect always added zest to their conversations. Quite possibly these widening intellectual interests were beginning to divert Lipchitz from his intense preoccupation with cubism and to prepare the way for new subject matter in his sculpture — although the change did not become visible in his work for several years.

The interchange of ideas and images with others in the circle gave some of his work the collective quality of the movement. Occasionally his gouaches and polychromed reliefs, done mostly in 1918, resembled the work of the painters ("that's the closest you ever came to Picasso," Gris once remarked to his infuriated friend).

But, always the sculptor, Lipchitz soon returned to his stone figures in the round. The group of clowns, musicians and bathers produced between 1917 and 1919 marks this period as one of the most brilliant in his career. There is a poetic quality in these faceted harlequins, as in the architectonic shafts which preceded them. They are images without explicit connotations; their beauty exists in the matter itself and its exciting configurations, as it does in certain word patterns of Mallarmé or Apollinaire.

4 Toward a New Sculpture, 1920-1927

The year 1920 saw a general diminishing in the cubist effort. Since the war's end there had been much talk about a return to nature, to the classic, to Ingres. Lipchitz had never accepted the idea of a cubist portrait; it seemed to him a contradiction of purpose ("I often disputed this point with Gris"). In the fall of the year he modelled a number of more or less naturalistic portraits — *Radiguet, Cocteau, Gertrude Stein* (p.40), and later a commissioned head of Gabrielle Chanel. Although he continued to make cubist sculpture too, there was now a much freer use of curved lines and less emphasis upon angles and flat planes. The change first appears in a pair of andirons made in 1922 for Mlle Chanel, who wanted something to look well in a room decorated in the style of Louis XV. On a larger scale this new manner can be seen in the curving patterns of the *Seated Man with Guitar* (p.38).

Since the war's end there had been so many visitors in his Montparnasse studio that his work was often interrupted. Then, in 1922, an important purchase and commission from Dr. Albert Barnes made him affluent for the first time. Therefore, after completing the Barnes reliefs, Lipchitz commissioned Le Corbusier to build a house and studio in Boulogne-sur-Seine, at the west end of Paris. Moving, in early 1925, he was elated by the tranquility of his new environment and began to work with more energy and enthusiasm than he had felt in many months.

Why does the year 1925 seem so important to Lipchitz? Because after gradually becoming aware of cubism's limitations, he now began to find his way out. Most of his sculpture since 1916 had been conceived for stone, and although at first he had pierced some of these statues with small openings, his later tendency had been to avoid holes or protruding parts. With so much energy in his broken surfaces, it had seemed desirable to maintain the solidity of the stone mass. Now that this effort had been realized, and he was groping for a freer form, he felt an urgent need to break into the mass, to loosen the tight, well-disciplined planes. His drawings and clay reliefs of 1925 have a sketchiness that is almost impressionistic. He was obsessed with the need for a much looser handling of the clay; furthermore he hoped to find some way of opening up its solid core to penetrations of light and space.

As so often happens when new ideas come to Lipchitz, he experienced a sudden revelation. "I was attending a lecture at the Sorbonne when it came to me, and I hurried back to my studio." The solution — or rather the first step toward it — was a cutout cardboard shape, pierced with openings (nothing new about that), which he then transferred to wax stiffened with resin. This he tried to cast in bronze by the *cire-perdue* process (therein was both the novelty and the difficulty).[3]

Persistent trials at the foundry finally brought success. The *Pierrot* completed in 1925 is just a flat little manikin, but others followed with larger openings, grids and ribbons of metal. In 1926, except for the handsome sculpture-in-the-round, *Ploumanach* (p.47), he devoted all his time to the new technique. Soon he was producing airy and *transparent* metal sculpture that has a wholly different effect upon the observer than the traditional sculpture of weight and support. "I soar with this heavier-than-air which is sculpture," wrote Lipchitz.[4]

Most of the early "transparents," as he began to call them, got their titles from the cubist repertory of harlequins and musicians, but one, representing a little clown before an unlocked gate, was called *Pierrot Escapes* (p.43). "This is myself escaping from the imprisonment of cubism."

Pierrot. 1925. Bronze, c.5″ high. Owned by the artist

5 The Emergence of his Monumental Sculpture, 1927 to World War II

Commissioned by Charles de Noailles to make a garden sculpture for his house at Hyères, Lipchitz saw an opportunity to expand the pattern of the transparents to monumental scale. He planned a dancing couple of cubist design, large enough to be seen against the sky, and placed it on a slowly rotating turntable (p.48). When first exhibited in Paris, it carried an inscription paraphrasing Baudelaire, "J'aime le mouvement qui déplace les formes." In this sense it might be called a forerunner of actual motion in sculpture. However, this innovation was of no real interest to Lipchitz; it was the *illusion* of movement that he sought.

Few knew at the time that the title, *La Joie de Vivre,* meant more to Lipchitz than the usual gaiety of cubist subject matter, but a serious change was taking place in his attitude toward his art. Until then, except for a few sorties into the world of affairs, he had kept to his ivory tower ("my Olympian period," he calls it). Now he found himself beset by worries and sorrows. Domestic problems had become acute; his father was ill, his favorite sister dying. With troubles all around him, he delib-

---

[3] *Cire-perdue* or lost-wax is a method of casting dating back to antiquity. In making the "transparents" Lipchitz modeled the original in wax without armature. At the foundry a plaster mold, containing a network of ducts, was built around it, so that the wax, when melted, could be drained off. Molten metal was then poured into the space left by the "lost" wax.

[4] Quoted by Roger Vitrac in bibl. 36, p.14.

erately chose to express his idea of happiness in defiance of these challenges.

Thus, in terms of content, *La Joie de Vivre* is the turning point toward his later sculpture. This confrontation of man and woman dancing in ecstatic happiness is the forerunner of the embracing couples, the violent conflicts and the grandiloquent themes that appear in his later sculpture.

Abstract patterns were still prominent in his work of the next two or three years, especially in two of his finest sculptures: the elegant *Reclining Nude with Guitar* (pp.50-51), whose harmonious counterpoint of solids and voids sparkle in polished black basalt; and the great bronze *Figure* of 1930 (p.53), which stands like a totem, with a stare that is almost hypnotic. (It was so overpowering to the original purchaser that she sent it back.)

To judge by surface appearances alone, one would say that after 1929 or 1930 Lipchitz had begun to replace cubism by something else, for the sharp contours and geometric patterns become rare. Instead, there is fluidity of line, emphasis upon bosses and recessions, and in general a return to naturalistically rendered anatomy.

Yet Lipchitz was never to abandon cubism. When he says today, "I am still a cubist," he means that what he learned in cubism remains the "grammar and syntax" of his art. From the collective experience of those years his personal language of form gradually emerged. Part of what he learned came from Picasso and Gris. He absorbed it from the particular milieu in which he lived and worked, just as he gradually became a Frenchman, assimilating the speech, customs, habits of thought and expression of his adopted country. As he began

Retrospective exhibition, Galerie de la Renaissance, Paris, 1930

to conceive of cubist aims in three-dimensional terms and later invented the transparent, his language grew more and more personal. Simultaneously his ego was aroused by a desire for self-expression. When this happened, the line of separation between form and content began to disappear — they tended to become one, each influencing the other. This, it seems to me, is the significance of the new developments in the art of Lipchitz between the twenties and the thirties.

In 1928 one of the transparents led the way to a further development. Lipchitz has described the vivid impression made on him by the harps at the Salle Pleyel ("... Invariably — the music contributing — the peculiar shapes of the harps, their strings vibrating in the light, veritable columns binding earth to heaven, transported me into a world from which I, in turn, had to make my way back ...")[5] Thanks to the transparent he had discovered a way of transmitting his vision directly into sculpture, *without being aware of the intervening discipline of cubism*: in *The Harp Player* (p.54).

During the next four or five years, perhaps inspired by Rodin, he made a very large number of small clay sketches. They differ from Rodin's in being modelled almost entirely from the imagination — Lipchitz had not sketched from the living figure since art school. One, for example, is a hollowed out *Head* of 1932, presenting a series of contrasts in solids and voids. These rough clay models were the direct response to the imagery that existed in his mind — some are clear and definite, others vague as if just emerging from his subconscious. Often he did not begin to grasp the meaning of the latter until they had appeared in the clay. (Lipchitz has repeatedly attested to this phenomenon.)

The Harp Player, once created out of the substance of his reverie, inspired new and more monumental work: first the double version, *The Harpists* (p.58), and finally one of his greatest monuments, the *Song of the Vowels* (p.59). Just as the original modest form became a huge transparent which seems to magnetize the surrounding space, so the original theme was transformed to symbolize the will of man asserting itself over supernatural forces. Lipchitz himself has said that the title was derived from a legendary prayer called "The Song of the Vowels" which the priests and priestesses of ancient Egypt used to conjure up the forces of nature.[6]

In the midst of these large sculptures came a small group of very lyrical transparents: *Chimène* (p.54), which refers to the first name of a beautiful woman, *Elle* and *Melancholy* (p.55). In revealing something of the intimate and romantic background of the artist they will

Head. 1932. Bronze, 9″ high. Owned by the artist

[5] Quoted by James Johnson Sweeney in bibl. 57, p.24.
[6] *Ibid.,* p.26.

perhaps help us to understand the presence of these same qualities in his larger sculptures. At this same time he was at work on a series of large groups related to the theme of the family: *The Couple,* an intimate expression of physical love, and the *Mother and Child* (p.56), probably a reference to his own mother toward whom he had always felt a deep attachment. But why does the mother have a birdlike head? Could this be a reference to his maternal grandmother whose name was Chaia Fegel (animal bird)? Or is it a reference to subconscious associations with birds and flight, for the bird image reappears frequently in his sculpture after the thirties? Such explanations are speculative at best but, as his work progresses from now on, it seems to me to demand interpretation on some such personal grounds if its total significance is to be fully appreciated. Another in this series is *The Return of the Prodigal Son* (p.57). Finished just before the *Song of the Vowels,* it suggests the return to the village, to the earth, to the spring at which the youth restores his energy ("While making this, I felt a curious sensation of thirst").

Jacob Wrestling with the Angel is the first work based on a theme of heroic conflict which appears frequently in his later work. Like the *Song of the Vowels,* its subject is both literary and personal in reference. All his life Lipchitz has read the Bible — especially the Pentateuch. "It is not impossible that I associated, subconsciously, Jacob's name with my own. But the real story is for mankind. Man is wrestling with the angel; it is a tremendous struggle but he wins, and is blessed."

While Lipchitz was conceiving these allegories in large sculptures, Europe was threatened by the political and economic disturbances of the thirties: the great depression, the rise of Hitler, the political tensions in France, the fear of war. That they would color his thinking was inevitable, and we must look for evidence of their impact in his subsequent sculpture.

The struggle of Prometheus with the vulture was probably the first great theme having a symbolic reference to contemporary events, and in Lipchitz' optimism he chose to represent Prometheus freed from the rock and strangling the vulture which had attacked his vitals. The theme first appears in 1933 in a small rough sketch (reproduced opposite) and again a few years later.

Finally in 1937 Prometheus became the subject of his large commission for the Palace of Discovery and Inventions at the 1937 World's Fair in Paris. This hall of science was housed in the Grand Palais where Lipchitz had already admired the huge neo-baroque chariots, above the cornice, by a forgotten sculptor named Recipon. In keeping with the environment, his new Prometheus was baroque in conception. Designed to be placed eighty feet above the ground[7] over one of the entrance

[7] John Rewald in bibl. 53, p.7.

portals, this son of the Titans is a colossal figure of tremendous energy and threatening pose, a direct heir of Bernini and Puget. He chose this subject because it seemed especially appropriate for an exhibition of scientific progress, but, in the forbidding atmosphere of threats between the totalitarian powers, he began to conceive of Prometheus less as the giver of fire than as the victor in a Promethean conflict (pp.60-1). The victory over the vulture symbolized for Lipchitz "the victory of mankind over these terrible forces." Ironically enough, after the sculpture was unveiled, the artist became the victim of a vicious newspaper attack, which continued in one form or another until the beginning of the war.

The last major work before Munich and the war is the *Rape of Europa* (p.62). Here again, Lipchitz found in classical mythology another symbol for the agony of Europe. The theme, however, is heralded by the *Bull and Condor* (p.62) of 1932.

6 Lipchitz in America, 1941 to the Present

Before settling down to make sculpture in America, Lipchitz suffered a prolonged interruption in his work, for since the start of the war he had scarcely been able to concentrate on any major piece. When finally he was able to take up sculpture again, he did so with a formidable spurt of energy that lasted well into his second year in this country.

Two small sculptures serve as a prelude to his American period: the *Flight* (p.65), modelled just before departure from Europe and carried here in his hand baggage, and the *Arrival* (p.65). Like the large *Prometheus,* they are in the baroque manner, turbulent figures expressing intense emotion. In the *Arrival* a man and woman are running wildly with a child thrust out before them as if to protect it from unseen dangers.

"What is the meaning of this thrust-forth child?" muses the sculptor. "Is it symbolic of my desire to beget a child? — or is it perhaps my sculpture which I feel must be saved?" The image later passed into a larger piece, the *Return of the Child,* and also, somewhat modified, it was transformed into one of his most dramatic sculptures, the *Mother and Child* of 1941 (pp.64, 66-7).

This huge, powerful torso, with every muscle flexed, head thrown back and arms raised in supplication, is a tortured prayer for the salvation of Europe — of the beautiful land of Ile de France and of the distant village of Druskieniki. Working in emotional tension, it was only after the sculpture was completed that Lipchitz discovered the source of his image — hidden until then in his subconscious mind: "In 1935 while visiting a sister in Russia, we had come out of a theatre late at night in the rain, and hearing the voice of a woman singing in a loud, hoarse voice, traced it through the darkness until suddenly she appeared

First sketch for *Prometheus.* 1933. Terra cotta, 8″ high. Owned by the artist

under a street lamp, a legless cripple in a little cart, with both arms raised and with her wet hair streaming down her back as she sang."[8]

Other large sculptures followed in rapid succession, a *Theseus,* a larger version of the *Rape of Europa,* and then the rounded, swollen forms of the *Benediction* (p.69), which Lipchitz explains as a prayer for the preservation of France. His energy was seemingly inexhaustible. "Throughout this period I was in a state of physical excitement."

Suddenly he began a series of transparents of the most rhapsodic character. It was as if he had rediscovered the feelings of love, its swelling passion and orgiastic desire, but also its tenderness. The lost-wax technique of the transparent was perfectly suited for the new imagery that followed. Stems, leaves, tendrils and buds entwined the male and female symbols and created an erotic botany of strange beauty. The sequence of bronze includes *The Promise* (p.71), *The Fiancée, The Bride, Blossoming* (p.72), and *Spring* (p.70).

Then, as if the rhapsody had ended, these bronzes were followed by more somber subjects: *Myrrah,* a terrifying disembowelment of the pelvic structure, and *The Pilgrim* (p.74), a tragic figure with exposed entrails whose body is clad in fluttering leaves, his pilgrim hat a coxcomb, his staff a budding branch.

While brooding over the mass tragedy of the Jews in Europe, Lipchitz conceived the *Prayer* (p.74), derived from the figure of *The Pilgrim.* Here the ancient sacrificial ceremony, in which each man of the community kills the cock by whirling it above his head, is represented by a solitary old man in a dishevelled cloak quivering in terror as the cock wildly flaps its wings. The hollowed-out anatomy and chaotically broken contours give a feeling of hysterical pathos. Yet the sculpture is not without beauty, beauty of a weird and unprecedented kind commemorating terror.

In 1948, relieved from the war's tensions and hopeful for the restoration of peace and the dignity of man, Lipchitz took up once again the theme of an ancient Hebraic rite and produced the *Sacrifice* (frontispiece). Here both spirit and content are totally different. In place of frenetic pathos there is solemnity and fatality. This huge and venerable patriarch is a Prometheus of the Old Testament, and to express him adequately, Lipchitz developed a new figure style, as impressive as the figure of the *Benediction,* yet less gigantic.

In the meantime, Lipchitz had received in 1944 one of those rare opportunities that sculptors dream of: to design a major sculpture for a specific architectural setting — the new Ministry of Education and Health building in Rio de Janeiro. At the suggestion of the architect, he

---

[8] This experience was first recounted by the artist to Alfred H. Barr, Jr. about 1942 and retold subsequently to the writer. The quotation above combines details of both accounts. The image first appears in drawings of 1939-40.

Ministry of Education and Health Building, Rio de Janeiro, with superimposed photograph of Prometheus sculpture in scale of original design

was assigned the great, convex, exterior wall of the auditorium wing.

Returning to the Prometheus theme, Lipchitz designed what, if properly executed, would have been one of the finest unions of sculpture and architecture in modern times. He conceived the group as if poised in space before the convex wall so that the perforated, space-defining sculptural mass and the unbroken wall surface would harmonize in a resounding chord.

Unfortunately, due to some misunderstanding, the seven-foot model Lipchitz sent to Brazil was poorly cast and in the same size, instead of

Five sketches for *Notre Dame de Liesse*. For the Church of Assy. 1947-1950.
Bronze, from 8½ to 10½ ″ high. Owned by the artist

being enlarged to twenty feet as the sculptor had intended. As a result
the scale of sculpture is wholly inadequate in relation to the wall. A
recent bronze, cast under the supervision of the sculptor for the Philadelphia Museum of Art, reveals its magnificent quality (pp.76-7).

While working on the Prometheus, Lipchitz produced in 1944 another architectural sculpture, a Pegasus, based on a transparent he
had done in 1929. The new Pegasus was designed for a projected
museum building. The subject was an appropriate one for a museum,
since according to one antique legend Pegasus is said to have given birth
to the Muses by striking his hoofs on a rock on Mount Olympus. This
project never got beyond the planning stage. However, from the several
Pegasus studies completed in 1944, Lipchitz later derived his design for
a *Birth of the Muses* relief which was commissioned as a decoration for
the fireplace of Mrs. John D. Rockefeller, 3rd's Guest House, where it
was installed in 1950 (p.79).

During the next year or two, Lipchitz worked on several lesser
themes: *The Rescue, The Joy of Orpheus* and *Song of Songs* (p.80),
Happiness. Then, following a visit to Paris in 1946, he accepted a commission from the late Father Couturier to make a baptismal font for the
little church of Notre-Dame-de-Toute-Grâce at Assy, a mountain village
above Chamonix in the French Alps. The font was to incorporate the
figure of the Virgin. Lipchitz stipulated that it should be joyous in con-

20

cept and proposed that it be called *Notre Dame de Liesse,* Our Lady of Joy.

The image was slow in coming, and for several months he turned to other works, such as *The Cradle, Miracle, Exodus 47, Sacrifice,* several of them related to the problems of the Jews in the postwar world. Then one day "I was riding in the subway when the idea for the *Virgin* appeared. I pulled out a pocket notebook and began sketching." Some of the details, we can see now, were related to various works in progress, particularly to the *Sacrifice* and *The Cradle,* but the total image is like the vision of a saint. The dove of the Holy Ghost, flying in space, plucks in his beak the three parts of heaven which form a starry canopy. Here stands the Virgin Mary, her palms spread toward the earth, while beneath her are three archangels and the lamb. This concept made no provision for the baptismal font; hence the added table in his first sculptural sketches (p.20). Later it was agreed to omit the font and place the Virgin in the choir.

The large model of *Notre Dame de Liesse* was destroyed in the studio fire of 1952. But this tragic loss gave the sculptor the image for one of his finest small bronzes, the *Virgin in Flames* (p.85), in which he imagined how the model must have looked as it was consumed in the fire.

While making various small sketches for the Virgin of Assy, Lipchitz one day picked up one of his sculptor's tools which had lost its wooden handle. With this as a basis he created several priest-like figures, by the addition of arms, legs, girdles or mantles, which were later cast in bronze and called *Variations on a Chisel* (p.86). After the fire, while working at the foundry he again returned to the chisel theme, and for nearly a month made one each day — small delightful inventions — a dancer, a centaur and many others which, like the transparents, reveal a lighter, more playful spirit, unexpected when seen against the high seriousness of his monumental works.

The burning of his studio was a severe blow — yet Lipchitz will not concede that it was altogether a loss. By now, several of the damaged pieces have been repaired, the new model of the Virgin of Assy is almost finished and — most important of all — he has a spacious new studio near his home in Hastings.

Above all, the challenge of the fire stimulated a fresh stream of ideas and images. Today at 63, with amazingly youthful energy Lipchitz is overflowing with plans for new sculpture — serenely confident that he will continue to grow with his work.

Woman and Gazelles. 1912. Bronze, 46½" long. Owned by the artist

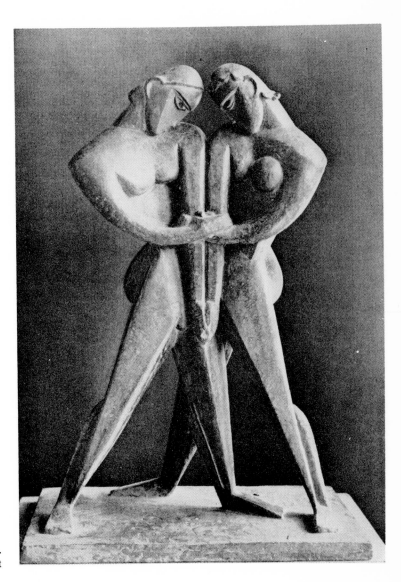

The Meeting. 1913. Lead, 32″ high.
Owned by the artist

Acrobat on Horseback. 1914. Bronze, 21½" high. Curt Valentin Gallery, New York

24

Woman with Serpent. 1913. Bronze, 25″ high. Collection Emil J. Arnold, New York

Sailor with Guitar. 1914.
Bronze, 30″ high.
The Philadelphia
Museum of Art

Bather. 1915. Bronze, 31⅝″ high.
Owned by the artist.

Figure. 1916. Oak, 26½″ high. Owned by the artist

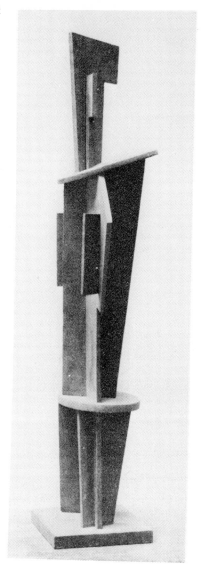

Pierrot. 1916. Drawing with color crayon, 22 x 14¾″. Collection Mr. and Mrs. Burton Tremaine, Meriden, Conn.

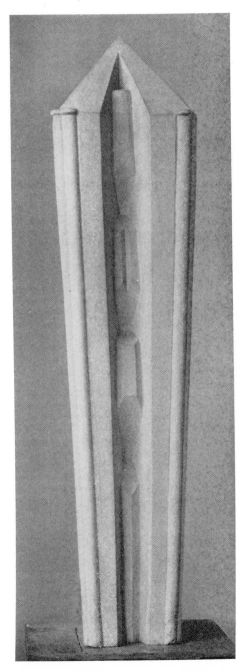

Figure. 1916. Lead, 49½″ high. Owned by the artist. *Stone reproduced*

Standing Personage. 1916. Stone, 43¾″ high. Owned by the artist

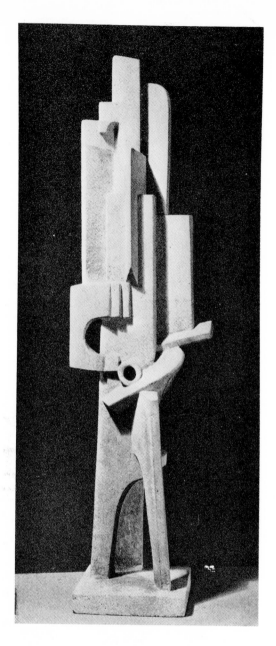

Man with a Guitar. 1916. Stone, 38¼" high. The Museum of Modern Art, New York, Mrs. Simon Guggenheim Fund

Bather III. 1917. Bronze, 24¾″ high.
Owned by the artist. *Stone, Barnes
Foundation, Merion, Pa., reproduced*

Back view. *Bather III.* 1917

Man with Mandolin. 1917. Stone, 29¾″ high. Yale University Art Gallery, New Haven, the Société Anonyme Collection

Side view of above

Seated Guitar Player. 1918. Bronze, 23⅝" high. Owned by the artist. *Stone, private collection, Switzerland, reproduced*

Seated Figure. 1918. Drawing with color crayon, 19½ x 12½". Farnsworth Art Museum. Wellesley College

Still Life with Musical Instruments. 1918. Stone relief, 23⅝ x 29½". Owned by the artist

Oval Polychrome Relief. 1918. Stone, 27½ x 18⅞".
Owned by the artist

Still Life. 1918. Gouache, 21¾ x 13".
Collection The Miller Company, Meriden,
Conn.

Pierrot with Clarinet. 1919. Stone, 31″ high. Collection
G. David Thompson, Pittsburgh

Seated Man with Guitar. 1922. Granite, 15⅞″ high. Collection Nelson A. Rockefeller, New York

Left. *Repentant Magdalen.* 1921. Right: *Seated Woman.* 1922. Both terracotta sketches, 6″ long and c.4″ high. Owned by the artist

Seated Man. 1922. Granite, 20″ high. Virginia Museum of Fine Arts, Richmond

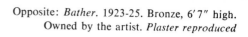

Opposite: *Bather*. 1923-25. Bronze, 6' 7" high.
Owned by the artist. *Plaster reproduced*

Gertrude Stein. 1920. Bronze, 13½" high.
Curt Valentin Gallery, New York

Berthe Lipchitz. 1922. Bronze, 19¾" high.
Owned by the artist

40

Pierrot with Clarinet. 1926. Bronze, 14¾″ high. Curt Valentin Gallery, New York

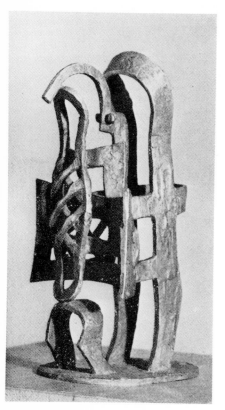

Mardi Gras. 1926. Gilded bronze, 10½″ high. Curt Valentin Gallery, New York

Pierrot Escapes. 1926. Bronze, 18¼″ high. Formerly collection
Mme de Mandrot, Paris. *Not in the exhibition*

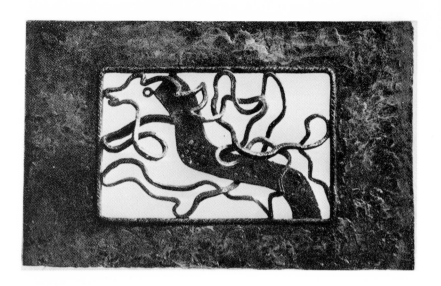

Circus Scene. 1927. Gilded bronze, 12 x 19½″. Collection Mr. and Mrs. Bernard J. Reis, New York

Harlequin with Guitar. 1926. Bronze, 13¼″ high. Private collection, New York

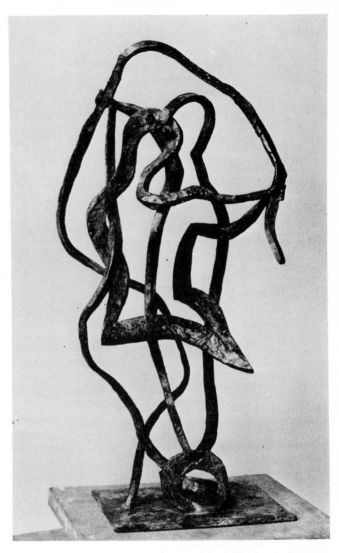

Acrobat on Ball. 1926. Bronze, 17¼" high. Collection the Baroness Gourgaud, Yerres, France

Guitar Player. 1925. Stone, 23¼" high.
Owned by the artist

Seated Man. 1925. Bronze, 22" high.
The Museum of Modern Art, New York

Ploumanach. 1926. Bronze, 31″ high. Private collection

La Joie de Vivre. 1927. Bronze, 7′ 4″ high. Installed in the garden of Vicomte Charles de Noailles at Hyères, on the Mediterranean. House designed by Mallet-Stevens, garden by Gevrekian

La Joie de Vivre. Three views: original plaster opposite page;
bronze above and right. *Not in the exhibition*

Reclining Nude with Guitar. 1928. Basalt, 26⅞″ long. Collection Mrs. John D. Rockefeller, 3rd, New York

Terracotta sketch for above

Back view

Sketch for unexecuted garden sculpture II. 1921.
Terra cotta, 5″ high. Owned by the artist

Two sketches for *Figure,* a garden sculpture. 1926.
Terra cotta, 8½″ high and 10″ high. Owned by the artist

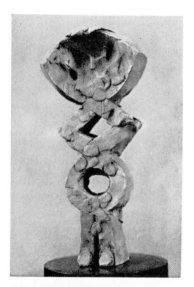

52

Opposite: *Figure.* 1926-30. Bronze, 7′ 1¼″ high.
The Museum of Modern Art, New York,
Van Gogh Purchase Fund

Chimène. 1930. Bronze, 18″ high. Curt Valentin Gallery, New York

The Harp Player. 1928. Bronze, 10½″ high.
Collection Mrs. T. Catesby Jones, New York

Melancholy. 1930. Bronze, 11½ ″ high. Collection Mr. and Mrs. Bernard J. Reis, New York

Mother and Child. 1929-30. Bronze, 51¼″ high. Owned by the artist

Above: *Return of the Prodigal Son.* 1931. Bronze, 47¼" long.
Owned by the artist. *Plaster reproduced*

Left: Terracotta sketch for above

Study for *Song of the Vowels*. 1931.
Terra cotta, 14½″ high. The Museum
of Modern Art, New York, gift of the sculptor

Opposite: *Song of the Vowels*. 1931-53. Bronze, 10′ high. Collection Nelson A. Rockefeller, New York.
Another cast, photographed in the garden of Mme de Mandrot, at Le Pradet, France, reproduced

The Harpists. 1930. Bronze, 17″ high.
Collection Mr. and Mrs. Bernard J. Reis,
New York

Opposite: *Prometheus Strangling the Vulture*. Final clay model, about 46′ high. Photographed with the sculptor before its installation over a portal of the Grand Palais for the Paris World's Fair, 1937. *Not in the exhibition*

Prometheus with Vulture. Study. 1936. Bronze, 16¼″ high. Collection Mr. and Mrs. Sam Jaffe, Beverly Hills, Calif.

Rape of Europa II. 1938. Bronze, 23⅛″ long. The Museum of Modern Art, New York

Bull and Condor. 1932. Bronze, 12¼″ long. Curt Valentin Gallery, New York

Study for *Rape of Europa IV*. 1941. Gouache, 26 x 20″. The Museum of Modern Art, New York, Mrs. Simon Guggenheim Fund

Study for *Mother and Child*. 1939. Gouache, 21½ x 14½ ″. Private collection, New York

Flight. 1940. Bronze, 14½″ high.
Private collection, New York

Arrival. 1941. Bronze, 21″ high.
Owned by the artist

Mother and Child II. 1941-45. Bronze, 50″ high. The Museum of Modern Art, New York, Mrs. Simon Guggenheim Fund

Opposite: An earlier cast in the collection of Edgar J. Kaufmann, photographed at *Falling Water,* Bear Run, Pa., architect Frank Lloyd Wright

Theseus. 1942. Wash drawing, 13¾ x 10½". Collection John S. Newberry, Jr., Grosse Pointe Farms, Mich.

Benediction I. 1942. Bronze, 42″ high. Collection Mr. and Mrs. Bernard J. Reis, New York

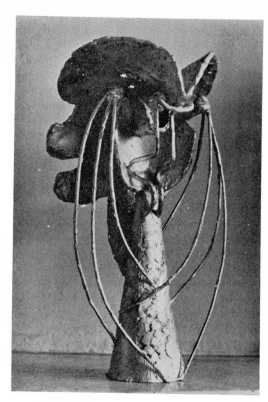

Barbara. 1942. Bronze, 15⅝″ high.
Smith College Museum of Art, Northampton, Mass.

Spring. 1942. Bronze, 14″ high.
Collection Mr. and Mrs. Bernard J. Reis, New York

70

The Promise. 1942. Bronze, 18″ high. Curt Valentin Gallery, New York

Blossoming. 1941-42. Bronze, 21½ " high. The Museum of Modern Art, New York

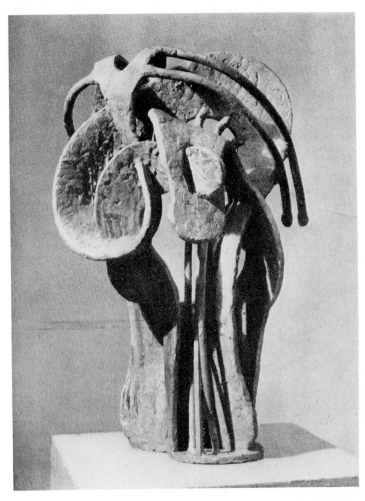

Trentina. 1946. Gilded bronze, 20″ high. Collection Mrs. Orswell Dailey, Pomfret Center, Conn. *Not in the exhibition*

Prayer. 1943. Bronze, 42½" high.
Collection Mr. and Mrs. R. Sturgis Ingersoll,
Penllyn, Pa.

The Pilgrim. 1942. Bronze, 31½" high.
Owned by the artist

74

Study for *Sacrifice*. 1946. Ink drawing, 22 x 17″. Collection
Mr. and Mrs. Morton G. Neumann, Chicago

Prometheus Strangling the Vulture II. 1944-53. Bronze, 8½' high. Owned by the artist

Back view

Birth of the Muses I. 1944. Bronze, 5″ high.
Collection Mr. and Mrs. Thomas J. Rosenberg, New York

Opposite: *Birth of the Muses.* 1944-50. Photographed after installation
at Guest House of Mrs. John D. Rockefeller, 3rd. *Not in the exhibition*

Pegasus. 1944. Bronze, 20″ high.
Curt Valentin Gallery, New York

Song of Songs. 1945-48. Bronze, 36″ long. Curt Valentin Gallery, New York

Hagar. 1948. Bronze, 30″ long. Curt Valentin Gallery, New York

Mother and Child. 1949. Bronze, 46½" high. Curt Valentin Gallery, New York

Miracle II. 1947. Bronze, 30¼″ high. The Jewish Museum, New York

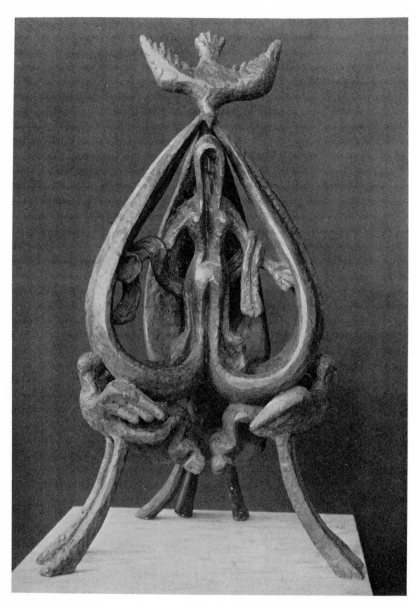

Study for *Notre Dame de Liesse*. For the Church of Assy. 1948. Bronze, 33″ high. Owned by the artist

Virgin in Flames I. 1952. Gilded bronze, 13½″ high.
Collection Mr. and Mrs. Leigh B. Block, Chicago

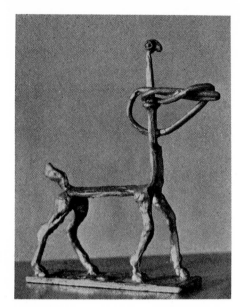

Three Variations on a Chisel. 1951-52. Bronze, from 8¾″ to 7½″ high. *Left* and *center,* Curt Valentin Gallery, New York; *right,* Private collection, New York

Opposite: Jacques Lipchitz in his studio at Hastings-on-Hudson,
New York. Photograph Paul Weller

Chronology

1891 Born August 22 at Druskieniki, small health resort (Lithuanian, *druskos:* salts) on river Niemen in Lithuania, then in possession of Tsarist Russia. Given name: Chaim Jacob (later changed to Jacques because thus inscribed on French identity card). First of six children of Abraham Lipchitz, young building contractor from Grodno, whose father was a wealthy banker. Lipchitz' mother, Rachael Leah Krinsky Lipchitz, daughter of a local hotel keeper.

1892-1902 Lived in large house with garden. Quiet, introspective child, vivid imagination. Liked to shape objects in clay. Early belief that he was destined for fame, fostered by mother for whom child felt strong attachment.

1902-1909 Local school being inadequate, entered commercial school at Bialystok. A pogrom, in June 1906, frightened parents into moving boy to Vilna, where he tutored and entered state high school. Father urged that he prepare for engineering school, opposed career in the arts, hoped son would join family business. Left school in fall of 1909, determined to go to Paris and study sculpture. In father's absence, mother consented and gave money.

1909-1910 Arrived Paris October, 1909, was admitted as *élève libre* in atelier of Jean Antoine Injalbert at Ecole des Beaux-Arts. Father forgave and started generous allowance. Lived at Hôtel des Mines, Boulevard St. Michel. Distracted by incessant hazing soon left Injalbert atelier, entered small class in direct carving at same school. In early winter enrolled also in sculpture class of Raoul Verlet at Académie Julian. Spent evenings at sketch classes in Montparnasse (Colarossi, Cours Municipal). For two years attended lectures on anatomy by Dr. Richet at Ecole des Beaux-Arts. Frequently visited Louvre and other art collections of Paris. Acquired wide knowledge of art — especially primitive. Preferred archaic Greek, Egyptian and Gothic. Began collecting.

1911 Allowance stopped due to failure of father's business. Found part-time job. Developed mild case of tuberculosis. Aided by wealthy fellow-student, Bernard Szeps, was hospitalized. Convalesced in Belgium during summer. Returned to art school in fall. Still aided by Szeps, rented small studio at 51 rue du Montparnasse. Met fellow-student, Cesare Sofianopulo, and modelled his portrait.

1912 Returned to Russia for military service. Rejected because of health. Back to Paris in autumn. Rented studio adjoining Brancusi at 54 rue du Montparnasse.

1913 Friendly with Diego Rivera who introduced him to Picasso. At first unsympathetic to cubism, especially to Picasso's sculpture. Exhibited the more conservative *Woman and Gazelles* at Salon d'Automne.

1914 In summer went with friends to Mallorca. After outbreak of war, moved to Madrid. *Sailor with Guitar* more radical than his sculpture of previous year. Returned to Paris at end of year.

1915 Met and later married Berthe Kitrosser.

1916 Became close friend of Juan Gris. Contract with Léonce Rosenberg Gallery.

1918 Spent spring and summer at Beaulieu-près-Loches with Gris and others.

1920 First one-man exhibition at Léonce Rosenberg Gallery in spring. Later broke contract with Rosenberg, borrowed money and bought back entire production. Illustrated monograph by Maurice Raynal published in May. Beginning of his fame. Henceforth, his work frequently published in periodicals.

1922 Dr. Albert C. Barnes purchased several sculptures and commissioned five reliefs for installation on exterior of new Barnes Foundation building, Merion, Pa.

1925 Moved to Boulogne-sur-Seine. At end of year began experiments with small cardboard shapes transferred to bronze by lost-wax process. These soon led to "transparents."

1926 Series of "transparents."

1927 *La Joie de Vivre* commissioned by Vicomte Charles de Noailles for garden at Hyères on Mediterranean. First large-scale group composition.

1928 Pink stone mantelpiece and gilded bronze andirons on theme of hounds and doves for house of Jacques Doucet, Auteuil. *Reclining Woman with Guitar* installed in garden of Mme de Mandrot at Le Pradet.

1930 First large retrospective exhibition, Galerie de la Renaissance (Jeanne Bucher), Paris in May.

1931 *Song of the Vowels,* garden sculpture in bronze begun for Mme de Mandrot (finished in 1932 and installed in the garden of her villa at Le Pradet; moved after her death to Kunsthaus, Zurich).

1935 First important exhibition in the United States, Brummer Gallery, New York.

1936-1937 Awarded gold medal for Prometheus sculpture, commissioned for Paris World's Fair. During Fair entire gallery devoted to his sculpture in exhibition, *Les Maîtres de l'Art Indépendant,* at the Petit Palais.

1939-1940 During unsettled period before fall of France made many drawings but few sculptures. Fled Paris in May, 1940. Settled in Toulouse, made a few portraits.

1941 Warned not safe to remain in France; at initiative of friends in U.S.A., came to New York in June. Rented studio on Washington Square South.

1942 First exhibition Buchholz Gallery, January, sculpture done since arrival in U.S.A. Continued to live at Washington Square South but rented studio at 2 East 23rd Street, overlooking Madison Square.

1943 Began work on monumental sculpture *Prometheus Strangling the Vulture* for Ministry of Education and Health building, Rio de Janeiro.

1944 Completed large plaster model of *Prometheus Strangling the Vulture.*

1946 Returned to Paris in spring. Exhibition at Galerie Maeght. Commissioned by Father Couturier to make baptismal font for church of Notre-Dame-de-Toute-Grâce, Assy, Haute Savoie, France. Received Legion of Honor decoration. After seven months decided to return permanently to the U.S.A.

1947 Acquired house at Hastings-on-Hudson. Subsequently married Yulla Halberstadt. First child, Lolya Rachael.

1948 Began sketches for Assy commission.

1950 Spent much of year on preliminary studies and large relief *Birth of the Muses* for Mrs. John D. Rockefeller, 3rd's Guest House, New York.

1951 At work on large plastelene model of Virgin of Assy. Received important commission from Fairmount Park Association, Philadelphia.

1952 Fire in January destroyed contents of 23rd Street studio, including models of Virgin of Assy and Fairmount Park commission. Committee of aid set up to help him build studio by advancing money on his work. Worked in temporary studio at Modern Art Foundry, Long Island City. Executed several commissioned portraits.

1953 In May, moved into new studio at Hastings-on-Hudson, designed with help of Philip L. Goodwin and local architect, Martin Lowenfish. Now rebuilding large plastelene model of Virgin of Assy and model for Fairmount Park group.

Exhibitions: Catalogs and Reviews

1920 Paris. Galerie Léonce Rosenberg.

1930 Paris. Galerie Renaissance. Catalog.
Reviewed in bibl. 39 and in *Formes* (Paris) no. 7, July 1930, p.17.

1935 New York. Brummer Gallery. Catalog with text by Elie Faure.
Reviewed in *Art Digest* (New York) v. 10, Dec. 15, 1935, p.10; in *Art News* (New York) v. 34, Dec. 14, 1935, p.20; in *Magazine of Art,* (Washington, D.C.) v. 20, Jan. 1936, p.38-9, and in bibl. 44.

1937 Paris. Petit Palais. Catalog *(Les Maîtres de l'Art Indépendant)* includes 36 works by Lipchitz.

1942 New York. Buchholz Gallery, Curt Valentin. Catalog.
Reviewed in *Art Digest* (New York) v. 16, Feb. 1, 1942, p.22; in *Art News* (New York) v. 40, Feb. 1, 1942, p.25.

1943 New York. Buchholz Gallery, Curt Valentin. Folder.
Reviewed in *Art Digest* (New York) v. 17, May 1, 1943, p.14; in *Art News* (New York) v. 42, Apr. 15, 1943, p.19.

1946 New York. Buchholz Gallery, Curt Valentin. Catalog.
Reviewed in *Nation* (New York) v. 162, Apr. 13, 1946, p.444; in *Art Digest* (New York) v. 20, Apr. 1, 1946, p.18.

1946 Paris. Galerie Maeght. Catalog with text by Jean Cassou, Camille Soula, Jacques Kober.

1948 New York. Buchholz Gallery, Curt Valentin. Catalog.
Includes excerpt from bibl. 50. Reviewed in *Art News* (New York) v. 47, Apr. 1948, p.60; in *Art Digest* (New York) v. 22, Apr. 1, 1948, p.13.

1950 Portland, Ore. Art Museum. Catalog with text by Andrew C. Ritchie.
Also shown at San Francisco Art Museum and Cincinnati Art Museum in 1951. Reviewed in *Art Digest* (New York) v. 25, Oct. 15, 1950, p.12; and in *Cincinnati Museum Bulletin* n.s. v. 1, Feb. 1951, p.12-13.

1950 Brussels. Petite Galerie du Séminaire.
Reviewed in *Beaux-Arts* (Brussels) no. 486, Mar. 17, 1950, p.7.

1951 New York. Buchholz Gallery, Curt Valentin. Catalog.
Includes list of sculptures by Lipchitz owned by American museums. Reviewed in *Art Digest* (New York) v. 25, May 15, 1951, p.18; in *Art News* (New York) v. 50, June 1951, p.46; in *Werk* (Zurich) v. 38, Oct. 1951, sup. p.136.

1951 New York. Exhibition circulated by Museum of Modern Art: "Birth of the Muses."
Reviewed in *Interiors* (New York) v. 111, Sept. 1951, p.12, 14.

1952 Venice. 26th Biennale. Catalog includes 22 works by Lipchitz.

1952 Beverly Hills, Cal. Frank Perls Gallery. Folder.
Also shown at Santa Barbara Museum.

Catalog of the Exhibition

LENDERS

Emil J. Arnold, New York; Mr. and Mrs. Lee A. Ault, New Canaan, Conn; Mr. and Mrs. Leigh B. Block, Chicago; Mme Pierre Chareau, New York; The Baroness Gourgaud, Yerres, France; Mrs. Henry R. Hope, Bloomington, Ind; Mr. and Mrs. R. Sturgis Ingersoll, Penllyn, Pa; Mr. and Mrs. Sam Jaffe, Beverly Hills, Calif; Mrs. T. Catesby Jones, New York; Mrs. Gertrude Lenart, New York; Jacques Lipchitz, Hastings-on-Hudson, N.Y.; The Miller Company, Meriden, Conn; Mr. and Mrs. Morton G. Neumann, Chicago; John S. Newberry, Jr., Grosse Pointe Farms, Mich; Mr. and Mrs. Bernard J. Reis, New York; Mrs. John D. Rockefeller, 3rd, New York; Nelson A. Rockefeller, New York; Mr. and Mrs. Thomas J. Rosenberg, New York; G. David Thompson, Pittsburgh; Mr. and Mrs. Burton Tremaine, Meriden, Conn; Mr. and Mrs. Hudson D. Walker, Forest Hills, Long Island.

Albright Art Gallery, Buffalo, New York; Yale University Art Gallery, New Haven; The Jewish Museum, New York; The Museum of Modern Art, New York; Whitney Museum of American Art, New York; Smith College Museum of Art, Northampton, Mass; Philadelphia Museum of Art; Virginia Museum of Fine Arts, Richmond; Farnsworth Art Museum, Wellesley College.

Carlebach Gallery, New York; Curt Valentin Gallery, New York.

CATALOG

The Museum of Modern Art, New York: May 18-August 1, 1954

Walker Art Center, Minneapolis: October 1-December 12, 1954

The Cleveland Museum of Art: January 25-March 13, 1955

Items marked by an asterisk are illustrated

*Head of Mlle S. 1911. Bronze, 19¾" high. Owned by the artist. Ill. p.9

*Woman and Gazelles. 1912. Bronze, 46½" long. Owned by the artist. Ill. p.22

Two Heads. Study for The Meeting. 1912. Ink drawing, 9 x 12". Curt Valentin Gallery, New York

*Woman with Serpent. 1913. Bronze, 25" high. Collection Emil J. Arnold, New York. Ill. p.25

*The Meeting. 1913. Lead, 32" high. Owned by the artist. Ill. p.23

*Acrobat on Horseback. 1914. Bronze, 21½" high. Curt Valentin Gallery, New York. Ill. p.24

*Sailor with Guitar. 1914. Bronze, 30" high. The Philadelphia Museum of Art. Ill. p.26

Dancer. 1915. Ebony and oak, 39⅜" high. Owned by the artist

*Bather. 1915. Bronze, 31⅝" high. Owned by the artist. Ill. p.27

*Man with a Guitar. 1916. Stone, 38¼" high. The Museum of Modern Art, New York, Mrs. Simon Guggenheim Fund. Ill. p.30

*Figure. 1916. Oak, 26½" high. Owned by the artist. Ill. p.28

*Pierrot. 1916. Ink drawing with color crayon, 22 x 14¾". Collection Mr. and Mrs. Burton Tremaine, Meriden, Conn. Ill. p.28

*Figure. 1916. Lead, 37½" high. Owned by the artist. Stone ill. p.29

*Standing Personage. 1916. Stone, 43¼" high. Owned by the artist. Ill. p.29

Seated Figure. 1916. Pencil, 18½" x 12¼". Curt Valentin Gallery, New York

*Bather III. 1917. Bronze, 24¾" high. Owned by the artist. Stone ill. pp.31-2

*Man with Mandolin. 1917. Stone, 29¾" high. Yale University Art Gallery, New Haven, Société Anonyme Collection. Ill. p.33

Seated Figure. 1917. Stone, 30" high. Curt Valentin Gallery, New York

*Seated Guitar Player. 1918. Bronze, 23⅝" high. Owned by the artist. Stone ill. p.34

*Seated Figure. 1918. Drawing with color crayon, 19½ x 12½". Farnsworth Art Museum, Wellesley College. Ill. p.34

*Still Life with Musical Instruments. 1918. Stone relief, 23⅝ x 29½". Owned by the artist. Ill. p.35

*Oval Polychrome Relief. 1918. Stone, 27½ x 18⅞". Owned by the artist. ill. p.36

*Still Life. 1918. Gouache on canvas, 21¾ x 13". Collection The Miller Company, Meriden, Conn. Ill. p.36

Bather. 1919. Bronze, 28" high. Collection Mrs. Gertrude Lenart, New York

Pierrot with Clarinet. 1919. Stone, 31″ high. Collection G. David Thompson, Pittsburgh. *Ill. p.37*

Portrait of Gertrude Stein. 1920. Bronze, 13½″ high. Curt Valentin Gallery, New York. *Ill. p.40*

Round Polychrome Relief. 1921. Stone, 24⅜ x 23⅝″. Owned by the artist. *Ill. p.11*

Sketch for unexecuted garden sculpture I. 1921. Bronze, 4″ long. Owned by the artist

*Sketch for unexecuted garden sculpture II. 1921. Bronze, 5″ high. Owned by the artist. *Terra cotta ill. p.52*

Repentant Magdalen. 1921. Bronze, 6″ long. Owned by the artist. *Terra cotta ill. p.38*

Portrait of Berthe Lipchitz. 1922. Bronze, 19¾″ high. Owned by the artist. *Ill. p.40*

Seated Man. 1922. Granite, 20″ high. Virginia Museum of Fine Arts, Richmond. *Ill. p.39*

Seated Woman. 1922. Bronze, c.4″ high. Owned by the artist. *Terra cotta ill. p.38*

Seated Man with Guitar. 1922. Granite, 15⅞″ high. Collection Nelson A. Rockefeller, New York. *Ill. p.38*

Musical Instruments. 1923. Bronze, 19½″ high. Curt Valentin Gallery, New York

Bather. 1923-25. Bronze, 6′7″ high. Owned by the artist. *Plaster ill. p.41*

Reclining Woman with Guitar. 1924-25. Bronze, 8½″ long. Owned by the artist

Two Figures with Violincello. 1925. Terracotta relief, 25⅝ x 19¾″. Owned by the artist

Woman with Mandolin. 1925. Bronze, 7½″ long. Owned by the artist

Seated Man. 1925. Bronze, 13½″ high. The Museum of Modern Art, New York. *Ill. p.46*

Guitar Player. 1925. Stone, 23¼″ high. Owned by the artist. *Ill. p.46*

Pierrot. 1925. Bronze, c. 5″ high. Owned by the artist. *Ill. p.13*

Woman with Guitar. 1925. Charcoal drawing, 14 x 10″. Curt Valentin Gallery, New York

Standing Woman with Guitar. 1926. Bronze, 11″ high. Collection Mme Pierre Chareau, New York

Pierrot with Clarinet. 1926. Bronze, 14¾″ high. Curt Valentin Gallery, New York. *Ill. p.42*

Mardi Gras. 1926. Gilded bronze, 10½″ high. Curt Valentin Gallery, New York. *Ill. p.42*

Harlequin with Guitar. 1926. Bronze, 13¼″ high. Private collection, New York. *Ill. p.44*

Acrobat on Ball. 1926. Bronze, 17¼″ high. Collection the Baroness Gourgaud, Yerres, France. *Ill. p.45*

Ploumanach. 1926. Bronze, 31″ high. Private collection. *Ill. p.47*

*Sketch for *Figure*, a garden sculpture, I. 1926. Bronze, 8½″ high. Owned by the artist. *Terra cotta ill. p.52*

*Sketch for *Figure*, a garden sculpture, II. 1926. Bronze, 10″ high. Collection Mr. and Mrs. Lee A. Ault, New Canaan, Conn. *Terra cotta ill. p.52*

Figure. 1926-30. Bronze, 7′ 1¼″ high. The Museum of Modern Art, New York, Van Gogh Purchase Fund. *Ill. p.53*

Circus Scene. 1927. Gilded bronze, 12 x 19½″. Collection Mr. and Mrs. Bernard J. Reis, New York. *Ill. p.44*

Reclining Nude with Guitar. 1928. Basalt, 26⅞″ long. Collection Mrs. John D. Rockefeller, 3rd, New York. *Ill. pp.50-1*

The Harp Player. 1928. Bronze, 10½″ high. Collection Mrs. T. Catesby Jones, New York. *Ill. p.54*

Mother and Child. 1929-30. Bronze, 51¼″ high. Owned by the artist. *Ill. p.56*

Melancholy. 1930. Bronze, 11½″ high. Collection Mr. and Mrs. Bernard J. Reis, New York. *Ill. p.55*

Chimène. 1930. Bronze, 18″ high. Curt Valentin Gallery, New York. *Ill. p.54*

The Harpists. 1930. Bronze, 17″ high. Collection Mr. and Mrs. Bernard J. Reis, New York. *Ill. p.58*

*Study for *Song of the Vowels*. 1931. Terra cotta, 14½″ high. The Museum of Modern Art, New York. Gift of the sculptor. *Ill. p.58*

Return of the Prodigal Son. 1931. Bronze, 47¼″ long. Owned by the artist. *Plaster ill. p.57*

Song of the Vowels. 1931-53. Bronze, 10′ high. Collection Nelson A. Rockefeller, New York. *An earlier cast ill. p.59*

Jacob Wrestling with the Angel. 1932. Bronze, 47¼″ long. Owned by the artist

Head. 1932. Bronze, 9″ high. Owned by the artist. *Ill. p.15*

Bull and Condor. 1932. Bronze, 12¼″ long. Curt Valentin Gallery, New York. *Ill. p.62*

*First sketch for *Prometheus*. 1933. Bronze, 8″ high. Owned by the artist. *Terra cotta ill. p.17*

Woman Leaning on Elbows. 1934. Bronze, 29½″ high. Owned by the artist

Study for *Prometheus*. 1936. Ink wash with watercolor, 16⅝ x 12⅛″. Collection Mr. and Mrs. Bernard J. Reis, New York

Prometheus with Vulture. Study. 1936. Bronze, 16¼″ high. Collection Mr. and Mrs. Sam Jaffe, Beverly Hills, Calif. *Ill. p.60*

Rape of Europa II. 1938. Bronze, 23⅛″ long. The Museum of Modern Art, New York. *Ill. p.62*

*Study for *Mother and Child*. 1939. Gouache, 21½ x 14½″. Private collection, New York. *Ill. p.64*

Flight. 1940. Bronze, 14½″ high. Private collection, New York. *Ill. p.65*

Arrival. 1941. Bronze, 21″ high. Owned by the artist. *Ill. p.65*

*Study for *Rape of Europa IV*. 1941. Black ink, red chalk and gouache, 26 x 20″. The Museum of Modern Art, New York, Mrs. Simon Guggenheim Fund. *Ill. p.63*

Blossoming. 1941-42. Bronze, 21½″ high. The Museum of Modern Art, New York. *Ill. p.72*

Return of the Child. 1941-43. Granite, 46″ high. Owned by the artist

Mother and Child II. 1941-45. Bronze, 50″ high. The Museum of Modern Art, New York, Mrs. Simon Guggenheim Fund. *Ill. p.66*

Portrait of Marsden Hartley. 1942. Bronze, 14″ high. Collection Mr. and Mrs. Hudson D. Walker, New York

Benediction I. 1942. Bronze, 42″ high. Collection Mr. and Mrs. Bernard J. Reis, New York. *Ill. p.69*

Sketch for *Spring*. 1942. Ink and pencil, 13½ x 10⅞″. Private collection, New York

Spring. 1942. Bronze, 14″ high. Collection Mr. and Mrs. Bernard J. Reis, New York. *Ill. p.70*

Barbara. 1942. Bronze, 15⅝″ high. Smith College Museum of Art, Northampton, Mass. *Ill. p.70*

The Promise. 1942. Bronze, 18″ high. Curt Valentin Gallery, New York. *Ill. p.71*

The Pilgrim. 1942. Bronze, 31½″ high. Owned by the artist. *Ill. p.74*

Theseus. 1942. Wash drawing, 13¾ x 10½″. Collection John S. Newberry Jr., Grosse Pointe Farms, Mich. *Ill. p.68*

Theseus. 1943. Etching, 13¾ x 11″. Curt Valentin Gallery, New York

The Couple. c. 1943. Ink with stick and brush, 24 x 25″ Carlebach Gallery, New York

Prayer. 1943. Bronze, 42½″ high. Collection Mr. and Mrs. R. Sturgis Ingersoll, Penllyn, Pa. *Ill. p.74*

Prometheus Strangling the Vulture II. 1944-53. Bronze, 8½′ high. Owned by the artist. *Ill. pp.76-7*

Birth of the Muses I. 1944. Bronze, 5″ high. Collection Mr. and Mrs. Thomas J. Rosenberg, New York. *Ill. p.78*

Pegasus. 1944. Bronze, 20″ high. Curt Valentin Gallery, New York. *Ill. p.78*

Song of Songs. 1945-48. Bronze, 36″ long. Curt Valentin Gallery, New York. *Ill. p.80*

*Study for *Sacrifice*. 1946. Ink with stick and brush, 22 x 17″. Collection Mr. and Mrs. Morton G. Neumann, Chicago. *Ill. p.75*

Sketch for *Rescue II*. 1947. Bronze, 6″ high. Collection Nelson A. Rockefeller, New York

Miracle II. 1947. Bronze, 30¼″ high. The Jewish Museum, New York. *Ill. p.83*

*Five sketches for *Notre Dame de Liesse*. For the Church of Assy. 1947-50. Bronze. Heights: 9½″, 8¾″, 10½″, 8½″, 9¾″. Owned by the artist. *Ill. p.20*

Hagar. 1948. Bronze, 30″ long. Curt Valentin Gallery, New York. *Ill. p.81*

Sacrifice II. 1948. Bronze, 49¼″ high. Whitney Museum of American Art, New York. *Frontispiece*. First cast, 1948, owned by Albright Art Gallery, Buffalo, shown in Cleveland and Minneapolis

*Study for *Notre Dame de Liesse*. For the Church of Assy. 1948. Bronze, 33″ high. Owned by the artist. *Ill. p.84*

Mother and Child. 1949. Bronze, 46½″ high. Curt Valentin Gallery, New York. *Ill. p.82*

Study for *Mother and Child*. 1949. Ink and wash, 25½ x 19¼″. Curt Valentin Gallery, New York.

Variation on a Chisel I. 1951. Bronze, 8⅛″ high. Curt Valentin Gallery, New York. *Ill. p.86, left*

Variation on a Chisel III. 1951. Bronze, 8¾″ high. Curt Valentin Gallery, New York. *Ill. p.86, center*

Centaur. 1952. Gilded bronze, 7½″ high. Private collection, New York. *Ill. p.86, right*

Centaur Enmeshed. 1952. Bronze, 7½″ high. Curt Valentin Gallery, New York

Oriental Dancer. 1952. Bronze, 9″ high. Collection Mrs. Henry R. Hope, Bloomington, Ind.

Virgin in Flames I. 1952. Gilded bronze, 13½″ high. Collection Mr. and Mrs. Leigh B. Block, Chicago. *Ill. p.85*

Virgin in Flames II. 1952. Bronze, 20″ high. Curt Valentin Gallery, New York

Portrait of Gertrude Stein. 1953. Bronze, 20″ high. Owned by the artist

Bibliography

Compiled by Hannah B. Muller, *Assistant Librarian*
The items are arranged chronologically

STATEMENTS AND WRITINGS BY LIPCHITZ

1 [Statement] *Valori Plastici* (Rome) v. 1, no. 2-3, Feb.-Mar. 1919, p.3
  Brief quotation in letter from Léonce Rosenberg to the editor of *Valori Plastici* explaining cubism.

2 "Answer to a Questionnaire," *Little Review* (New York) v. 12, May 1929, p.47-8, port.

3 [Statement] in *Omaggio a Modigliani,* Milano, 1930

4 "Réponse à une enquête sur l'art d'aujourd'hui," *Cahiers d'Art (Paris)* v. 10, 1935, p.68, illus.

5 "The Story of My *Prometheus,*" *Art in Australia* (Sydney) ser. 4, no. 6, June-Aug. 1942, p.28-35, illus., port.

6 "Foreword," in catalog: Buchholz Gallery, Curt Valentin, New York: *Bronzes by Degas, Matisse, Renoir,* New York, 1943

7 "Juan Gris," in catalog: Buchholz Gallery, Curt Valentin, New York: *Juan Gris,* New York, 1944

8 "Remarks [on Picasso's *Guernica*]" In Museum of Modern Art, New York: *Symposium on "Guernica" ... November 25, 1947,* New York, 1947
  Unpublished typescript in Library of Museum of Modern Art, New York.

9 "I Remember Modigliani," As Told to Dorothy Seckler, *Art News* (New York) v. 49, Feb. 1951, p.26-9, 64-5, illus.

10 [Statement] In *Fourteen Eyes in a Museum Storeroom,* Philadelphia, The University Museum, University of Pennsylvania, 1952
  Lipchitz selects anthropological objects from the Museum storeroom. Also published in *University Museum Bulletin* (Philadelphia) v. 16, no. 3, Feb. 1952, p.12-17, port.

11 *Amedeo Modigliani,* New York, Harry N. Abrams, 1952, 22 pp., illus. (some col.) (Library of great painters. 4)

12 [Statements] In "What in the World? Identification of Archaeological Objects: a Television Broadcast" *Archaeology* (Cambridge) v. 6, Mar. 1953, p.18-23, port.
  —See also 36, 49, 55, 57, 58, 60, 67

BOOKS AND ARTICLES ABOUT LIPCHITZ

13 Raynal, Maurice. *Lipchitz,* Paris, Action, 1920, 15 pp. plus 21 plates. (Art d'Aujourd'hui)
  Illustrations cover the period 1915 to 1919. Extracts from the text appear in Italian in *Valori Plastici* (Rome) v. 2, no. 7-8, 1920, p.90-1.

14 Salmon, André. "Des Indépendants au Louvre," *Europe Nouvelle* (Paris) v. 3, Feb. 14, 1920, p.281
  Discusses the work of Lipchitz shown at the Salon.

15 Dermée, Paul. "Lipchitz," *Esprit Nouveau* (Paris) no. 2, Nov. 1920, p.169-82, illus., port.

16 George, Waldemar. "Jacques Lipchitz," *Amour de l'Art* (Paris) v. 2, 1921, p.255-8, illus.

17 George, Waldemar. "La sculpture de Jacques Lipchitz," *Vie des Lettres* (Paris-Neuilly) v. 4, Apr. 1921, p.490-1, illus.

18 George, Waldemar. "Jacques Lipchitz," *Sélection* (Brussels) v. 2, Nov. 1921, p.16-21, illus.

19 Cocteau, Jean. "Jacques Lipchitz and My Portrait Bust," *Broom* (Rome) v. 2, 1922, p.207-9, illus.

20 "The Technique of Jacques Lipchitz," *Broom* (Rome) v. 2, 1922, p.216-19, illus.

21 George, Waldemar. "Jacques Lipchitz," *Das Kunstblatt* (Berlin) v. 6, 1922, p.58-64, illus.

22 Kuhn, Alfred. *Die neuere Plastik,* München, Delphin-Verlag, 1922, p.126-7, illus.

23 George, Waldemar. "Jacques Lipchitz," *Feuilles Libres* (Paris) v. 4, Dec. 1922-Jan. 1923, p.429-30.

24 George, Waldemar. "La Fondation Barnes," *Amour de l'Art* (Paris) v. 4, 1923, p.601-4, illus.
  Bas-reliefs by Lipchitz described, p.604. Reprinted in *Arts à Paris* (Paris) no. 7, Oct. 1923, p.11.

25 Hildebrandt, Hans. *Die Kunst des 19. und 20. Jahrhunderts,* Waldpark-Potsdam, Akademische Verlags-Gesellschaft Athenaion, 1924, p.443, illus.

26 Parkes, Keneton. "The Constructional Sculpture of Jacques Lipchitz," *Architect* (London) v. 114, Sept. 18, 1925, p.202-4, illus.

27 George, Waldemar. "Bronzes de Jacques Lipchitz," *Amour de l'Art* (Paris) v. 7, 1926, p.299-302 illus.

28 Salmon, André. "Jacques Lipchitz," *Art d'Aujourd'hui* (Paris) v. 3, no. 10, 1926, p.21-3, illus.
  Reprinted in *Cahiers d'Art* (Paris) v. 1, 1926, p.163-5, illus.

29 Einstein, Carl. *Die Kunst des 20. Jahrhunderts,* Berlin, Propyläen-Verlag, 1926, p.173, 547-9, 570, illus.

30 Stein, Gertrude. "Lipchitz," *Ray* (London) no. 2, 1927, p.1
Reprinted in Yale University Art Gallery, New Haven: *Collection of the Société Anonyme: Museum of Modern Art 1920,* New Haven, 1950, p.132. This volume also contains a statement on Lipchitz by Marcel Duchamp dated 1945.

31 George, Waldemar. *Jacques Lipchitz,* Paris, Le Triangle [1928?] 17 pp. plus 18 plates
Text in Yiddish.

32 Huidobro, Vicente. "Jacques Lipchitz," *Cahiers d'Art* (Paris) v. 3, 1928, p.153-8, illus.

33 Ozenfant, Amédée. *Art,* Paris, Budry, 1928, p.112-13, illus.
Most recent English edition published under title: *Foundations of Modern Art,* New York, Dover Publications, 1952.

34 Lozowick, Louis. "Jacques Lipchitz," *Menorah Journal* (New York) v. 16, 1929, p.46-8, illus.

35 Zervos, Christian. "Notes sur la sculpture contemporaine," *Cahiers d'Art* (Paris) v. 4, 1929, p.465-73, illus. Lipchitz, p.470-2.

36 Vitrac, Roger. *Jacques Lipchitz,* Paris, Nouvelle Revue Française, 1929, 63 pp., illus. (Les sculpteurs français nouveaux. 7)
Includes statements by Lipchitz and reprints of comments by critics.

37 Colrat, Bernard. "Jacques Lipchitz," *La Renaissance* (Paris) v. 13, June 1930, p.149-54, illus.

38 Baron, Jacques. "Jacques Lipchitz," *Documents* (Paris) v. 2, no. 1, 1930, p.17-26, illus.

39 Tériade, E. "A propos de la récente exposition de Jacques Lipchitz," *Cahiers d'Art* (Paris) v. 5, 1930, p. 259-65, illus.

40 Huidobro, Vicente. "Lipchitz," in Edouard-Joseph: *Dictionnaire biographique des artistes contemporains, 1910-1930,* Paris, Art & Edition, 1931, v. 2, p.398-9, illus.

41 Guéguen, Paul. "Jacques Lipchitz; ou, L'histoire naturelle magique," *Cahiers d'Art* (Paris) v. 7, 1932, p. 252-8, illus.

42 Fierens, Paul. *Sculpteurs d'Aujourd'hui,* Paris, Editions des Chroniques du Jour, 1933, p.14-15, illus.

43 Benson, Emanuel Mervin. "Seven Sculptors," *American Magazine of Art* (Washington, D.C.) v. 28, Aug. 1935, p.454-81, illus.
Lipchitz, 455-8.

44 Craig, Martin. "Jacques Lipchitz," *Art Front* (New York) v. 2, Jan. 1936, p.10-11, illus.
Occasioned by exhibition held at Brummer Gallery, New York.

45 Giedion-Welcker, Carola. *Modern Plastic Art,* Zurich, H. Girsberger, 1937, p.44-7, 155
Includes excerpt of statement by Lipchitz from bibl. 4. New, revised edition to be published 1954.

46 Zervos, Christian. *Histoire de l'Art Contemporain,* Paris, Editions "Cahiers d'Art," 1938, p.297, 305-6, 308, illus.

47 *12 Dessins pour Prométhée, 1940,* Paris, Jeanne Bucher [1941?]
Portfolio of color plates

48 Schwartzberg, Miriam B. *The Sculpture of Jacques Lipchitz,* New York, 1941, 136 pp. plus 56 plates
Thesis. Unpublished typescript in Library of Museum of Modern Art, New York.

49 Georges-Michel, Michel. *Peintres et sculpteurs que j'ai connus, 1900-1942,* New York, Brentano's, 1942, p.282-3
Report of a conversation with Lipchitz.

50 Hartley, Marsden. "Letter to Jacques Lipchitz," In the author's *The Spangle of Existence* [1942] p.194-7.
Unpublished typescript in the Library of the Museum of Modern Art, New York.

51 Gómez de la Serna, Ramón. "Lipchitzmo," in the author's *Ismos,* Buenos Aires, Editorial Poseidon, 1943, p.231-6, illus.

52 Buchholz Gallery, Curt Valentin, New York. *Twelve Bronzes by Jacques Lipchitz,* New York, 1943, 2 pp. plus 16 plates

53 Rewald, John. "Jacques Lipchitz's *Struggle,*" *The Museum of Modern Art Bulletin* (New York) v. 12, Nov. 1944, p.7-9, illus.

54 Buchholz Gallery, Curt Valentin, New York. *The Drawings of Jacques Lipchitz,* New York, 1944, 3 pp. plus 20 plates.

55 Sweeney, James Johnson. "An Interview with Jacques Lipchitz," *Partisan Review* (New York) v. 12, Winter 1945, p.83-9
Reprinted in Spanish in *Revista Belga* v. 2, June 1945, illus.

56 "Jacques Lipchitz: Sculptures exécutés aux Etats-Unis," *Cahiers d'Art* (Paris) v. 20-1, 1945-6, p.394-404, illus. Illustrations only.

57 Sweeney, James Johnson. "Eleven Europeans in America . . . Jacques Lipchitz," *The Museum of Modern Art Bulletin* (New York) v. 13, Sept. 1946, p.24-7, 38, illus.
Includes interview with Lipchitz.

58 Warnod, André. "Jacques Lipchitz," *Arts* (Paris) no. 95, Nov. 29, 1946, p.5
An interview.

59 Rewald, John. "Lipchitz retourne en France," *Arts* (Paris) no. 73, June 21, 1946, p.4

60 "A Little Song," *Time* (New York) v. 47, Feb. 18, 1946, p.63, illus.
Includes statement by Lipchitz explaining his sculpture: *Benediction.*

61 Raynal, Maurice. "La Sculpture de Jacques Lipchitz," *Arts de France* (Paris) no. 6, 1946, p.43-50, illus.

62 Guéguen, Pierre. "Retour d'un sculpteur," *Architecture d'Aujourd'hui* (Paris) v. 16, May-June, 1946, p.92-3, illus.
Lipchitz's sculpture discussed in relation to architecture.

63 Pach, Walter. "Lipchitz and the Modern Movement," *Magazine of Art* (Washington, D.C.) v. 39, Dec. 1946, p.354-9, illus.

64 Cassou, Jean. "Lipchitz," *Horizon* (London) v. 14, Dec. 1946, p.377-80, illus.

65 Raynal, Maurice. *Jacques Lipchitz,* Paris, Editions Jeanne Bucher, 1947, 17 pp. plus 72 plates, port.
Reproductions cover the period 1911 to 1945.

66 "Lipchitz," in *Current Biography, 1948,* New York, H. W. Wilson, 1949, p.378-80, port.

67 Sweeney, James Johnson. "Two Sculptors: Lipchitz and Arp," *Theatre Arts* (New York) v. 33, Apr. 1949, p.52-6, illus.
An interview. Includes statements by Lipchitz.

68 Frost, Rosamund J. "Lipchitz Makes a Sculpture," *Art News* (New York) v. 49, Apr. 1950, p.36-9, 63-4
Description of the artist's technique.

69 Weller, Paul. "Jacques Lipchitz: a Portfolio of Photographs," *Interiors* (New York) v. 109, May 1950, p. 88-95, illus.

70 Slusser, Jean Paul. "Sculptures by Arp and Lipchitz," *Bulletin, University of Michigan, Museum of Art* (Ann Arbor) v. 1, no. 1, May 1950, p.9-12, illus.
Discussion of Lipchitz's *Happiness.*

71 Couturier, M-A. "Assy," *Art Sacré* (Paris) no. 1-2, Sept.-Oct. 1950, p.1-20, illus.

72 Faure, Elie. "Jacques Lipchitz et le cubisme," *Arts Plastiques* (Brussels) no. 2, 1950, p.117-22, illus.

73 George, Waldemar. "Jacques Lipchitz, père légitime des transparents," *Art et Industrie,* Paris, v. 27, no. 24, 1952, p.28-9, illus.

74 "Fire [in Studio]" *Art Digest* (New York) v. 26, Feb. 1, 1952, p.14

75 Bouret, Jean. "Lipchitz, le constructeur," *Arts* (Paris) no. 345, Feb. 8, 1952, p.4

76 "Another Phoenix," *Art Digest* (New York) v. 26, Feb. 15, 1952, p.13, illus.
Sacrifice by Lipchitz acquired by the Albright Art Gallery.

77 Kelleher, P. J. "*Sacrifice:* Bronze Acquired by the Museum," *Buffalo Gallery Notes* (Buffalo) v. 16, May 1952, p.2-3

78 Hope, Henry R. "La Scultura di Jacques Lipchitz," *Biennale* (Venice) no. 10, Sept. 1952, p.8-11, illus.

79 Veronesi, Giulia. "Jacques Lipchitz," *Emporium* (Bergamo) v. 116, no. 691-2, July-Aug. 1952, p.53-6, illus.

80 Auerbach, Arnold. *Sculpture: a History in Brief,* London, Elek Books, 1952, p.85-7, 101, illus.

81 Ritchie, Andrew Carnduff. *Sculpture of the Twentieth Century,* New York, Museum of Modern Art, 1953, p.32, 42-3, 178-81, illus.

82 Goldwater, Robert. *Jacques Lipchitz,* Amsterdam, Allert de Lange, 1954
Dutch, English, French, and German editions.

83 Couzijn, W. "In de Werkplaats van Lipchitz," *Kroniek van Kunst en Kultuur* (Amsterdam) v. 14, Jan. 1954, p.1-2, illus., port.

84 Braat, L. P. J. "Lipchitz: het Wezen van zihn Werk," *Kroniek van Kunst en Kultuur* (Amsterdam) v. 14, Jan. 1954, p.2-3, illus., port.

Photograph Credits

Main Brothers, London: p.56

Philadelphia Museum of Art: pp.76-7

John D. Schiff: Frontispiece

Adolph Studley: pp.15, 20, 23, 26, 28 below, 34 below, 36 below, 38 above, 40 above, 42, 46 above, 47, 55, 60, 62, 63, 64, 65 below, 69-75, 78, 80-86

Soichi Sunami: pp.30, 51, 53, 65 above, 66, 68

Marc Vaux, Paris: pp.7, 9, 11, 13, 14, 17, 22, 24-5, 27, 28 above, 29, 31-33, 34 above, 35, 36 above, 37, 38 below, 39, 40 below, 41, 43, 44, 45, 46 below, 48, 49, 50, 52, 54, 57, 58, 59

William Vandivert: pp.79

Paul Weller: p.87

This reprinted edition was produced by the offset printing process. The text and plates were photographed separately from the original volume, and the plates rescreened. The paper and binding were selected to ensure the long life of this library grade edition.

THIS BOOK WAS PRINTED IN APRIL 1954
FOR THE TRUSTEES OF THE MUSEUM OF MODERN ART
BY THE PLANTIN PRESS, NEW YORK